Dirt

In memory of Dame Mary Douglas (1921–2007)

New Geographies of Cleanliness and Contamination

Dirt

Edited by Ben Campkin and Rosie Cox

I.B. TAURIS

LONDON · NEW YORK

New paperback edition published in 2012 by I.B.Tauris & Co Ltd
6 Salem Road, London W2 4BU
175 Fifth Avenue, New York NY 10010
www.ibtauris.com

Distributed in the United States and Canada Exclusively by Palgrave Macmillan
175 Fifth Avenue, New York NY 10010

First published in hardback in 2007 by I.B.Tauris & Co Ltd

ISBN 978 1 78076 417 7

A full CIP record for this book is available from the British Library
A full CIP record is available from the Library of Congress

Library of Congress Catalog card: available

Printed and bound in Great Britain by TJ International Ltd, Padstow, Cornwall from
camera-ready copy copy-edited and typeset by Oxford Publishing Services, Oxford

Contents

CONTENTS

Figures

Acknowledgements

The editors would like to thank everyone who has made the production of this collection possible.

A number of the chapters included were first presented at the Association of American Geographers Annual Meeting in Denver in 2005. Two sessions on 'Geographies of dirt and purity' were organized by Rosie Cox and Laura Venn who received support from the British Academy Overseas Conference Grant Scheme.

We would like to thank the Architecture Research Fund of the Bartlett School of Architecture, UCL, for a grant to assist with costs related to the book's production. We are particularly grateful to Jane Rendell for her advice and support for this project.

Our thanks also go to David Stonestreet and Jayne Hill at I.B.Tauris and Selina and Jason Cohen at Oxford Publishing Services for their contributions to the book's editing and production.

Introduction: Materialities and Metaphors of Dirt and Cleanliness

BEN CAMPKIN AND ROSIE COX

All of us conceive of 'dirt', and attempt to avoid or eliminate it on a daily basis. The word has a broad range of associations, yet we seldom question what precisely we mean by it, or why exactly dirt needs to be cleaned. Materially, it refers at once to the mundane matter under our finger nails, down our toilets, on and under our streets – hardly the reified substance of conventional academic enquiry, one might think. However, it is the everyday nature of dirt and cleaning, and their apparently 'natural' delineation, that make them so important as objects of study. This volume of new work addresses the themes of dirt and cleanliness in relation to domestic, urban and rural space. Dirt is considered at a theoretical level, but also as that which slips easily between concept, matter, experience and metaphor. Collectively, the authors demonstrate the importance and potential of understanding dirt and cleanliness, and of acknowledging that they are located within and constitutive of space and social relations. In this introduction we outline the possibilities of these themes as a focus of investigation and analysis, before proceeding to introduce the structure and range of the following chapters.

The spatialities of dirt and cleanliness are revealed when we reflect on the history of concepts of cleanliness and cleaning practices.[1] In the 'modern' West it is generally assumed that such practices, and acceptable standards of cleanliness, have been developed in a linear fashion in response to scientifically informed 'germ theory', which unquestionably explains what is hygienic or unhygienic, and which chemicals, technologies and behaviours will banish the microscopic organisms that threaten to spread disease. However, when cleaning practices are examined closely we find that the daily processes intended to keep bodies, houses or cities free of dirt are not organized in direct relation to unquestionable scientific evidence. Scientific definitions of 'dirty' and 'clean' are produced within particular historical and cultural contexts, rather than standing as objective truths. As sociologist Elizabeth Shove asserts, such 'concepts of cleanliness are of surprisingly limited value in understanding contemporary conventions of bathing and laundering'.[2] We clean because we believe dirt exists and because an ever increasing range of technologies and products promise us distance from it, playing upon individual and collective desires and anxieties.

The strength of emotional reactions to perceived dirt and emotive prompts to clean are not new. Adrian Forty has argued that modernist hygiene reformers in early twentieth-century Britain used a combination of scientific and emotive arguments to press for change. He concludes that 'on the whole, the arguments based upon scientific logic were less effective than those which appealed to emotion.'[3] The use of a guilt-inducing rationale for increased hygiene required dirt to be considered as simultaneously a moral and physical problem. In contemporary society, at both an individual and collective level, we are driven to eradicate dirt by a complex and often contradictory web of scientific and cultural, rational and emotional, physiological and psychological prompts.

The historian Georges Vigarello has argued that to understand changing notions of cleanliness we need to examine historical conceptions of the human body.[4] For example, in the sixteenth century the body was popularly believed to contain humours that needed to be kept in a state of relative equilibrium. It was thought to be permeable to heat and water, which could unbalance the humours and let in pestilence and disease. Bathing was thought to be dangerous to health – letting vital substances seep out and dangerous ones in.[5] The result was that people rarely washed their bodies or clothes thoroughly and considered filth in public spaces to be aesthetically displeasing, perhaps, but not a threat to health.

The miasmatic theory of disease, popular in eighteenth and nineteenth century Europe, posited that foul air transmitted pestilence. The mind-set that accompanied this theory imagined the danger to lie with the smells and gases arising from filth and decay, rather than with the matter of dirt itself. As a result, an emphasis was placed on the importance of air circulation, on the avoidance of stagnant air inside and outside buildings, and on 'purifying' the air with perfumes.[6] For some, dirty skin was seen as a protection against miasmas just so long as sufficient perfume covered worrying smells. Personal cleaning was not, therefore, prioritized. However, the cleansing of streets and other public areas started to be addressed as early sanitizers sought to banish the sources of foul smells.[7]

More recent thinking about dirt and the body has been influenced by bacterial explanations of the spread of disease, accompanied by the rise of invisible 'dirt'. Anxieties about such invisible threats can be seen in part to have prompted an obsessive attention to eliminating visible dirt – also thought lethal at the end of the nineteenth and beginning of the twentieth centuries – in the form of dust.[8] Shove comments that

> Germs cannot be seen so there are no obvious indicators of their effective elimination. ... If germs cause disease and if they can be killed by scrupulous hygiene, it is reasonable to interpret the visitation of illness not as accident of fate but an indication of domestic failure and lax standards.[9]

Since the nineteenth century, manufacturers and advertisers of cleaning products have grasped this logic firmly and have used it to market increasingly diverse products that promise to eliminate ever more germs from ever more places around the house and in the public sphere.[10]

In *History of Shit*, Dominique Laporte remarks: 'that which occupies the site of disgust at one moment in history is not necessarily disgusting at the preceding moment or the subsequent one. There are even instances of micro variations, whereby the attitude toward waste reverses, reinstituting previous practices within the space of a few short years.'[11] An examination of the substances used for washing laundry provides an everyday example of how concepts of dirt and cleanliness in popular circulation have changed over a relatively short period of time. Until the mid-nineteenth century, in much of Europe, linen was cleaned by soaking it in stale urine.[12] This illustrates that urine was seen as simultaneously contaminating and cleansing and reveals 'human ambivalence to bodily wastes and discontinuity in our systems for dealing with them'.[13] In some urban areas of Britain urine was collected in a common barrel from which each house on the street would take its supply on washday. The poor used the collected urine to wash themselves too, apparently with excellent results. Other cleansing agents used in Britain included 'lye', made by steeping wood ash in water, to which could be added bran, stale urine or chicken or pigeon dung steeped in water.[14] These methods produced the desired result – visibly whiter clothes – using materials that were freely available.

Changes in thinking about the nature of the body and the threats posed to it have driven, and been driven by, changes in the spaces, systems and technologies of cleansing at every scale, from the intimate design of the domestic bathroom, to gargantuan public works such as subterranean sewer networks. Ideas about dirt are so pervasive that they frequently seem to dictate a benchmark of 'normality'.[15] As such, beyond the specific architectures of hygiene, notions of dirt and cleanliness can be said directly or indirectly to influence the arrangement and occupation of all interior and exterior space, informing the minutiae of human behaviour and actively influencing relations between people.

Dirt and cleanliness in theory

It is with the historically, geographically and culturally specific nature of dirt and cleanliness that theorists have been particularly concerned. In 1966, social anthropologist Mary Douglas (1921–2007) published the first edition of her groundbreaking book, *Purity and Danger: An Analysis of Concepts of Pollution and Taboo*.[16] In this work, which introduced the topic to a wide academic readership, Douglas cites a definition of dirt as 'matter out of place',[17] and argues that cleanliness and contamination, pollution and prohibition, are part of a classificatory system, used by all cultures, to police boundaries. Dirty things, she argues, are those that transgress established borders, confound order and disrupt dominant belief systems. The prohibitive structures and pollution behaviours evidenced in modern Western, scientifically informed cultures were no different in this sense, Douglas asserted, from those used by the 'primitive' societies that were the main focus of her work as a social anthropologist. *Purity and Danger* announced that dirt, purity, and 'pollution behaviours' related to these categories, are socially constructed, culturally and historically specific.

As well as legitimizing the analysis of pollution systems and their accompanying rituals and symbols in the context of religion and culture, through the domestic metaphors that she uses to elaborate her arguments, Douglas suggests that the study of dirt and hygiene at this grounded and everyday level is an important pursuit. Though Douglas's broad category of 'dirt' may inadvertently have led to the blurring of categorical boundaries between different types of dirt, it is interesting that a number of cultural, anthropological and philosophical surveys have recently appeared that examine specific material forms of dirt and pollution such as dust, odour, earth and garbage.[18]

Understandings of dirt and pollution have advanced conceptually through contributions from the fields of post-Freudian – particularly Lacanian – psychoanalytic theory and feminist theory, often building directly on Douglas's work. The powerful notions of the 'abject' and 'abjection' have helped to elucidate the subtle interactions between pollution beliefs and behaviours at a social level, emphasized in Douglas's anthropological work, as well as at a psychological level, as they influence and are experienced by the individual subject.[19] In turn, the idea of the abject has influenced recent

4

anthropological work, as well as other disciplines interested in questions of space and society. The abject, as that which is both familiar and alien, also provides a conceptual link to Freud's 'uncanny', a term more frequently used in recent art, architectural and urban discourses.[20]

In Kristeva's theory abject matter is the cause of a combination of physical, moral and psychological reactions, operating through different though interconnecting registers. For example, feelings of disgust at a rotting object;[21] or of moral repulsion to an horrific crime. The sense in each case is of a strong and apparently 'natural' reaction: a 'revolt of the person against an external menace from which one wants to keep oneself at a distance – it may menace *from inside*'.[22] As with Douglas's dirt and pollution behaviours, Kristeva's abject is articulated and interpreted through spatial metaphors, and abjection refers to spatialized processes, the interactions between material, corporeal, environmental, psychological and social realms and systems through which the subject or society attempt to impose or maintain a state of purity. As anthropologists Victor Buchli and Gavin Lucas suggest, the abject accounts for a greater level of ambivalence on the part of the subject towards the pollutant or potentially pollutant object than Douglas's theory accounts for. In addition, through the notion of 'spaces of abjection' Kristeva's concept may be put to use to highlight with greater clarity the relationships between marginalized people and their spatial and material contexts. The abject may therefore be seen as a more overtly political theoretical tool than Douglas's concept. While in geography writers such as David Sibley and Jenny Robinson have used both Douglas's and Kristeva's theories to develop studies of politically and culturally isolated communities,[23] in architectural and urban discourse these theories have largely been employed in relation to hygiene aesthetics.[24]

Dirt, cleaning and socio-spatial relations

Theories of dirt and the abject are, therefore, useful tools for understanding and confronting inequality or marginality. As Shove argues, 'describing people, things or practices as clean or dirty is not a socially neutral enterprise.'[25] The perception of the dirtiness of others, whether they be 'the great unwashed' or 'smelly foreigners' reinforces dominant value systems and social boundaries. The ordering of people in terms of their proximity to dirt operates both in relation to perceived personal dirtiness and responsibilities for cleaning dirt away. Dealing with physical dirt is both mundane and messy. Cleaning is a continual activity, yet not something we all do. In fact the doing, or not, of dirty work is divided down lines of class, ethnicity and gender – the most powerful social divides in contemporary life. It is those on the 'losing' sides of those divides who clean most – the poor, women and people of colour – while those with the social and economic power to avoid it attempt to do so. The ability of dirt to act as a means of social classification is revealed vividly in the organization of paid domestic labour. Paying others to deal with the most intimate forms of dirt reinforces social status and signals it to others. Dirt and cleaning exist within and constitute social relations both within and outside domestic environments.

Distinctions between dirt and cleanliness are also used in racist constructions of others. Non-white and immigrant groups' habits and practices have frequently been labelled as unhygienic and used to justify denigration and the interference by dominant authorities in the most intimate areas of life. Historian Suellen Hoy has argued that teaching particular methods and standards of cleaning was an important part of the Americanization project in post-Civil War USA. Black Americans and newly arriving immigrants were subject to lessons in school and from community social workers about 'American' standards of cleanliness. The attainment of these standards was the sign they had truly become a part of American society.

Concepts of cleanliness have also been part of the 'civilizing' mission of empire. Visual culture theorist Anne McClintock has argued that through instilling routines of personal hygiene, and marketing British-manufactured soap, the management of cleanliness in newly colonized areas was a means of imposing social order and control.[26] In a similar vein historian Timothy Burke has detailed how the widespread penetration of manufactured toiletry products into colonial Zimbabwe was achieved through advertising campaigns that associated cleanliness with whiteness and 'civilization'.[27] These studies reveal that dirt is not only a structuring concept of racial prejudice when individuals sling insults, but the association of denigrated Others with dirt is also used on an international scale by multinational companies and governments attempting to control markets and nations.

New geographies of cleanliness and contamination

One of the potentials of dirt as the focus of critical academic research and writing is its potential to link theoretical work, physical spaces and environments and their representation, the world of material objects, communities and individuals. As William Cohen has recently written: 'filth represents a cultural location at which the human body, social hierarchy, psychological subjectivity, and material objects converge. Standing at a theoretical crossroads, filth is at once figurative and substantive.'[28] This spatial metaphor of dirt at a theoretical crossroads seems especially appropriate. The nineteenth century expression 'dirty work at the crossroads' referred to underhand activities, and suggests the association of urban intersections with accumulations of unwanted people and material. Cohen's 'theoretical crossroads' is suggestive of the potential for the themes of dirt and cleanliness to drive interdisciplinary and comparative work. However, to date, much of the literature on these topics seems introspective, or when drawing on other disciplines does not fully exploit the transformative possibilities of an inter-disciplinary approach.[29] Although Douglas's work bridges many of the existing studies, surprisingly, theoretical work on dirt has in the main remained distinct from literature on its materialities and on cleaning practices. While relevant theoretical work has emphasized psychological states and their correspondent social contexts, it has largely ignored cleaning itself. Studies of cleaning tend to emphasize histories of housework and servants, and technologies of cleaning, focusing on material practices, with little attempt to elucidate the broader meanings of dirt. This volume brings these literatures together to emphasize culturally, spatially and socially pro-duced understandings of dirt and hygiene, arguing against any notion of objective, scientific definition that exists outside those contexts.

We use the prefix 'new geographies' to denote an emerging range of studies on this topic in disciplines that are concerned with spatial matters. The contributors, not all geographers by academic discipline – though all engaged with questions of space relating to domestic, urban or rural environments – include those who work in the fields of anthropology, architecture, architectural history, art history, geography, literature, policy studies, sociology and urban planning.[30] Their points of reference represent an even more diverse range of disciplines, interests, questions, sources and methods.

The collection is by no means intended as a comprehensive survey, but rather a snapshot of emerging work, which particularly reflects the editors' and authors' research interests. The book is organized into three sections – 'Home', 'City and Suburb' and 'Country' – each with a brief introduction. These categories provide a useful way of negotiating the distinct but interrelated geographies of pollution and cleanliness. The boundaries between each section are porous as, for example, issues of domesticity in 'Home' connect with discussions of suburbanization in 'City/Suburb', and food growth and consumption practices in 'Country'. The majority of the book's contributing authors are concerned with dirt and cleanliness in a contemporary setting in the global North, though there are important contributions from South America and Asia. The 'City' section includes historical geographies of the physical and social sanitization of cities. However, in contrast with more conventional studies within, for example, the canon of environmental history, here the authors who explore historical material do so in relation to contemporary theories of dirt and space, reworking the conventional narratives of urban hygiene and sanitization in innovative ways.

Mirroring the central themes of Douglas's *Purity and Danger* – everyday and symbolic dirt, its socio-cultural contexts, and its formal, visual and spatial consequences – the collection brings together new work on dirt and cleanliness in disciplines concerned with questions of space. The authors elucidate abstract concepts and conventions through reference to grounded practices and examples, extending our understanding of a range of different material, social and symbolic manifestations of dirt and cleaning, and suggesting a rich territory for future interdisciplinary enquiry.

Section 1

HOME: DOMESTIC DIRT AND CLEANING

Introduction

ROSIE COX

The contributors to this section explore the meanings of dirt and cleanliness in domestic and quasi-domestic settings. They raise new questions about how we understand the categories of 'dirty' and 'clean' both on physical and metaphorical levels. The first and last chapters show how ideas about the home, and domestic social relationships, can be used to understand notions of pollution and purity in other settings. The remaining authors focus on practices within the home that define who and what are considered 'dirty'. The chapters range widely in their geographical locations and objects of study – from care workers in the USA to domestic employees in Brazil, to families in England and funeral homes in New Zealand. Together, they suggest both the social importance of ideas of pollution and purity, and the cultural and geographic specificity of concepts of dirt and cleanliness and associated practices.

The authors offer new arguments about cleaning and cleanliness in the domestic sphere that require moving beyond traditional discussions of domesticity, dominated by a focus on gender in relation to responsibilities for reproductive work. Feminist writers and activists have firmly established the importance of women's responsibility for reproductive labour to their position in society and oppression.[1] In academia this has meant that domestic cleaning and childcare have become recognized as valuable topics for social research and a large literature now exists on reproductive labour.[2] More recently, studies of paid domestic work and the workers who do it have supplemented this work – bringing ethnic and class-related aspects of reproductive labour into focus.[3] While there is now a diverse and thorough literature on both paid and unpaid domestic work, the majority of studies are on the organization of housework and relations between those who do and do not do the cleaning. Little attention has been paid to the physical matter being dealt with – dirt – and cleaning practices themselves. The implications of working with 'polluted matter', and the culturally defined nature of cleaning and values attached to cleanliness have yet to be as thoroughly explored.

Bringing together these distinct literatures reveals the importance of dirt and cleanliness in the construction of social relations. The organization of paid domestic labour vividly illustrates how dirt can act as a means of social classification. Employing servants was the primary indicator of middle-class standing in Victorian Britain and elsewhere. When industrialist and social reformer Seebohm Rowntree conducted his survey of York in 1899, he took the 'keeping or not of servants' as the dividing line between 'the working classes and those of a higher social scale'.[4] To remain 'respectable', the impoverished middle classes would struggle to keep a single servant. Those who could not even afford this would attempt to disguise their situation and hide their labours, particularly those that involved the closest contact with dirt.

At this point in history there was a clear and widely acknowledged correlation between class, cleanliness and cleaning work. Historian and heritage consultant Pamela Sambrook argues in relation to her examination of British country house servants between the seventeenth and nineteenth centuries, that a primary purpose of cleaning was to indicate status. Cleanliness marked higher status in a world where being clean was difficult, and the purpose of servants was to deliver that cleanliness, so demonstrating their employer's standing to the world.[5] Household servants were employed to create an environment that was comfortable and that would clearly signal a householder's high standing, both through ensuring cleanliness and by caring for all the employer's goods, which were such important markers of rank. Therefore, it was not only the ability to afford to employ domestic servants that marked status, but also the actual product of their work.

For most of the last 500 years having a clean house, as well as visibly clean and well-kept clothing and household linen, was a mark of high status because a clean habitat was so difficult to achieve. Cleanliness demonstrated how many servants were employed and how well those servants worked. The use of open fires, the difficulties of heating water and the lack of modern cleaning products, such as soap or washing powder, all meant that houses were dirtier and cleaning was more time consuming and difficult. Poor people could not maintain their houses and linen to the same standards as people who had servants to work for them, so cleanliness was a sign of wealth and status. Being able to maintain a distance from the dirt, which was everywhere, both inside and outside houses, was something that was only possible for the privileged few.

The relationship between dirt and social status is an aspect of domestic labour that is rarely mentioned today. However, much paid domestic labour (like its unpaid counterpart) still reflects differences in status. Having a beautifully kept home and time for leisure can be an indicator of high status for the owner; being actively involved in dealing with dirt means low status for the worker who does it.[6]

INTRODUCTION

Through their investigations of how and why cleaning is performed, and how working with dirt defines workers' identities and contributes to the social construction of domestic spaces, the authors of the following chapters offer a view of relationships between home, dirt and cleaning that differs from the majority of existing accounts. They reject 'common sense' understandings of dirt and cleanliness as concepts that are objective and known to everyone to explore how these categories are created through everyday practices and within hierarchical social relations.

In the opening chapter Carol Wolkowitz explores conceptualizations of dirt and looks at their usefulness in social theory. Drawing on examples of work with 'real dirt' – such as care work and garbage handling, and work that is constructed as abject, such as prostitution – Wolkowitz examines whether the linguistic focus of postmodern social theory can be reconciled with real dirt to provide a critical realist sociology of dirt with political relevance for workers involved in dirty work. Wolkowitz asks us to move beyond symbolic constructions of dirt and to 'focus instead on how lived experiences of dirt are underpinned by the powers, strategies and constraints available to different social groups' (page 16). Rather than a conventional understanding of the domestic, in this chapter she extends to commoditized forms of domestic activity.

Following this, Lívia Barbosa offers a detailed view of how concepts of pollution shape the experiences of one group of workers who deal with dirt every day. She examines how paid domestic workers in Brazil are subject to widespread practices and forms of behaviour that segregate them from their employers in myriad ways. Such practices include requiring domestic workers to use different cutlery and crockery from the rest of the household, and prohibiting them from washing their clothes in their employers' washing machines. Barbosa argues that the design of Brazilian houses and apartment blocks builds such practices into the domestic environment because both the physical environment and the habits and actions of employers separate domestic workers within the home.

Continuing with the theme of interior domestic cleaning, Lydia Martens uses detailed empirical research with families in Britain to examine decisions about what cleaning needs to be done and when. The author argues that during the postwar period a shift took place from temporally-structured practices, such as the emphasis on seasonal (spring) cleaning and the weekly wash, to visually-determined forms of behaviour that prioritize the appearance of dirt rather than cleaning routines. The visual impetus to clean may have driven standards of cleanliness upwards, for householders no longer wait for it to be 'time' to clean, while they may also have an effect on the choice of surface materials and other features of interior decoration given that certain materials reveal dirt more easily than others.

13

In the final chapter of this section Kyro Selket explores the ways in which ideas of home are used in the funeral industry in Aeoteroa, New Zealand. Selket argues that the associations in funeral home design with the middle-class home, and with order and cleanliness, act to disassociate death from disease and contamination. She reads this as a process of metaphorical sanitization for the benefit of the recently bereaved. The chapter traces how modern funeral homes have been carefully designed to echo the respectability and calm of upper-middle-class dwellings; from their location in suburban neighbourhoods to the choice of décor and furniture. However, inside they are laid out so that the living can move through them without coming into proximity with the corpse. It is only through the process of embalming that the dead body is considered to be cleansed and is then permitted into the more public spaces of the home.

Chapter 1

Linguistic Leakiness or Really Dirty? Dirt in Social Theory

CAROL WOLKOWITZ

In this chapter I consider several different conceptualizations of dirt and 'dirty work' and their place in social theory.[1] At first sight, one can identify two leading trends in the literature. Postmodern and/or poststructural dirt is purified through abstraction, prettified, much like old neighbourhoods. The apparently polar opposite is the idea of 'real dirt' – one can smell it, feel it, it is undeniably disgusting. Although people can become acclimatized, one has an 'instinctive reaction'. Real dirt is credited with an objective status, for instance as an agent of infection, and is removable only by physical means.

Here I argue that this simple, binary way of categorizing conceptualizations of dirt may hide a more complex and interesting array of theoretical postures. In particular, critical realism can help to prise apart the binary between linguistic leakiness and the 'really dirty', making a space for a sociology of dirt that does not have to choose. Critical realists argue that we can, and indeed must, recognize that social phenomena 'really' exist, even while being ready to acknowledge that their construction inevitably depends on human activities, including the use of language.

After outlining the binary between naturalistic and social constructionist views of dirt and dirtiness in more detail, I consider two areas of research and debate in which dirt features as a central axis of analysis and debate. My first example is research on how gender divisions influence the strategies of people whose paid work involves contact with disgusting substances. Second, I go on to another example of work that is frequently characterized in terms of its 'dirtiness', prostitution, and consider differences between feminist commentators in how they deal with this. Both examples suggest that rather than highlighting the symbolic construction of dirt in culture, we should focus instead on how the powers, strategies and constraints available to different social groups underpin lived experiences of dirt.

Naturalistic accounts

In what Mick Smith and Joyce Davidson call 'naturalistic' or 'evolutionary' accounts, 'dirt' is found in nature rather than defined by human societies.[2] According to Smith and Davidson, such accounts focus on what is taken to be the natural aversion to the objective characteristics of the offending articles and their biological significance. Research in biology and neuroscience emphasizes the universality of disgust as an innate response to relatively similar objects across cultures, including bodily excretions and body parts, decay and spoiled food, particular living creatures, certain categories of outsiders and violations of morality or social norms.[3] Stimulated by sensory cues, such as smell, feel and sight, material that is 'dirty' or contaminated naturally excites disgust and avoidance. Disgust is especially evident in situations in which contamination might take place through ingestion or touch. The universality of these responses is explained by the evolutionary advantages of disgust in protecting ports to the body, such as the airways, the gut, the genitals and the skin. Even moral disgust is seen as having evolutionary benefits because it leads to the avoidance of outsiders who are likely to carry germs or viruses to which one does not already have some resistance. Such arguments for the universality and evolutionary benefits of disgust are now being reinforced by evidence that the disgust response is rooted in brain chemistry.[4]

Whatever their merits (surely many emotional reactions are registered 'in' the brain, but this does not explain them), such naturalistic views have had little role in feminist scholarship or sociology, which usually cite Mary Douglas's *Purity and Danger*, discussed further below, as a foundational text.[5] A recent article by Tim Dant and David Bowles, however, asks social scientists to pay more attention to the 'natural', as against the symbolic, qualities of dirt.[6] In the abstract of their article, which is based on research on the way that car repair workers deal with dirt, Dant and Bowles suggest that a 'common sense' approach to dirt – as naturally unpleasant and to be avoided if possible – may be more useful in understanding how dirt is dealt with than the historical and anthropological analyses of dirt that predominate. They say that the workers they observed displayed a rational attitude towards the causes of dirt and dealt with it in an instrumental, flexible and matter-of-fact manner. They recommend we be cautious of any reduction to culture that overlooks prior bodily and material concerns. While we may want to take this point on board, Dant and Bowles's failure to discuss properly the distinctions between nonorganic and organic dirt, which as they say in a footnote were pointed out by a reader, the gendering of different kinds of 'dirty work', or the gendering of attitudes to (different kinds of) dirt suggests that one cannot simply put social constructions of dirt to the side.

We should be careful not to conflate a critical realist account, which I think is what Dant and Bowles are actually after, with naturalism, since the first neither seeks the positivist certainties of evolutionary laws nor sees the social as explicable in terms of biological universals. As Andrew Sayer argues, critical realism highlights the distinctiveness of social phenomena.[7] Social phenomena are emergent phenomena in the sense that they have properties that are irreducible to their constituents. While 'social phenomena are emergent from biological phenomena, which are in turn emergent from chemical and physical strata', we cannot explain social life simply in terms of biology or physiology. However, this 'does not mean that we can ignore them' either; since we are embodied beings 'the interactions between the social and physical needs to be acknowledged'.[8] Critical realism is thus compatible with phenomenological understandings of our interactions,[9] including aversion to dirt, for human bodily morphology lends itself to particular ways of experiencing our being in the world, for instance our sense of the interior and exterior of the body, even if it does not determine it.[10]

Symbolic dirt

Social constructionist notions of dirt of the kind Dant and Bowles criticize are associated most closely with Mary Douglas, and, in feminism, their further development by Julia Kristeva and Elizabeth Grosz.[11] For Douglas social constructions of dirt are intertwined with social constructions of the body in particular societies. The body is taken as a symbol for any bounded system and, by the same token, bodily orifices and fluids (blood, milk, urine, faeces, sweat and tears) stand for potential threats to the social collectivity, namely transgressions of the social order. This is because margins and borders are so problematic – messy and untidy – for societies. Reflections about purity and pollution are actually reflections about order and disorder, form and form-lessness, being and nonbeing.[12] Hence, nothing is dirty in itself; dirt only exists because, as matter out of place, it lies outside and threatens the social system.

The French feminist theorist Julia Kristeva builds on Douglas in formulating her concept of abjection. The abject provokes fear and disgust because it exposes the fragility of the border between self and others,

17

threatening to dissolve the self. The abject is also a source of fascination, and hence a source of pleasure, as in the case of the horror genre in literature or film that Kristeva uses as an example.[13] UK reality television programmes such as *How Clean is Your House?* or *All New Cosmetic Surgery* might be seen as further examples of the pleasure we derive from teasing our tolerance for dirt. (*How Clean is Your House?* features two professional cleaners who attack the dirtiest homes viewers can nominate, while *All New Cosmetic Surgery* is one of many UK programmes broadcasting cosmetic surgeons at work.)

Sexual difference is not actually very important to Douglas, since although she recognizes that the perception of pollution – especially clinging viscosity – is linked to a rejection of the female body, as a natural symbol the body (and the difference between male and female bodies) only stands in for anxiety about other social divisions. In contrast, for French corporeal feminists and those whose work has developed within the frameworks they established, sexual difference is at the heart of the social distinction between clean and dirty. Fluids and 'leakiness' are associated with femininity, the solid and concrete with the masculine. Where Freud saw civilization founded on the repudiation of pre-Oedipal attachments, for French feminists this repudiation is profoundly gendered, since the formation of the 'proper' adult male – clean, decent, obedient, law-abiding – involves the abjection of the open, fluid female body.[14]

Although Grosz uses Kristeva to help her link women's experiences of 'corporeal flows' and the culturally specific meanings of sexed bodies, others stress that the categories to which much of this commentary refers are linguistic categories and gendered speech, rather than 'real' bodies or (clean or dirty) objects.[15] As in poststructuralist thought more generally, meanings in language are unreliable, with no reliable referent: in post-Derridian thought there is no 'originary source for what exists in language/ representation'.[16] Binary oppositions like 'clean' and 'dirty' or 'pure' or 'impure' exist in language, not the empirical world. Hence, according to Kristeva, it is not lack of cleanliness that causes abjection but what does not respect borders, rules and identities.

There has been a (very) recent move against the excesses of this 'linguistic turn'. As Alexandra Howson argued in a recent review of the literature on gender and embodiment, academic feminism often 'forget[s] the body as an experienced material and sensible medium',[17] but not much has been written as yet about what this turn might mean for rethinking the place of 'dirt' or 'disgust' in social life. If there is a problem in reducing the body to little more than what Robyn Longhurst calls 'linguistic territory',[18] is the same true of 'dirt'? Longhurst's response is an empirical sociological study of Australian men's perception of bathroom hygiene and their attitudes towards cleaning up after themselves and others. The examples I explore briefly below go to show that, even as constructed in language, constructions of dirt and dirtiness operate within social relations and not just the symbolic realm.

The first example reviews some English-language sociological research on people's experiences of employment involving contact with polluting substances, especially in the context of the recent growth in paid care work in the West. The second example relates to contact with activities that are seen as *morally* repellent. It considers recent feminist debate on prostitution in the USA and Britain, in which the perception of prostitution as a form of dirty work plays a large rhetorical role in both academic and activist accounts.[19]

Rationalizing dirty work

Since E. C. Hughes[20] considered the rationalizations adopted by people who undertake the dirty work of their societies, namely work seen as morally or physically repellent, it has been clear that people frequently conceptualize their involvement in dirty work in ways that help foster or maintain self-esteem. Even though Hughes did not really locate these rationalizations sociologically, that is he did not consider how they related to how people are simultaneously positioned in class, gender, 'race' or other social hierarchies, we should recognize them as aspects of the social relations of dirt. The materiality of dirt lies not simply in its physical manifestations, smells or stickiness, but as importantly in its embeddedness in paid work and social hierarchies. Because dirt is created and cleaned up within social relations its social character goes much beyond its existence as a symbolic representation of social relations of the kind that interested Douglas.

For reasons of space I identify constructions of dirty work that are strongly related to gender, leaving aside for the present their articulation with other social divisions. For example, Dant and Bowles's[21] car repair workers' outlook – their rational explanation of the dirtiness of car repair work (due to the design of cars) and their pragmatic attitude to cleaning up – is surely best seen as a particularly masculine construction, not necessarily a natural one. Dirt created by or in the process of manly work is perceived to be cleaner than, for instance, bodily fluids, which are associated with the feminine. Moreover, one wonders whether car repair workers insist on maintaining their strikingly pragmatic attitude to cleaning up partly because of the absence of women workers in the body repair shop. Because there are no women working in the repair shops onto whom responsibility for dirt can be projected, exclusion of any hint of the potentially polluting, degrading connotations of (cleaning up) dirt may be essential to the maintenance of the shop's egalitarian, all male, comradely ethos.

An even clearer account of the masculinization of dirty work comes from Tony Horowitz's Pulitzer Prize-winning New York newspaper article about the working conditions and attitudes of waste handlers in the recycling trade.[22] According to Horowitz, worker turnover in some materials recovery facilities (MuRFs) reaches 100 per cent annually, but those workers who remain shrug off the health risks, having 'made their peace' with the stigma of 'working in garbage'. Interviewed while flies swarm on his face and hands as he sifts raw trash on a hot September day, Travis Foley remembers his first day at work at a MuRF in Iowa: 'I threw up three times. Didn't stop working, though, I just stepped back and vomited in the nearest can.' The place of this comment as part of a discourse concerning male workers' ability to sustain dirty work becomes even clearer when the worker adds that 'there's stuff here that would make even Superman sick.' Another worker conceptualizes his dirty work as dollars in the pocket, clearly rationalizing the work in terms of his role as male family breadwinner. Maurice Davis says that 'It used to bother me that I'd get home and my kids would say, "Daddy, you stink"... Now I tell them, "Yeah, but you never say that on Fridays when I come home with a pocket full of cash."' We might take this also as an example of what Grosz sees as men's tendency to deal with their anxieties about bodily fluids by converting them imaginatively into solids (for instance semen = child) that do not run or seep.[23] In any case such rationalizations help these workers accommodate and even disclaim the objective health hazards presented by the work, along with its low status.

Dealing with bodily hygiene is another kind of work in which dirtiness provokes disgust, but one strongly associated with women rather than men. Normally, adults do this work for themselves, but there are significant exceptions, especially people, often ageing or disabled, who require nursing or personal assistance. The dirtiness of body work, with its 'unsavoury secretions, smells and signs of bodily maturation', is insufficiently dealt with in most current research on the body.[24] Such work is highly racialized as well as gendered, marking the bodies of those who undertake the work as well as stigmatizing the dependence of those who are cared for.[25]

According to Lise Widding Isaksen, both formal and informal intimate care of the elderly, whose bodies are imagined as open and unlimited (namely unbounded), is almost entirely the responsibility of women, even though men may be involved in emotional and other practical forms of support. The 'unwritten rule saying that the more intimate the work is, the less likely it is that men are doing it' rests in part on normative associations between genders, bodies, spatial regulations – and dirt; old age in particular is perceived as dirty, representing not only a 'piling up of undischarged remnants of a lifetime of eating and drinking',[26] but also contaminated by its proximity to death (see Selket, Chapter 4 in this volume).

Although, according to Widding Isaksen, masculine dignity demands that men be protected from the leaky ageing body, according to Cinzia Solari some men with little choice in the labour market may be obliged, along with women, to accept paid care work as an occupation.[27] Their ways of maintaining self-esteem in the face of their involvement in dirty work do not simply reflect masculine (or feminine) identities but feed back into their reconstruction. Solari's research concerned recent migrants from Russia working as care workers in the USA, men as well as women. Their involvement in care work represents downward social mobility in occupational terms. She says that workers' self-concepts vary, as between the Russian Orthodox migrants, who negotiate their role through a discourse of saintly, personalized caring, and the Jewish migrants, who insist on distancing themselves from the clients' emotional concerns as a mark of the 'professional' status of carers. The workers' relationships with those they cared for were much influenced by the ways they rationalized their relation to dirt through the adoption of different strategic identities.

Although we usually think about how the performance of dirty work affects the identities (and stigmatizes the bodies) of the workers concerned, it is important to remember that the employers' identities are also affected. For instance, in her examination of the American paid domestic cleaning industry, Ehrenreich argues that the increasing use of paid cleaners in the home legitimizes social hierarchy, since it is usually only done under the assumption that the employers have 'something better' to do with their time, as do their children, who a generation ago would have helped with the chores. She adds that to 'be cleaned up after' is to achieve 'a certain magical weightlessness and immateriality',[28] namely recognizing that the relation of the worker to dirt and the body in turn enables the employers to enjoy a different one.

Campaigns by organizations representing disabled people have put a lot of emphasis on how care and its conceptualization affect their identities. Many argue that they can best retain their independence if paid personal assistants, rather than family members caring on an unpaid basis, meet their needs, and if the work is construed as a purely instrumental activity rather than as a form of emotional labour.[29] This strategy is rightly concerned about the fact that being 'cared for' is experienced as disempowering, but it says little about the implications of different conceptions of the work, and the work relations involved, for the personal assistant's social visibility and social esteem. Lynn May Rivas suggests that although good quality care allows the disabled person to feel that 'I am doing this', a construction that may reflect the (masculine) ideals of self-reliance privileged in American culture, it also relies on and may contribute to the social invisibility of the care worker.[30]

Surely if the shift to thinking about disabled people as employers, rather than as the recipients of 'care', is not accompanied by social recognition of the personal assistant, and the worth and dignity of their work, then we are just replacing one injustice with another. Moreover, recognition and respect for personal assistants that is not accompanied by (much) higher pay is toothless. Whatever else might be debatable, the bottom line should be that 'dirty' work should always be well-paid work.

Prostitution and/as dirty work

Another area in which the meaning of dirt and dirty work is to the fore is in feminist controversies over the legitimacy of sex work and the social position of prostitutes. In the public imagination nothing is as dirty as the work of the prostitute and the prostitute herself, who is figured as the dregs of society and 'regarded as a kind of sponge or conduit of other's men's "dirt"'.[31]

There are real contradictions when disgust-provoking rhetoric creeps into progressive social critique. As Martha Nussbaum argues, the emotiveness of disgust is deployed most often by conservatives, for instance against same-sex civil partnerships, on the grounds that same-sex sexual activity is disgusting and unnatural. She suggests that, like erotic love, disgust is too unreliable and idiosyncratic an emotion to adopt as a guide to just law.[32]

The use of graphic imagery of disgusting acts, especially those involving the penetrability and leakiness of the body celebrated by French feminists, is particularly evident in the writings of feminists seeking to make tangible the wrongs of prostitution. Take for example this observer's account: 'This was the first occasion that the reality of what being a prostitute entails had been made starkly apparent – alone, on your knees, with a client's penis in your mouth. It is difficult to say why, but it was incredibly shocking to see that reality.'[33] Sheila Jeffreys's other examples convey the oppression suffered by what she terms 'prostituted women' through depictions of feelings of uncleanliness, citing for instance the woman who has come to feel 'as if she is moving through life inside a boil or clothed head to toe in a rash'.[34] Another woman says that she uses tampons all the time, even when she is not menstruating, and that 'because I'm afraid of stinking I never sit too close to people, I wash my ears ten times a day because I'm afraid guck is running out of them.'[35] Kelly Holsopple continues this strain in depicting the work of lap dancers, who must deal with customers and staff who 'smell so sour, they breathe very heavy and kind of wheeze when women are near'.[36] Although such images of the wounded, wronged body of the prostitute see the prostitute as a pristine body tarnished by working in the sex trade, rather than as inherently dirty, they cannot help but cement wider associations between prostitutes and moral and physical contamination.

However, it is not clear that commentators who challenge this discourse take sufficient account of the underlying social relations within which most prostitution takes place, and the consequent dangers to which sex workers are exposed. For instance, Wendy Chapkis, who defends prostitution as a legitimate choice, thinks feminist attacks on sex work are guided mainly by what she terms the 'ick factor'.[37] Postmodernists hint that the prostitute body can be seen as a challenge to the closed, 'proper' body of masculinist thought, its openness a welcome transgression of the social order.[38] Some such commentators may suggest that the problem of prostitution can be resolved at the discursive level, by resignifying its meaning.[39]

Is any use of graphic imagery ruled out on the grounds that it may perpetuate the association between prostitution and dirtiness? Julia O'Connell Davidson's account of the relation between prostitution, power and freedom is as graphic as anything produced by radical feminists. She suggests that the social transaction that defines prostitution gives the user the (temporary) right to 'command the prostitute to make bodily orifices available to him, to smile, dance or dress up for him, to whip, spank, massage or masturbate him, to submit to being urinated upon, shackled or beaten by him, or otherwise submit to his wishes and desires'.[40]

For O'Connell Davidson the use of such imagery seems to stem not so much from repugnance at the 'ickiness' of particular sexual acts but anger at the extent to which the prostitute is subjected to the will of the prostitute user. The power relations of prostitution compel prostitutes to relinquish control over their bodily boundaries, dignity and personal safety, a control that is constructed as a cornerstone of individual sovereignty, while the clients use prostitutes as a way of evading 'the complex web of rules, meanings, obligations and conventions which govern noncommercial sexuality'.[41] The focus is on the incommensurability of the transaction.

In principle, O'Connell Davidson's analysis is not confined to prostitution, but applies to other kinds of work that depend on the misrecognition of the Other. It makes it possible to consider similarities between sex work and paid domestic labour, for instance, wherein some employers may also seek 'a person who is not a person' to do work they consider too dirty or humiliating to do themselves,[42] that is where the connections between dirt, dirty work and power are also central to the work relationship. It goes along with her and others' research on the factors that affect sex workers' differential capacity to adopt strategies to protect themselves and to define access to their bodies, or to maintain their self-esteem in the face of stigma.[43]

Conclusions

Dant and Bowles say that Douglas's anthropological views have overly influenced recent explorations of dirt in the context of the sociology of work (they cite, for example, Anderson's *Doing the Dirty Work*).[44] But, while such writers may cite Douglas, my brief discussion of the gendering of 'dirty work' would suggest that Anderson's or Solari's understanding of the relation between dirt and the social order is actually different from Douglas's, as in their writing on care work and other forms of paid domestic labour they see 'dirt' as constructed in relation to, and within, social relations, and not simply as representing them symbolically. The emphasis is on gender as a social relation rather than sexual difference.

The example of debate on heterosexual prostitution is much more complicated, since 'dirtiness' and disgust are invoked in many different ways. I suggest that while rejecting radical feminist views that seem to rest on the presumed purity of the female body, which is seen as defiled by involvement in commercial sex, we also need to question accounts that presume that the problem of prostitution will be resolved by rejecting discursive constructions of commercial sex as dirty or sordid. More preferable is O'Connell Davidson's account, which is guided by anger at the unequal power relations that underwrite sex work (including class and 'race', as well as gender), rather than disgust at the nature of commercial sexual activities, and which relates 'dirtiness' to issues of dignity and power, rather than purity and contamination. This does not exclude consideration of, and may even highlight, sex workers' risks of exposure to disease or violence and the variables that influence their ability to deploy strategies to resist them.

As Sayer argues, I think we should be wary of setting up a binary between poststructuralism and the sociological endeavour, since sociologists have much to learn from some versions of social constructionism about the role of language in the social world we study. We might want to reject Douglas's claim that 'dirt is essentially disorder', or that there is 'no such thing as absolute dirt: it exists in the eye of the beholder',[45] but we should not throw the baby out with the (dirty) bath water either. This is not just (or even primarily) a matter of bringing the tactile, physical qualities of 'dirt' back into the picture, as Dant and Bowles suggest. What is needed is theory and research that acknowledge that as social phenomena 'dirtiness' and 'cleanliness' are real social objects and do not exist only within discourse. In particular, we need to consider 'dirt' from the point of view of those whose work involves dealing with it.

Chapter 2

Domestic Workers and Pollution in Brazil

LIVIA BARBOSA

Brazilian middle-class families, like those in other South American countries, still enjoy the possibility of help with housework on a regular basis. This help comes predominantly in the form of live-in maids (*empregada que dorme*) or daily helpers (*diaristas* and *faxineiras*) who work once or twice a week or even every weekday in one house or in several different houses.[1]

Different and complex types of interpersonal relationships between employers and maids accompany these working and living arrangements. These vary enormously, ranging from very paternalistic to more professional ones when the maid enjoys the same legal and labour rights as any other worker.[2]

However, this variation in interpersonal relationships between employers and maids does not have a counterpart when we examine the material conditions of the maids' living quarters in the houses of their employers. Here we come across a high degree of homogeneity and material conditions can be characterized as very poor in most dwellings.

In this chapter I explore the physical and material conditions of domestic workers through the design, classification and use of space within Brazilian middle-class homes. The focus of attention is on the area purposely designed for domestic workers to sleep in and to use while at work. This area is clearly separated from the rest of the employer's house.

Existing discussions of the status of paid domestic workers and household tasks in Brazil have emphasized the racial, class and gender hierarchies that partially organize and govern relationships between domestic workers and their employers, as well as their status within the social structure of Brazilian society.[3] Another line of argument emphasizes the historically low social status attributed to domestic labour that affects whoever does it, whether housewife or maid. Although these variables play an important role in establishing the tone of relationships and in reproducing the low social status of domestic workers, I would argue that they are not sufficient to explain the physical separation of domestic workers within Brazilian homes and in the communal areas of condominiums. I argue that the idea of pollution in systems of classification in Brazil – organizing spaces, tasks, utensils and people in everyday life – is one of the key ingredients for explaining the physical separation and material conditions of the living quarters of domestic workers in Brazilian society.[4]

Dirt, pollution and physical spaces

The literature concerning dirt, cleanliness and pollution is vast and has increased in recent years. Traditional themes such as the symbolic significance of cleaning and personal toilet[5] and their relation with religion[6] now stand side by side with studies about the introduction of new technologies and industrial products for cleaning and how these affect household tasks, their social meanings and our patterns of hygiene.[7] Works about the construction of a 'culture' of de- and re-odorization in everyday modern life vie for our attention with others that emphasize the role and impact of taken-for-granted Western cultural habits of cleaning and personal hygiene on environmental sustainability.[8] Studies of the meaning of dirt, cleanliness and pollution over time and space have also taken new directions. Vigarello's[9] and Elias's[10] approaches, focused on the different cultural and historical conceptions of the body and cleanliness and the process that ended up privatizing these habits, have been complemented by the history of domestic appliances, scientific knowledge and technology and their silent relation to changes inside the house, in housework tasks and gender roles.[11] The feminist literature has also been active in contributing to an understanding of the role of cleanliness in the context of household tasks and their respective values from historical and sociological points of view.[12]

However, when we try to merge notions of cleanliness, dirt and pollution with spaces and the people who circulate within them, the literature is meagre, particularly when it is related to housework and domestic workers. Maybe the reason, as Cox suggests, comes from the idea that although dirt is both omnipresent and largely absent, it is not explicitly assumed as an important element of domestic labour, an aspect that sets it apart from other jobs. As the same author emphasizes, 'We seldom think about dirt and cleanliness as being an aspect of social status in modern societies.'[13]

Here I want to pursue the relationship between domestic workers and the idea of dirt, cleanliness and pollution in the context of the physical space of Brazilian homes from an anthropological point of view. Accordingly, I start with the 'structural' anthropological tradition of establishing homologies between symbolic values and physical/social spaces, as done by authors like Pierre Bourdieu,[14] Freyre[15] and Da Matta.[16] I shall follow this with an exploration of the relationship between these spaces and notions of cleanliness, dirt and pollution and with the categorization of domestic workers inside middle-class homes. Such notions restrict their behaviour while attributing and establishing clear physical separation between domestic workers and the rest of the house.

The first Brazilian author to explore the relationship between masters and servants was Gilberto Freyre in his two famous books *Masters and Slaves* and *The Mansions and the Shanties*. In both works Freyre described the living quarters of the master and his slaves in colonial Brazil and the pattern of relationships that developed between the two during colonial times and the early urbanization process of Brazil in the seventeenth and eighteenth centuries. Da Matta has worked along similar lines, focusing on the distribution of values of modernity within different spaces in Brazilian society and metaphorically expressed in the symbolic opposition between street and house; he has also shown how Brazilians manipulated these values in different spaces and contexts.

However, most social science literature ignores the relationship between employers and domestic servants in contemporary Brazil, or subsumes it as part of working-class, race or gender studies, displacing its specificity to other areas. None of this literature has explored the complex and diverse relationships between domestic workers and employers inside the home from the anthropological perspective used here.

The data employed in this chapter come from field work carried out in 2002 and 2004, based on a sample of 20 middle-income households in Recife (PE) and Fortaleza (CE) in the northeast, and in Rio de Janeiro (RJ) and São Paulo (SP), the urban centres of the southeast. This research covered matters of personal hygiene, laundering and house cleaning practices, notions of dirt, order, disgust and tidiness, as well as patterns of consumption of personal and cleaning products by both housewives and domestic workers. The field work included in-depth interviews, the observation of everyday household cleaning routines and a close inspection of closets, kitchen cabinets, laundry baskets and backyards.

The symbolic geography and cartography of the interior of Brazilian homes

Brazilian domestic architecture obeys the same general cultural patterns as Western houses as regards the disposition and definition of the rooms:[17] a living room for receiving people, dining room for eating, bedrooms for sleeping, kitchen for cooking and bathroom for personal hygiene. The activities are fixed and members of the household circulate through each room according to the time of day and the activity being performed.

It is this general cultural plan that lies behind all Brazilian homes, regardless of income or taste. Of course, this ideal plan varies according to income and the degree of individualistic ideology prevailing within the family, and as a consequence we find huge contrasts in the external physical appearance, internal material conditions, the distribution of rooms among people, and the size of homes among the different social segments of Brazilian society.

This general plan is customized in Brazil according to certain symbolic values that attribute different meanings and status to rooms and activities. Three pairs of symbolic oppositions appear to organize space inside Brazilian homes. The first is the distinction between street and house that objectifies the difference between the values that pervade everyday family life and those that operate within the public sphere.[18] The second is the distinction between 'masters' and 'servants' that is physically represented in all houses from those of the middle income up, but is also present in the houses of people in lower income groups. The third symbolic opposition is between the social and the service areas of the house. These three pairs of dualisms are important for understanding the symbolic geography of Brazilian homes. They are also key ingredients in comprehending the patterns and the logic of cleaning and its evaluation, the criteria of dirt and pollution that prevail in each room and how these criteria function in establishing boundaries, restricting behaviour and categorizing people.

Domestic workers in Brazilian homes

The layout of Brazilian houses and apartments reveals the permanence of the distinction between employers and domestic workers. This can be perceived in the distinction that is always made between the 'social' areas of the home – those used by the employing family and where visitors can be received – and the service areas where domestic workers live and work.

The service area, located in the back of the house, was the most secluded part of a Brazilian home and always hidden from the eyes of visitors and strangers. It was the place of the servants, the space of low-status activities like cooking, laundering and cleaning and, until recently, it was given no aesthetic consideration. However, in the last few years all that has changed, particularly with regards to the kitchen, part of which moved from its hiding place at the back of the house to emerge brand new and exposed to visitors' eyes. The kitchen has changed because of new meanings given to cooking and gastronomy, and through a general process of aesthetization undergone by everyday life within Western society.[19] The changes to the kitchen have also extended to the utility area in terms of 'modernization' and aestheticization.[20]

The last part of the service area of the house is the maid's living quarters. This is the area that has undergone no qualitative or aesthetic change, except for the use of new construction materials that usually emphasize the pragmatic aspects of cleaning, such as tiles on the bedroom floor instead of wood parquet blocks. The servants' living quarters are still the most secluded part of a Brazilian house. They are always kept away from the eyes of visitors and, although other members of the family will very seldom go to them, they are, from a certain perspective, public space, since no one who lives in the house has to ask permission to enter.

The maid's room is usually very small, sometimes without any kind of window or proper ventilation and light. Servants often have to share this small space with other objects that have no place within the house or with things that still do not have their final destiny sealed. So, they might have to share their living space with vacuum cleaners, suitcases, old raincoats, boxes and pets. Their rooms are a mixture of storeroom and bedroom. This conjugation of people, animals and objects means that their rooms are their master's property and that the maids only sleep there. It is their space of intimacy, but not of privacy. The maids have no power to use the space as would best fit their taste or comfort.

The servant's bathroom conditions are not very different from those in the bedroom. Usually the bathroom has a toilet, shower and sometimes a wash basin. In the absence of the latter (which is common), the maid has to wash her face and hands and brush her teeth in the sink located in the utility area, one of the most polluted and unclean spaces in the entire Brazilian house. The filth of the sink stems from all the impure activities that take place there. It is there where the floor mop is washed, where buckets of dirty water from cleaning the house are emptied, where the garbage can is washed on the days when the kitchen receives a good scrubbing, and where the dirt from cleaning utensils is removed every day. Even if it is white and shining bright, its everyday contact with filth makes it a permanently polluted artefact.[21]

Although most employers, when asked, would agree that these are poor living conditions that would seem inhuman for their own use, very few have plans to change them by redecorating the house. Changing the living conditions of maids is a low priority. One interviewee (a 50-year-old woman in Rio de Janeiro) commented: 'Now my husband and I are planning to renovate the entire kitchen and the service area. We want to make them more modern, change the floors, walls and the cabinets. ... No I have not thought about reforming the servants' living quarters.'

Maids also have a clear idea of the poor material conditions of their living quarters compared with the rest of the house, although some say that they are much better than in their own houses in the slums, since they are not exposed to sewage or any other kind of dirt. 'If we compare it to the rest of the apartment, it is bad, but compared with a lot of places in the slums, it is not that bad' (woman, 35 years old, Rio de Janeiro).

This, however, does not necessarily mean that they prefer their living quarters in their employer's home. To own a house, in whatever condition, is to be protected 'from life' and humiliation. There is a crucial difference between someone who is poor and someone who has 'a roof over my head that is mine'. Besides being located at the far end of the service area several other physical and symbolic boundaries and limitations restrict servants' movements inside Brazilian homes. For example, the maid's clothes are rarely washed with those of the other people in the house, and in some families maids are not even allowed to wash their clothes in the washing machine. The same is true of crockery, glasses and cutlery, for many employers keep specific sets just for the domestic workers.

This clear material and physical separation does not mean that maids are considered intrinsically dirty. On the contrary, to be personally clean and to maintain high standards of hygiene during the performance of household tasks are important criteria for hiring and keeping a person as a domestic servant. The opposite is also true. To be dirty, personally or at work, is a criterion for firing a maid. There is also no correlation between real dirt and the physical and material conditions of the living quarters of domestic workers. In fact, it is expected that they should be as clean as the rest of the house. So this separation does not have to do with the presence or absence of dirt itself, but with the idea of pollution.

Domestic workers and communal areas

This attitude of avoiding mixing what belongs to the servants with what belongs to other people in the house is extended and made public in the case of the communal areas of apartment buildings; the existence of a specific 'service entrance' and 'service elevators' are other good examples of this. Officially, both should be used for cargo, commercial deliveries, people with pets and people sweating from physical exercise. However, in everyday life, both the service entrance and elevator are used by all maids working or living in the apartment buildings, as well as cargo and commercial deliveries. Owners with their pets and/or smelling of sweat from physical exercise use the social areas of the building without being challenged by the other owners, even when they consider such behaviour improper or disgusting. Cases of maids being withdrawn from social elevators are very common and, as far as I know, not a single one has had any legal consequence. The same clear physical division between masters and servants applies to the leisure areas of apartment buildings. Servants are forbidden to use the swimming pools, sports areas or the keep-fit room. At most, they can sit on the benches outside the common areas.

Pursuing pollution

It was and still is difficult to talk to people about the physical separation and the material conditions of their maids' living quarters. This is a taboo subject. To avoid direct confrontation, which could sound like an inquisition to people who were amiably receiving me in their homes, I adopted a research methodology of posing problems and asking for their reactions. The first was how 'they' would react if they found their maids taking a shower in their private bathroom. The second was why they would allow a stranger (a visitor or a guest) to use their private bathroom, yet the same situation would upset them if it concerned their maids. And the third question was about inviting 'new friends' to their houses or swimming pools for entertainment, arguing that they would be total strangers in terms of hygiene habits. In the face of these questions/problems, some of the interviewees rose to a crescendo of irritability or irony against me. What lay behind their behaviour was the correct idea that my credentials to enquire about such practices were limited when I probably behaved the same way in my own house. However, after some stressful moments, people recognized that there was more to their attitude and to Brazilian attitudes in general towards the physical separation and material conditions of the living quarters of domestic servants, than we usually want to admit or understand.

There were several different lines of arguments offered by interviewees to explain why they kept these strict separations. Usually these arguments were a mixture of economic considerations, together with hygiene, contamination, 'civilization' and private property.

- 'I want to have my intimacy protected. I do not want the maids to see me and my family at ease in the swimming pool, sharing my intimacy.'
- 'They wouldn't feel comfortable since they wouldn't know how to behave.'
- 'We do not know who they are, their habits and so on.'
- 'We can't be sure if they have some kind of sickness, some kind of skin disease.'

When I asked employers why they would not wash their clothes in the washing machine together with their maid's clothes, which would save electricity, water and soap, those keener on economic reasons reacted with perplexity. And even more so when I pointed out to them that they probably would not separate a guest's or visitor's clothes so rigidly, although I was sure that they would not know their hygiene habits either, or whom they deal or live with. The same was true of crockery, glasses, knives and forks. Although they also would not know the habits and acquaintances of their guests and visitors, they would give them their best.

Some of these arguments would also apply to other categories of people, such as total strangers about whom they knew nothing at all. However, it is difficult to justify any of them as they are all easily forgotten when the maids share the intimacy of everyday family life, washing, cleaning and cooking for the whole family. Besides, many domestic workers live and work in a single house for many years, which allows for a great deal of mutual knowledge about their personal habits and families to develop.

It is important to note the independence of the explanations given for the physical division and material conditions of the living quarters of the maids and the size of the house or apartment, the income, the intellectual capital and the political ideology of the family.

Another important point to mention is the feeling of disgust that some maids expressed about certain of their employers' habits. Women were the main targets of the domestic servants in terms of their personal hygiene and also some of their cooking or cleaning practices. The maids were also very clear about their own standards of cleanliness in their homes, which matched the ideal ones required for them in their performance of household tasks at work. They were also very critical of other maids' cleaning standards and per-formance at work. However, some would agree that it was better for things to be separated since they would not feel at ease if they had to participate intimately in the family's life. This does not mean that the domestic servants in Brazil do not feel humiliated or that they are not conscious of the distance between them and the rest of the household. A good employer is a con-siderate one who treats them equally. What appears to be important is not the physical separation inside the house, but the interpersonal treatment received from employers, including their understanding of personal dif-ficulties and hardships, and the granting of all legal and labour rights. What is central here is the possibility that pollution criteria are so ingrained in Brazilian life that they have became a structural aspect of life for all social groups.

Final remarks

In two previous works I have argued that Brazilian practices of washing clothes, house cleaning and personal hygiene revolve around the idea of pollution in opposition to a practical, economic or 'efficient' criteria that prevailed predominantly in the USA and UK. This criterion of pollution could be seen in the innumerable classificatory categories of clothes that can and cannot be washed together, in the storage of cleaning utensils, in personal hygiene practices and in many other aspects of daily life, as well as in symbolic representations of what is and what is not disgusting.

The theoretical point made at that time was that the idea of pollution in modern society was alive and well. This point was in contrast to much of the literature that considers pollution mainly in relation to traditional societies, religion or the working classes in modern societies. Here I believe that I have demonstrated that pollution is not only alive and well and that, at least in Brazil, pollution is a criterion that concurs with others in organizing the social life of our society in certain spaces and contexts, a criterion that is used regardless of political ideology and level of education.[22]

What supports this criterion of pollution, particularly in the context of the relationship between employers and domestic workers are two different notions. First, there is a work ethic that historically devalues all manual and freelance work and values the social origin and stability of a person's income more than the individual capacity to earn a living. Second, there is an idea of pollution that combines feelings related to social contamination and fear of invasion of intimacy of one's own group that is not necessarily linked to dirt. Brazilian social hierarchy is then characterized by a combination of the physical proximity of people of different social origins at the same time as existential distance.

This leads to a possible different answer to the problem proposed by Douglas,[23] when she compared Indian and Western societies and asked which system of stratification is the more ruthless in exploiting human beings – one based on wealth and authority or one based on a system of purity rules? The answer is that they are not mutually exclusive. The tragic fact is that they can combine, as in the Brazilian case, to make the lives of the people at the base of social hierarchies even harder than they would otherwise be.

Chapter 3

The Visible and the Invisible: (De)regulation in Contemporary Cleaning Practices

LYDIA MARTENS

In her postscript to *Chasing Dirt*, Suellen Hoy asks: 'Are we as clean as we used to be? Probably not. At least, that's my quick and dirty answer to the one question I am most frequently asked.'[1] She then adds substance to her argument by alluding to some well-rehearsed characteristics of late modern households and their organization: more women are going out to work; few husbands help out at home; women refuse to be 'super moms' and learn to live with declining standards of cleanliness in their households while turning to commercial alternatives instead of utilizing old-fashioned elbow grease; and women realize that little satisfaction and status is to be derived from housework.[2] This passage exemplifies a trend in contemporary scholarship and popular commentary on domestic life and this is that the resonance of negative moralizations about everything domestic is accompanied by a general lack of understanding about domestic practices and practice cultures. Claims that all is not well in domestic life are accompanied by an acknowledgment that the organization of mundane practices in households, like domestic cleaning, has not inspired much scholarly curiosity.[3]

In this chapter I address this conundrum by offering an analysis of the organization of domestic cleaning and the ways in which contemporary practitioners talk about their practices. I am particularly interested in examining the idea that such practices have become deregulated. The notion of '(de)regulation' derives from the work of Émile Durkheim and has been utilized by social theorists commenting on the transformations that are said to have accompanied the rise to late modern society.[4] It implies that contemporary practitioners are guided less by traditional norms and values and that practices have consequently become more volitional – open to be 'filled in' by 'the individual'. Arguments that important social transformations are taking place frequently come with a note of criticism that the proclaimed changes are for the worse. There are intimations that because contemporary cleaning practices are deregulated, they lack the necessary routine and skill to make 'a good job of it'.

In examining claims of domestic deregulation, I draw on recently completed ethnographic research on cleaning and ordering practices in the kitchens of 12 households, diverse in terms of their life cycle stage and composition (see Table 3.1 for further details). Our research involved households in a variety of visual data generation methods, including CCTV recording, and qualitative interviewing to investigate sentiments around and representations of kitchen cleanliness.[5] My argument develops in two stages. I start by considering the notion of cleaning routines, as it was in relation to this concept that our practitioners voiced their awareness of, and response to a traditional understanding of domestic cleaning, which I unearth by interweaving the existing academic literature on the modern history of cleanliness with discourses on cleanliness found in the *Good Housekeeping* magazine in the early postwar years. In the second part, I argue that this traditional understanding is accompanied by another understanding for organizing domestic cleaning, and this is a method that relies on the visual monitoring of domestic material culture. I will discuss the consequences of a move towards such aesthetic concerns for claims about the (de)regulation of cleaning practices and the place of invisible dirt, like germs, in the hierarchy of cleaning priorities.

Routine and regularity in cleaning practices

The participants in our study discussed a series of kitchen related practices with us that included dish washing, cleaning the kitchen infrastructure and ordering its material culture, food related practices (including eating), shopping and other more miscellaneous practices. Participants talked about what they cleaned in the kitchen, what their priorities were and also about when and how cleaning activities were done. Part of the reason for generating ethnographic material through CCTV footage was our interest in routines in the kitchen. In the Findley household, doing the dishes, cleaning kitchen surfaces and the table, dusting the Rayburn,[6] emptying and cleaning the bin, and dealing with dirty and clean clothes were seen as priority tasks, some of

Table 3.1 Socio-demographic characteristics of participating households

Household name pseudonyms	First name pseudonyms	Priority HH?	Visual material	Life cycle stage
Allison	Sarah and Richard	Yes	CCTV, video tour & kitchen plan	Older couple
Potts	Catherine and Kevin	No	Video tour	Older couple
Lyle	Pamela and Bernard	No	Video tour	Older couple
Findley	Mandy and Sam	Yes	CCTV, video diary & photographs & kitchen plan	Couple with teenage children
Cooper	Fran and Marc	No	Kitchen plan	Couple with teenage children
Roberts	Judith and Alexander	Yes	Video diaries, video tour, photographs & kitchen plan	Couple with young children
Andrews	Janice and Simon	No	Kitchen plan	Couple with young children
Crammond	Gemma and Billy	No	Kitchen plan	Couple with young children
Stevens	Josie and Martin	Yes	CCTV, video tour & photographs	Couple with baby
Wise	Karen and Andy	Yes	CCTV & video trail	Couple only
Lowe	Maria and Robert	Yes	Video diary, video tour & kitchen plan	Couple only
Howard	Jenny	No	None	Single person

Household composition	Age of adults	Pets?	Employment
2 resident adults	60s	Dog	Sarah – housewife Richard – retired farmer
2 resident adults – grown up children living in own HHs	50s	Dog	Catherine – housewife Kevin – long term sick leave
2 resident adults	50s	No	Pamela – housewife (formally a teacher) Bernard – teacher
2 resident adults and teenage children, one child at college, one in own HH	40s	Cat, rabbits and chicken	Mandy – teacher (formally a housewife) Sam – health care worker
2 resident adults and teenage children	40s	Cats	Fran – call centre worker Marc – publishing
2 resident adults and young children	40s	Dog	Judith – housewife Alexander – police officer
2 resident adults and one young child	30s	No	Janice & Simon – social workers
2 resident adults and one young child	20s	No	Gemma – administrator (pt) Billy – mobile phone retailer
2 resident adults, one young child and a baby	30s	No	Josie – food production (pt) Martin – glass retailing manager
resident adults	20s	Cat, dog, guinea pig and fish	Karen – local authority Andy – unemployed
resident adults	20s	No	Maria – archivist Robert – IT
resident adult	30s	Cats	Jenny – researcher

which were done several times each day. These were contrasted with other cleaning tasks that were deemed important, but that would be done less frequently, like vacuum and wet cleaning the tiled floor, washing the kitchen doors, cupboards, walls and ceiling (because the Rayburn deposited a continuous layer of dust on everything) and cleaning the kitchen window. Additional daily tasks that are clearly not so much part of the discursive consciousness can be witnessed in the CCTV footage. These included setting and clearing the table, organizing the dishes waiting to be cleaned, and a variety of ordering practices. The CCTV video footage also illustrated *how* 'regular' tasks, like dish washing, ordering and wiping surfaces, get done.

But 'routine' was also a topic of conversation during interviews. The Findleys argued for instance that routines were prominently present in their kitchen and that this was not regarded as a problem. Quite the contrary! Routines were positively welcomed and adhered to, and this seemed to provide a sense of trust in their own practices. Anticipating the CCTV's presence in their kitchen, Mandy commented: 'We are always saying that, "oh we are so disorganized, we ought to have more routine," but you will probably find that we have got loads [laughs].' In contrast to the Findleys, some of our domestic practitioners asserted that they did not have a cleaning routine, providing early support for the notion that cleaning has become deregulated in at least some contemporary households. Sarah Allison provided the strongest denial of adherence to any sort of cleaning routine. This presented us with a conundrum, as CCTV footage of her kitchen activities clearly indicated the presence of routines. What exactly was she telling us with her denial?

To answer this question, we need to ask how cleaning has traditionally been understood and how it was 'regulated'. If we focus on cleaning as an aspect of domestic care taking, it could be argued that domestic cleanliness was premised on three main cultural priorities; countering germs, attaining the right domestic appearance, and concerns around efficiency and ease of cleaning. As Tomes pointed out, with the growing awareness that germs passed between human beings and spread disease 'by seemingly innocuous behaviours such as coughing, sneezing and spitting, sharing common drinking cups, or failing to wash hands before eating, the end of the nineteenth century saw the breakthrough of the germ theory of disease'.[7] Through a process of domestication, germ consciousness generated major shifts in thinking about disease, its prevention and cleanliness, leading to new and routine cleaning practices such as washing hands and bodies with water and soap; cleaning toilets, sinks and work surfaces with water and disinfectants; and killing flies that happened to find themselves in the house.

The establishment of home economics, the decline in domestic servants and the advent of advice manuals for middle-class women doing their own home-making for the first time historically all followed the discovery of germs. During the interwar years, home economists, female scientists, women's magazines and women's interest groups debated the efficiency of domestic work.[8] These interest groups shared a common vision about the role and purpose of women in the domestic sphere and together they significantly raised the profile of women's domestic role. Efficiency thinking was crucially about perfecting the housewifely role and attaining higher standards of cleanliness in conditions where making a home look and smell good were not what they are today. As discussed in Martens and Scott, discourses about efficiency and the ease with which cleaning could be accomplished continued into late modernity.[9]

By the middle of the twentieth century, we move into a period Hoy has called the 'culture of cleanliness', characterized by the high status of domesticity.[10] It would be inaccurate to argue that germs and efficiency thinking were the only stimulants to the development of such a culture, as germ awareness had declined in cultural prominence by this time and standards of cleanliness seemed symbolically increasingly associated with a domestic sphere that both looked and smelled good. This move may be seen as a consequence of the *invisibility* of germs. In a context where practitioners could not know that germs had been effectively eradicated, this priority merged and fused in complex ways with a specific domestic aesthetic of shiny, white, sparkling and pleasantly smelling interiors that was promoted in the pages of the *Good Housekeeping* magazine at this time. The priority of appearance in cleaning came forth from a complex mixture of cultural concerns that preceded germ consciousness.[11] In addition to the argument just made, it tapped into concerns about status and respectability, ideas about fashion and the trend towards modern décor as well as a desire to make the home a welcoming and cosy place to be.[12]

A reading of cultural texts, like *Good Housekeeping* magazine, during the period offers insight into the way these three cultural priorities were brought together in a discourse of 'best practice'. As discussed in Martens and Scott, the pedagogy of best practice proffered here was one that attained a high standard of cleanliness through the adoption of routine practices that were based in a specific temporal organization of cleaning work and that included the right types of household technology.[13] An example is the following quotation from a piece entitled 'A happy home for your family', which appeared in the April issue of 1961:[14]

Healthy homes go a long way towards being happy homes. First and foremost have a clean house, really clean. Get rid not only of obvious dirt but of the insidious underneath sort – and not just in great twice a year turnouts that leave your home disinfected like a hospital, but in *regular day to day chores that are second nature to you.* ... These days a routine of thorough cleanliness need not be hard work indeed there wouldn't be much joy in having a family bursting with good health at the expense of your own physical well-being. ... This high standard of hygiene is not something that has to be worked at too consciously ... it is simply a standard that can perfectly *easily be maintained in a daily routine*, that will not only keep your home fresh and gay, but a safe and sure place for the family to grow up in.

(emphasis added)

This type of discourse reappeared in other material in the magazine, like a piece called the 'Brides Homemakers Supplement' of March 1961, which advised newly weds to plan the cleaning work around daily, weekly and less frequent routines.

It is this cultural model of cleaning that was clearly still of relevance in the commentary of our participants. Such models of social organization and shared understandings have been identified as relevant in relation to other areas of domestic practice and Warde and Martens have explored how and when practitioners improvise on them and how that makes them feel.[15] In our study, Sarah Allison's denial that she adhered to any strict routine was evidence of her rejection of this cultural understanding of cleaning rather than evidence of the absence of routine in her everyday practices. Within the context of asserting that she did not like cleaning and housework, she described herself as follows:

I'm not the type of person who on April the 1st thinks 'Gosh I must spring clean'. ... I'm not fanatical about cleaning by any means. (Matt: Do you know anyone who is?) Oh yes. I've got a friend ... she only lives on her own ... and erm, she thinks that each week she has to pull all the furniture out, just in case she pops off, and somebody moves the furniture and says 'good grief, she hasn't Hoovered under here for a few weeks!' Well to me I'm sorry but that's not the way I work. I can't be governed by things like that you know! There is more to life than worrying about popping off.

It is clear, then, that when practitioners expressed aversion to having a 'cleaning routine', they were not necessarily communicating to us that their actual practices were deregulated, but instead voiced their awareness of 'expected norms' about how that work should be accomplished and delivered a judgement on them.

Contained within these judgements were statements on the level of practitioner satisfaction with their cleanliness practices. Sarah Allison for

40

instance seemed quite happy with her practices and could effectively reject what she believed to be the fanatical tendencies of cleaning.[16] Jenny Howard and the Findleys, whose cleaning was organized around some very specific temporal and organizational routines, also seemed quite happy. However, others perceived their routines to be unhappily disturbed or inadequate, and this seemed related to specific household circumstances, such as the presence of young children, moving home or being in the middle of major DIY jobs. In the Andrews household, for instance, the arrival of a baby had completely disrupted the organization of cleaning along rather strict temporal routines. In contrast to past practices, Simon described their current ones as 'as and when now', with Janice saying that she does what 'needs to be done'.

Janice: I think since we had Alice, I don't have the time to clean up as I used to. You know, where you used to think, 'Oh I have to do this because it's such and such, or I haven't done this.' I'm like, I do what needs to be done and at this minute in time, it doesn't look very much actually [laughs].

Simon: ... you used to have, I can't really say you washed on a Monday, but you used to have set days where you'd do certain tasks. And they've gone a bit out the window, [it's] as and when now. Erm. ... Rather than a particular day ... Or a particular day to wash or ...

Janice: Yeah it was like, ironing on a Sunday night. I don't do that now. I tried with the best will in the world, but it doesn't work very well with the little one at the moment.

Lydia: Does that worry you?

Janice: If you'd have asked me three years ago, I'd have said 'yes', it would. It really would've gotten me. ... I'm not saying it worries us, it just annoys us at the moment 'cos I think 'ee, I should be doing that'. But ... Alice is more important basically.

Contemporary households with young children indicated how they are subject to two opposing priorities – the cultural imperative to maintain a high standard of cleanliness and the importance of having time to spend with young children. This shows an interesting contemporary contradiction because, in advice given to families with young children, cleanliness is often stressed, especially through the recommendation to sterilize the equipment for the baby. In households with young toddlers, the salience of this was evident in discussions about germs. Yet, expectations of good contemporary parenting also demand that parents spend 'quality' time with their youngsters. In the Andrews and Stevens households, childcare was combined with paid work of both partners, and their discussions showed lucidly how these two priorities competed with each other.

41

Visual monitoring and the urge to clean

From our discussions it was apparent that a variety of situations and conditions triggered the urge to clean. The expected arrival of a stranger or a guest (including members of the research team) was for some a reason to clean. The presence of children and pets was a reason for more frequent cleaning and ordering, and indicated an implicit link to germ awareness and knowledge. For others, the decision to clean was associated with the arrival of specific times of the year, like Christmas and spring, suggesting that there is some adherence to traditional notions of *when* it is appropriate to clean. The degree to which the domestic environment had been shaped by the domestic practitioner and to what extent they regarded this as part of their 'self' formed a further dimension related to the urge to clean. Reflecting on her years of living in rented accommodation as a student, Karen Wise said there was a greater incentive to imbue the domestic material world with care and attention if there was evidence that it had been well looked after. The reverse was also true: where the domestic world is seen as alien or other or not well cared for, the incentive to clean was not as great, and at times led to replacement practices. In this study, an excellent example of this was the renewal of the kitchen shortly after moving into a new home, something that the Andrews, the Coopers and the Lowes had done:

> The kitchen when we first moved in was just not useable at all. It was very, very old; it was an old lady who used to live here. ... It was very old units, everything was dirty; the floor was horrible. Everything was horrible in the kitchen. There was no way we could cook in this kitchen. It was like having no kitchen. When we saw the state of the kitchen it was like 'no way! I am not going to cook anything in here!' We needed to er, to remove all the rubbish, to clean everything, to redo everything.
>
> (Robert Lowe)

These examples speak to the strength of personalization rituals and how emotions of disgust may be generated through the confrontation of different domestic cleanliness cultures, generating claims to difference in standards.[17]

One of the striking findings of our analysis of contemporary cultures of domestic cleanliness is how strongly cleaning is motivated by sensory stimuli. Corbin and Pink have outlined the historical and contemporary significance of smell in cultural constructions of the foul and the fragrant.[18] It is clear that smell and sight operate as powerful triggers in the creation of an urge to clean. How visible dirt stimulated cleaning was the subject of discussion around cleaning the kitchen floor. Sam Findley said that their tiled floor was wet cleaned once every three days, indicating that the household had adopted a temporal routine around floor cleaning in the kitchen. Even so, the exact timing of a cleaning episode was influenced by how it looked. In wet weather, it tended to 'get a bit muddy and it doesn't look very nice' and this would be the stimulus to clean it earlier and hence more frequently than at other times.

What is evident in these discussions is how the kitchen's material culture is seen to take on agency; through its very qualities it takes on a 'dirty' appearance, generating the need to clean.[19] The Crammonds and Judith Roberts lamented that their kitchen floors had a habit of taking on the appearance of being dirty rather easily. The Crammonds' laminate flooring, in particular, was a bone of contention because it constantly communicated the message: 'I'm dirty, clean me!'

Gemma: We're always having to brush up round here as well ... the kitchen, 'cos of the ...
Bill: The floor!
Gemma: We never used to ... The floor and ... 'cos it's not carpet and it's a nightmare. I mean as you can see, it needs brushing now it's just that it, especially with Sophie [their young daughter].
Bill: Yeah ... Everyday ... we need to brush it. It's terrible, eh, this mess on the floor, I mean, we did that at the weekend didn't we? Brushed it.
Gemma: We did it yesterday.
Bill: Did we do it yesterday? [Laughs]
Gemma: And it's like this again.

The Crammonds had wanted laminate flooring before they moved into their current home because of its aesthetic appeal. Yet, living with it in the context of the realities of their everyday lives, their wish had quickly turned to disappointment, for their flooring hardly ever adhered to the pleasing aesthetics it had promised. The couple was now discussing replacing it with carpets. What seemed interesting here was their acknowledgement that carpets were easier to live with because, by harbouring dirt, they also obscured it, thereby ameliorating the need to clean as frequently. This was tentatively seen as a problem for kitchen flooring, but not for other areas of the ground floor.[20] What is clear, however, is that participants were thinking creatively about how the material culture of their homes fitted into their everyday lives, and that when they indicated 'problem' areas, this was often with a view to making changes if possible.

The prominence of the visual in contemporary cleanliness was emphasized in other ways, too. There was some discussion about products that had recently come onto the market that showed how 'dirty' things are or were. In addition to the laminate flooring discussed above, examples included Janice

Andrews's steam cleaner, which showed the water getting dirtier as cleaning tasks progressed. Another example was the Coopers' Dyson vacuum cleaner, which showed the muck that came up from the floor through a window display on the machine. One of the consequences of this technology is that it had a tendency to make their users feel that they had inadequate cleaning practices, simply because they found it hard to cope with the amount of dirt that evidently came from bouts of cleaning activity:

Fran: Well we are forever emptying it so it makes you wonder where it all comes from.

Marc: We thought we were quite a clean household until we got this Dyson and dear me, it is erm, it does, it sucks.

Sue: So does it make you feel that the house is dirty?

Marc: Well, you would think ... I was talking to someone about it and they said it must be coming from under the floor boards. And that is where I thought, well the house can't be that dirty!

Another way in which the prominence of the visual in contemporary cleanliness came to the fore was in relation to germs. In a cleaning culture where sensory stimuli are important, invisible and odourless 'entities' like germs may easily slip down the hierarchy of domestic priorities. On the other hand, it may be argued that because 'they' are invisible, germ anxieties are more potent – after all, given that they cannot be seen, the domestic practitioner does not know whether there are harmful germs in their environment and whether their cleaning activities successfully remove them. Nevertheless, it is clear that health educationists and marketers eager to proclaim the salience of germs have resorted to media campaigns in which germs are made visible, which some of our participants, like Sally Findley and Mary Lowe, accounted as having made them more keenly aware of germs. The invisibility of germs is clearly regarded as a challenge by those who perceive germs to be met with cultural indifference. It is interesting how these same people make the invisible visible by utilizing the techniques of a culture where 'looks' clearly matter.

Notwithstanding these concerns, our research showed clearly that domestic aesthetics did not always win it over germ consciousness. Interestingly, in some households, where cleaning had been relegated to the lower ranks of the domestic priority task list, there was a concomitant reorganization of the priority placed on germs and aesthetics. Health educationists will be pleased to hear that in our discussions with Janice and Josie, both working mothers with very young children, cleaning to counter germs remained of significant importance, with the maintenance of an ordered appearance relegated to second place:

Let's put it this way, if it's a choice between having the ironing done and knowing that the toilets are clean … is much more important to me … in terms of kitchens and bathrooms and things, if there's gonna be germs there then you're going to end up picking them up. I think there's a risk that people could become ill with it.

(Janice Andrews)

Another example was that of dish drying. Jenny Howard, whom we introduced earlier as someone who liked things tidy, spoke about her friend being appalled by the idea that she was drying her dishes:

My friend from Canada is horrified if I dry them because of all the germs on the tea towel! And I say 'well I change my tea towels every couple of days so there's not a lot of germs on there you know.' I could understand if the tea towel had been there for a week but it's not so. … But she always air dries and doesn't dry anything so.

A similar discussion occurred with Janice and Simon Andrews, who reasoned that their own change in practices from towel drying to leaving the dishes to dry on the surface was most certainly related to countering germ cross-contamination. They then spoke about how Simon's mum found this practice hard to accept. The shift to leaving dishes to dry may also tap into the priority of making cleaning less time consuming and therefore easier, and it may in fact have been this that irked Simon's mother most. Clearly, for her the task of tidying the kitchen was not complete until everything had been tidied away into cupboards.

Balancing on the dirt threshold

'I have a tolerance threshold I think. And when I hit that threshold I have to have a good blitz and that will hit at random times every week basically' (Karen Wise). As discussed earlier, there is evidence that our practitioners still engaged to some extent with a cultural understanding of cleanliness that has its roots in a bygone era of housewifely care and attention. However, it could be argued that evidence of its general cultural consequence was lacking and that an alternative notion; that of the tolerance threshold, otherwise called the cleanliness or dirt threshold, suggests that a 'new' cultural standard based on domestic aesthetics is taking root. Discussions about reaching the tolerance or dirt threshold seemed to affect a similar discourse as that related to the traditional notion of cleaning as attached to temporal ordering in the sense that participants used it in self-judgement.

Two models of cleanliness seemed to indicate how practitioners balanced on and around the tolerance threshold. The 'right' side of this threshold spoke to a notion of 'keeping on top' and of being in control of things; the 'wrong' side of the threshold indicated that things were out of control, with cleaning tasks building up – as evidenced by the Andrews' third bedroom resembling a pile of washing waiting to be ironed – and resulting in an emotional reaction of annoyance that something needed to be done about it. It was in relation to this that some respondents spoke about engaging in a cleaning blitz to get back in control of things. Sarah Allison used another concept, that of 'bottoming out', to refer essentially to the same thing, and related this to being stimulated by finding something in the kitchen cupboard to be out of date to start a thorough check of all the cupboard's contents.

While model one embodies the late modern desire for 'being in control', model two symbolizes 'lapse of control'. Even so, these models embodied another late modern ethos that reflects on the self, and this is the disjuncture between being too strict and uptight as opposed to being relaxed in one's everyday life and practice. In a compact passage, indicating her shift from model one to model two, Judith Roberts explained how her cleaning practices were a lot more relaxed these days than they had been in the past.

> It's [cleaning] when I can fit it in. That sounds terrible doesn't it! I did used to have routines. I did used to do everything properly! [laughs] Until the children came along [laughs], erm and I remember when I had my first one and my mother said 'Oh my God, I never thought I would see your house looking like this!' 'cause it was like a show house. I am not saying that it wants to be like that but I worked in show houses at the time so I suppose it was what I was used to seeing every day. Erm, but I am a lot more relaxed these days.

Various research participants raised the theme of being relaxed about cleaning in the discussion. For some, like the Andrews, Roberts and Potts, this indicated a shift from model one to model two through stages of the life cycle. Whereas for the Roberts family, as Judith's discussion above indicated, this shift happened when her children arrived, Catherine Potts's cleaning activities relaxed as a consequence of ill health associated with her age, which made her no longer physically capable of maintaining high standards. Others, on the other hand, simply did not think cleaning was important enough to dictate their activities. The Lowes were a case in point, indicating that here, too, cleaning was stimulated by reaching a level beyond which 'things' became impossible, and action had to be undertaken.

Marie: No, there is not really a routine but I think it's more, we are more functioning in a way where we have to reach, you know, a level, and say 'Oh my God, it's not possible any more, we have to clean that!' to do the washing up. I think we are working more in this way. We're trying to have a routine and, say maybe once a week clean the floor and once a week clean the bathroom. But I find it very hard to have an established pattern to fit into it. And I think we are both functioning the same way.

Robert: Yeah, there is some sort of routine but the routine is sort of adaptable to the ...

Marie: Yes, it's between once a week and once a fortnight to have a good cleaning in the kitchen but if we have something planned or if we are staying longer outside or we are feeling tired, we are not doing it and saying 'Let's do it tomorrow' then yeah [laugh].

Conclusion

The claim that domestic life has become deregulated is in need of critical appraisal. Within it resides the idea that there has been a shift from regulation towards deregulation, and that this change is for the worse: that, as Hoy suggested, homes are now sadly dirtier than they used to be.[21] In this chapter, I have argued that the remnants of a now somewhat outdated cultural understanding of domestic cleanliness, which connects high standards to a specific temporal ordering of cleaning work, still exists, and that this needs to be seen as the model of cleanliness that approximates the notion of regulated domestic activity. There was evidence in our research that this culture impacted on the thinking patterns of some of our respondents. Indeed, through expressions of dissatisfaction with existing practices, some domestic practitioners worried about the absence of routine in their practices, while others indicated that their household's visual cleanliness moved frequently beyond their own tolerance levels.

The prominence of visual monitoring of cleanliness in the domestic sphere could also be taken as evidence that cleaning is deregulated. After all, it suggests that the decision to clean is based more on 'how things look' than on 'the time has arrived to do it'. In addition, the idea that contemporary households are dirtier than they used to be suggests that the traditional culture of cleanliness, with its temporal routines, is more effective in keeping the domestic sphere clean than practices that result from visual monitoring. Yet, adhering to a temporal routine of cleaning may not necessarily result in 'the best' cleanliness. The example of kitchen floor cleaning discussed above suggests that when contemporary cleanliness is connected with visual monitoring, cleaning practices may become more rather than less frequent as practitioners chase the dirt that is visible in their homes; indicating that there is perhaps less cultural tolerance of visible dirt in today's society than there was in the past.

In some respects, it is hardly surprising that the visual plays such an important role in stimulating cleaning practices in today's households. The prominence of the visual in late modernity is not specific to domestic cleanliness practices, but finds an extension in other contemporary practices and preferences, such as fashion and the desire for aesthetically pleasing objects.[22] In this sense, the visual adds to our sense of civility and symbolizes more generally a shift towards a 'cleaner' and visually pleasing everyday environment. It is probable, too, that because of interior design changes during the twentieth century, the home has become 'better' at showing up dirt, while at the same time offering inventions that reduce the presence of traditional forms of dirt, like soot from solid fuel stoves. It was clear that some domestic materials were more 'effective' at communicating 'dirt' to the domestic practitioner than others. While products like the Dyson vacuum cleaner are sold as modern inventions that clearly 'show' dirt, it is clear from the discussion of the diverse qualities of floor covering in this study that household objects that obscure dirt may be welcomed precisely because they diminish the urge to clean. The relationship between visible and invisible dimensions of dirt in cultures of contemporary cleanliness no doubt warrants more attention than I have managed to give it here, for one because it connects in interesting ways with the boundaries domestic practitioners create around aspects of the home about which they are and wish to be aware and those of which they wish to remain ignorant.[23] Germs may rightly be seen to pose a problem in relation to this because, through their invisibility, they may be the easiest form of dirt to ignore and de-prioritize. Our evidence suggests, however, that in those households where it is said to matter most, germ dangers gain priority over visible and perhaps more innocent forms of dirt.

A shift towards the visual monitoring of dirt in the home may be a direct consequence of the decline in the temporal ordering of cleaning practices. If an organization along specific temporal routines is rejected, perhaps because other household priorities do not allow them to be organized in that way, domestic practitioners need to have a means of judging when it is time to clean what. By 'showing' dirt, household objects and surfaces more or less effectively communicate with the practitioner when it is time to clean. Lastly, the diversity of households included in this small ethnographic study nevertheless shows that opportunities and constraints for 'filling in' everyday life vary significantly. Given this diversity it would be strange to find that cleaning was regulated in a sense that everyone followed the same temporal and practice routines. In fact, we should expect to find that practices vary between households, but this is not the same as arguing that routines do not exist in people's practices, or that today's households are necessarily dirty.

Chapter 4

Bring Home the Dead: Purity and Filth in Contemporary Funeral Homes

KYRO SELKET

In 2001, television viewers from around the world were welcomed into the home of Nathaniel and Ruth Fisher, a fictitious North American family who owned and operated Fisher & Sons Funeral Home, located in present day Los Angeles, California. *Six Feet Under*[1] took viewers behind the scenes of a seemingly typical American family's life, and merged their daily life with the morbid business of death.

What made this programme particularly interesting for viewers, especially in places such as Aotearoa New Zealand,[2] was that the Fisher family home was located above their funeral business. This fusion of family and funeral home is rarely, if ever, experienced in Aotearoa New Zealand. Nevertheless, contemporary Western funeral services draw heavily on conservative notions of 'home' to promote their professional image.

The promotion of this particular deathscape[3] as a home is said to provide the bereaved with a space where they can take time to reflect, grieve and say farewell to their dead. However, this engagement with death, which is upheld by the industry as being an important step in the grief process, can only be achieved if the body of the deceased is embalmed. Without embalming, viewing the dead is believed to be hazardous, for, 'even when the cause of death is known to be noninfectious, there may well be hidden or undiagnosed disease(s) present.'[4] Therefore, it is imperative that the corpse be excluded from the spaces of the living before being thoroughly embalmed. In fusing sanitary approaches to understandings of death with home, the funeral home becomes a site fraught with complex and contradictory relationships.

Little has been written specifically on the fusion between home and death. By exploring the physicality of the funeral home and the inclusion of the dead within this space, in this chapter I contribute to the growing body of literature on the geographies of cleanliness and contamination. By mapping the movements of the bodies of the living and the dead within the home, I highlight various maintenance and containment practices. These practices help maintain the borders between life and death, inside and outside, home and homelessness, and purity and filth.

Before looking specifically at the practices of maintenance and containment within the funeral home I want briefly to explore the transformation of the funeral parlour to the funeral 'home'. This helps set the backdrop for exploring how the idea of home has come to be important to the funeral business.

Death of the Parlour

Until the late nineteenth century, in Western countries such as Britain, the United States of America and Aotearoa New Zealand, the family home was the pivotal site for the care and disposal of the dead. Midwifes or female family members washed and prepared the dead for the wake, which was held in the home's front parlour. The modern funeral service is said to have had its origin in the friendly efforts of relatives and neighbours to aid people in distress. Through a process of evolution these neighbourly efforts eventually developed into a formal vocation.[5]

At the turn of the nineteenth century the funeral parlour replaced the family home as a funeral space. By expanding the carpenter's premises, by including a mortuary and viewing room, guardianship was removed from the family and placed firmly under the authority of the burgeoning undertakers.[6] The introduction of crude preservation practices and the increasing responsibility of registering and handling death certificates meant that the care of the dead was permanently transferred to the undertaker and contained within the funeral parlour.[7] This was further underpinned by new discourses about bacteria and death. Death came to be viewed as a health risk to the living, due in part to the spread of contagious diseases from crude burial practices.[8] Death was no longer central to people's daily lives. With the medicalization of death came a greater degree of anxiety and, in turn, death was shunned, depersonalized and excluded.[9]

Between the 1830s and 1840s the United Kingdom, the United States of America and Australia began to introduce new sanitary reforms in response to various public health concerns.[10] Similar sanitary reforms were implemented in Aotearoa New Zealand and, like their counterparts, these reforms focused on such things as water supply, sewage and burial practices. While these hygiene and sanitation approaches were viewed as a practical way of dealing with health concerns, many of the principles and practices underpinning hygiene became embedded in middle-class ideas of refinement. Therefore, practices associated with hygiene were further included in the daily lives of the middle classes.

Through new attitudes about appropriate or inappropriate bodily behaviour, including body odour, lack of odour became associated with the 'civilized' and clean middle and upper classes, while bodies that 'reeked', like the bodies of the working classes, racialized bodies or dead bodies, were no longer tolerated within the middle-class home. Instead, these bodies were segregated and in the case of the dead, permanently separated from the spaces of the living.[11]

As a result of these new understandings about disease and hygiene, the family parlour, once the pivotal site for bidding farewell to the dead, took on negative connotations as a death space and, in turn, lost favour among homeowners. Undertakers exploited these fears and began to offer mourners 'sanitary' practices. For example, in 1900 E. Morris and J. Flyger and Company, a funeral home in the Wellington region ran an advertisement in the Wellington newspaper offering 'sanitary' funerals to the citizens of the Wellington region.[12]

Consequentially, the family home took on new meanings and it was no longer an acceptable or desirable place temporarily to house the dead. The bodies of the dead, now viewed as unclean because of their potential danger from the threat of disease, had to be moved to the funeral parlour where it was understood that the undertaker, with his scientific knowledge of death, could adequately monitor not only the body but also the space within which these bodies were kept, thereby preventing the spread of contagious diseases.

The space of home and the funeral home

Eventually undertakers rejected the term 'parlour', transforming the parlour into a funeral 'home'. In using the term 'home', funeral directors drew on the qualities and virtues believed to be present in the family home. Incorporating these into the funeral space meant that the funeral service could offer the public a sanitized, safe and somewhat neutral space in which to engage with the dead.[13] Through the promotion of this deathscape as a 'home', as opposed to purely a business, funeral rituals were

4.1   Main funeral home, corner Willis and Aro Street, Wellington City.

transformed from merely bleak engagements with death, to specialized funeral rituals. This meant that the business aspect of funeral work became embedded within a discourse of homeliness, giving the bereaved a sense of place, a sense of home.

This sense of 'home' could be described as being similar to the home Gaston Bachelard described.[14] Bachelard's description of home is a place where the infant initially comes to understand the world. The funeral home then is a place where, in the presence of death, the living come to understand death.[15] While the home has come to represent a place of intimacy, a space to which people can withdraw, away from the hustle and bustle of the outside world, it is also a place fraught with complex, contradictory relationships;[16] because it 'touches so centrally on our personal lives, any attempt to dis-passionate social scientific analysis stimulates emotional and deeply fierce arguments and disagreement'.[17] In adding death to this mix of intimacy, filth, cleanliness and social interrelations, the funeral home becomes a complex and at times contradictory space worthy of exploration.

Funeral owners and operators attempt to incorporate all that is perceived as 'good' about home, thereby offering families refuge in their 'time of need'. Funeral homes embody and reflect all that is thought to be civil and middle

4.2 Beauchamp Funeral Homes exterior, Kimbolton Road, Feilding; interior, Morris Street, Marton.

class in a home. The majority of funeral homes in Aotearoa New Zealand are built with sturdy and/or classical designs.[18] For example, Lychgate Funeral Homes (see Figure 4.1), which has been part of the funeral industry since 1876, located its premises in a number of affluent residential areas in Wellington. This funeral home is described as a grand colonial residence, surrounded by rose gardens. The intention is to create a homely atmosphere, 'an environment where people feel relaxed at what can be a stressful time'.[19]

Like the ideal middle-class family home, the funeral home is situated unobtrusively and discreetly away from the public gaze at the end of a driveway or nestled behind vast lawns and hedges (see Figure 4.2).

This home offers the bereaved a certain level of privacy, respectability, and discretion. With its trimmed hedges, mowed lawns and cobbled driveway the funeral home speaks of order and with order comes a guarantee of cleanliness and, in turn, security.

I want to suggest that in locating funeral homes in middle-class suburban areas, as opposed to more commercial locations or working-class neighbourhoods, which are both viewed as less homely, less private, far more stark or public in character, funeral owners and operators are presenting the public with a home that speaks of order and luxury, a harmonious representation of home. It is a place where the bereaved can be at home with their grief, at home with their family and friends and, most importantly, at home with death.

To ensure that all interactions between the living and the dead are incident-free and meaningful for the bereaved, funeral directors operate within a highly regulated and 'proper' environment. This not only contains the borders of the home, but aids in the management of the bodies of the living and the dead. The most effective form of management within the funeral home is by means of separating the private (unclean) from the public (clean) spaces within the home.

Welcome to the funeral home: creating the public and private

To explore the various containment and separation practices employed by funeral directors, I have mapped the movements of both the living and dead bodies in and around the funeral home. In this way we can see how certain spaces within the funeral home have come to be defined as public (clean) and private (unclean). Figure 4.3 details the various rooms located within the funeral home. The plan shows the movement of mourners in and around the home, and the movement of the corpse into and out of the home.

Much of the professional work carried out in funeral homes is undertaken within a highly controlled and bounded space. The funeral home is designed to minimize any needless 'messy' encounters between the living and the dead.[20] This concern about presenting funerals without incident stems from society's concern about leaking bodies, and the dead body is the ultimate signification of this.[21]

Not only does death bring with it the frightening annihilation of the subject self, but with the onslaught of death comes the breaking down of the body's borders, bringing the insides out.[22] This appearance of disorder signifies that the corpse has 'come a cropper; is cesspool, and death; it upsets even more violently the one who confronts it.'[23] Therefore, like the acts of urinating or defecating, death must be contained not only behind closed doors but also through the retardation of the onslaught of decay.

In securing the orifices of the cadaver and temporarily reconstituting the body's borders the dead are believed no longer to offend or to be a threat to the living. Stripped of its difference the dead are forced to perform a 'fake death', 'maintained as a puppet within the orbit of the living in order to serve as an alibi and a simulacrum of their own lives'.[24]

Therefore the funeral director attends to ensuring that the borders between the inside and outside, and between the private and the public are both solid and impenetrable. However, any attempt truly to free oneself entirely of this cesspool is futile because death hovers at the threshold, lying dormant yet present 'beckoning the self to take up the place of abjection, the place where meaning collapses'.[25]

The importance of doors

On arrival, mourners come to the front door of the funeral home, which is rarely, if ever, allowed to stand open. On their arrival, the funeral director will promptly answer the door, for it is important never to leave the bereaved standing for long periods of time in any one place.

Visitors will become aware of a certain hushed silence, a hesitant atmosphere that permeates throughout the house. This muted silence works in conjunction with the opening and closing of doors. Together doors and

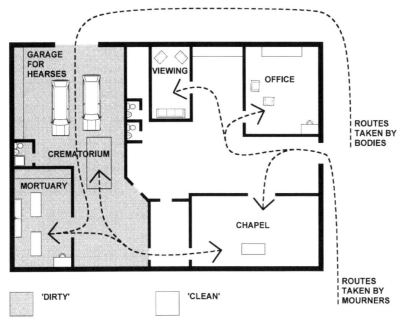

GARAGE
FOR
HEARSES

VIEWING

OFFICE

CREMATORIUM

MORTUARY

CHAPEL

ROUTES
TAKEN BY
BODIES

ROUTES
TAKEN BY
MOURNERS

'DIRTY'

'CLEAN'

4.3 Plan of a typical funeral home.

silence operate to temper the bodies of the living, creating not only a highly controlled space but a certain ambiance in which the management of bodies can be controlled.

The opening and closing of doors creates an orchestrated performance that is based on a need for privacy, aesthetics, timing and the seamless flow of both the living and dead bodies in and around the home. As I have suggested, doors are especially important in funeral homes as they are utilized to prevent incidents, seepages, and border crossings that may destabilize the operational aspect of providing a 'proper', 'incident-free' environment. Most importantly, doors separate and contain the public and privates spaces within the home until the appropriate time when the corpse, which has itself now been contained, can enter the public space of the home.

Front doors embody a degree of formality because they give people a sense of arrival, a ceremonial coming home.[26] Doors, particularly front doors, bridge the space between the public and private. They also signal beginnings or endings, changes in status and rites of passage.[27] Within the funeral home doors are extremely important, not only are they utilized to contain liminal spaces from more public space, but they also help the transformation of bodies from one state of being to another.

On opening the front door the bereaved are welcomed into the funeral home. This welcome forms the foundation of interactions between the funeral director and the bereaved. It is important to note that only the living ever use the front door. The corpse is relegated to entering the home either through the back door or via the garage. This restriction on the entry of the corpse into the funeral home can be compared with nineteenth-century etiquettes surrounding the entry of servants and tradesmen into the homes of the upper and middle classes (see also Barbosa in this volume). Servants and tradesmen were required to enter houses via the back door or trades door, thereby creating zones that were viewed as clean (the front door) and less clean (back entrances). Like the maid[28] who is also described as a doorway, a threshold, in that she exists between, as part of, yet outside the family, the corpse holds an ambiguous position. It sits between filth and purity, between life and death, and for this reason it must be excluded, while retaining its essential part of the family. Once transformed into a less contagious, less contaminating subject the deceased can depart via the front door. This makes the foyer an important threshold for defining cleanliness.[29]

In promptly opening the front door to the bereaved, the funeral director indicates that the bereaved are important visitors. Once inside, the bereaved will remain momentarily in the foyer area. The foyer, or hallway, is a transitional zone (see Figure 4.2). It is here that that the bereaved momentarily discard their social and public identities to take on the role of the bereaved. Like the foyer or hallway of the family home, the foyer is utilized as a 'protective and neutralizing zone to prevent or ease transition from the public to the private world'.[30]

The foyer will be subtlety decorated. Pot plants will be carefully placed giving the funeral home a sense of life, while subtle lighting and soft tones will be utilized to create a safe and calming environment. In some homes a plaque with a well known proverb, either about death or the home, might decorate a wall. One or two framed pictures may hang on the walls and there will be a few comfortable chairs or couches positioned close to the viewing rooms. Important information about the funeral and grief process will be laid out neatly on a small table. This need to present a clutter free space where everything is systematically arranged helps present a professional image to the bereaved. This is further highlighted by a funeral director who is not only stylish in his or her manner, but also well groomed.

On entering the family home, visitors are almost always placed in an inferior power position, as not everyone who enters the hallway can instantly proceed beyond it.[31] Similarly, the funeral home's foyer is used to identify the bereaved. Simultaneously, the roles of both the bereaved and the funeral director are established.

It is here that the funeral director 'directs' where the bereaved can and cannot go. This manoeuvring of the bereaved bodies is achieved through statements such as 'please follow me' or 'this way please'. Funeral directors will also place their body between mourners and doors they identify as being off limits to the living. In this way a funeral director politely manages and manoeuvres the bodies of the living around the funeral home, ensuring that the borders between the public and private spaces of the home are reinforced. On each and every occasion that the bereaved and the funeral director meet, these separations will be reiterated and re-enacted, ensuring that the overall process of the funeral is conducted 'without incident'.

As I have mentioned, the dead do not enter the funeral home via the front door. On arrival the deceased's body is driven directly to the rear of the funeral home, where it is immediately removed from the hearse and taken without delay to the mortuary (see Figure 4.3). The transferring of the deceased's body from the hearse to the mortuary must be undertaken in such a way as to ensure the dignity and respect of the deceased. This transferral must also be accomplished to prevent the general public or visiting mourners accidentally viewing an unprepared corpse.[32] It is for this reason that the mortuary is located at the rear of the funeral home (see Figure 4.3).

To ensure the separateness of the mortuary, it is deemed off limits to all but those directly qualified to work with the corpse. This separation of the mortuary from the public space at the front of the funeral home is upheld through a variety of health and safety regulations. However, the most important separation technique comes about through the construction of the corpse as a contagious object. As I have suggested, the funeral industry holds that no matter what type of death has occurred, all corpses are polluting dangerous objects. Therefore, within the hidden space of the embalmer's room the most abject of human fear exists, the decomposing corpse. This liminal zone and the decaying bodies that occupy it are, for many outside the funeral industry, an uncomfortable, unspeakable and mystifying space. It is here that the material and nonmaterial worlds are socially and historically constructed, simultaneously engaged, regulated and disciplined. Notions of the sacred and profane are negotiated and contained.

The correct atmosphere

To ensure that the borders between the living and the dead are enforced I have suggested that the funeral home is separated into public and private spaces. To guarantee this separation, funeral directors close doors between these two spaces. However, the mere closing of doors will not ensure that these borders remain intact. Therefore it is necessary for the funeral director to draw on various notions of correct behaviour or funeral etiquette, so as to create an atmosphere within which certain behaviour is performed.

Another way of ensuring that the borders between the public and private, clean and unclean, are separate is to create a well ordered public space. Some homes draw on a bygone era, using the décor of old Victorian homes. Leather chairs and couches, stained wooden tables will adorn the interviewing room, giving the bereaved a sense of order, harmony, and comfort. Most importantly though, presenting the bereaved with Victorian style décor creates solidity, which gives a degree of security embedded in what has come to be understood as representing 'old fashioned' values. Qualities associated not only with the Victorian era,[33] but also with middle-class civility.

While some homes prefer to create a more modern environment, similar to that found in Beauchamp's Funeral Home (Figure 4.2), which replicates an early 1970s living room, the rooms, whether old or new, will be simple and uncluttered, comparable with that of a more middle-class living room.

Although it is necessary for the funeral director to create a homely atmosphere, which helps place the bereaved at ease, they do not want to create an eerie illusion. While comfort is important nothing must deflect the bereaved from the purpose of their visit, which is, of course, dealing with death. For this reason funeral items will be discreetly placed around the room.

As I have previously suggested, the nineteenth century saw concepts about cleanliness become embedded in middle-class practices of refinement, which in turn were replicated in people's homes. In the funeral home, viewing and interviewing rooms, whether replicating a bygone Victorian era or a more modern period, are orderly, and order equates with safety, cleanliness and notions of comfort. With viewing rooms designed to allow for the open expression of emotions,[34] the bereaved can safely discuss death and express their grief. The ordered environment allows the bereaved to come back from the brink of the disorder that death has brought to their lives.

Until this moment the corpse has been segregated or stored in an adjoining corridor or holding room. The storage space lies behind the kitchen and beside the main viewing area. While this may appear to be contradictory in practice, housing the dead within close proximity of the kitchen is viewed as safe by those working in the funeral industry because the body has been thoroughly embalmed. Once embalmed and coffined the corpse is no longer considered a polluting object. It is at this point that the deceased can enter the public space of the funeral home. With its borders reconstituted and the signs of death eradicated, the corpse is no longer considered dangerous to the living. It is now at home with the living.

Conclusion

In this chapter I set out to examine how the establishment of the funeral 'home' and its association with purification and filth has led to contemporary funeral homes becoming necessary, yet marginal spaces. In Western societies, much of what has come to be understood about the disposal of the dead, and the need for funerals, has been constructed through varying discourses within the funeral industry. These discourses are, in turn, performed through the bodies of the living and the dead, within what have come to be known as funeral homes. By drawing on middle-class notions of home, and merging this with medical discourses around contagion and sanitation, the funeral home has come to offer mourners a sanitized and safer version of death, and a space within which to engage with death. However, the need for this space to be more than merely a business space means that the funeral director has to draw on notions of the home to minimize the harsh reality of death.

In tracing the movements of both the living and the dead through the funeral home and exploring various regulatory acts that contain and construct the private and public spaces of the funeral home, I have begun to highlight the borders between life and death, inside and outside, home and homelessness, and purity and filth as played out in this deathscape. In doing so, I have revealed the inseparability of the construction of the sanitized funeral 'home' and the discourse of the 'diseased' dead.

Acknowledgements

I would like to thank Keith Newell of Lychgate Funeral Homes in Wellington, and Julie Beauchamp of Beauchamp Funeral Home in Palmerston North.

Section 2

CITY AND SUBURB: URBAN DIRT AND CLEANSING

Introduction

BEN CAMPKIN

This section is concerned with the themes of dirt and cleanliness in relation to the urban environment, its spaces, infrastructures, representations and communities. The accounts range from studies of the contemporary city and suburbia, to historical geographies of urban spaces and societies. Given the long association of modern London with dirt in fictional representations and social science, a number of chapters focus particularly on that city. However, the discourses of dirt and purity that they illuminate are by no means specific to London, and the chapters that look beyond it pick up and develop similar threads – of class, sexual and racial politics; of moral, spiritual, corporeal and physical cleansing; of infrastructure and urban sanitation; of representation and aesthetics; and of socio-spatial processes of Othering through the segregation and zoning of marginal social groups. From studies of the Victorian city, insights about contemporary campaigns of urban cleansing and reform emerge, while other chapters address the shifting materialities, theorizations, representations and perceptions of dirt in the mid to late twentieth century and the present day.

There is by now a substantial body of literature on the environmental history of modern industrial cities in which waste, pollution, the sanitary reform movement and the development of urban infrastructures are examined.[1] A more limited selection of publications explores sanitation in relation to the pre-modern city.[2] However, as a whole, these historical accounts tend to be conservative in approach,[3] and do not meaningfully connect historical phenomena with the theoretical trajectories mapped, for example, by Mary Douglas, or with other more recent theorists of dirt and cleanliness cited above (see main Introduction, pages 4–5).

Furthermore, the majority of existing studies of urban dirt and waste have remained in an historical 'comfort zone' that deals with the history of urban hygiene in relation to modernism, focusing on the period from the mid-nineteenth to the early twentieth century, without reference to contemporary beliefs and practices. The predominance of such studies that particularly examine sanitation systems in the major European and North American capital cities,[4] is at least partly attributable to the historical context of a rapid growth in urban populations, and therefore of associated waste and dirt, during that period.[5] The formation of new attitudes to waste and dirt, at an individual and collective level, constituted an important ingredient of the development of the modern industrial city, and it is important to consider these new discourses. However, the increasing centrality of dirt and waste in contemporary theory, culture and public debate suggests a need for more work on this topic in relation to the late modern metropolis.

While a few recent accounts imaginatively revise the conventional histories of sanitation systems through re-evaluation of archival evidence and engagement with contemporary urban and spatial theory, they are by no means typical in these respects. Rather, as Matthew Gandy has argued, there are conceptual limitations in many accounts that are 'derived from the somewhat narrow theoretical base which has evolved within the subdiscipline of environmental history'.[6] Much potential exists for new interpretations of the spaces of urban sanitation, moving away from pure formal or technical analyses, and historical accounts of the key individuals and organizations involved, towards an enquiry that questions how such spaces were conceived, experienced and represented by the urban populations whose lives they affected.

We can look to work on the modern city in literature to take us beyond the possibilities of a narrow technical history of urban sanitation, and provide a cultural context in which to consider the development of urban responses to dirt. For example, in their discussion of some classic nineteenth-century accounts of urban dirt and filth, Peter Stallybrass and Allon White explore metaphors of height and visibility in the mapping of the city by writers such as Chadwick, Mayhew, Marx, Engels, Freud, Baudelaire and Dickens. The hidden underground is seen to equate to the lowliest matter, while above ground purity is reflected through height in, for example, civic and religious architecture. In this context, as Stallybrass and White argue: 'the axis of the body is transcoded through the axis of the city, and whilst the bodily low is "forgotten", the city's low becomes a site of obsessive preoccupation, a preoccupation which is itself intimately conceptualized in terms of discourses of the body.'[7] In this period, as evidenced through the texts of reformers, novelists and other urban commentators, new social hierarchies and spatial boundaries in urban space (high/low, suburb/slum) are both instituted and transgressed.[8]

Recent work has problematized the tendency to overemphasize the vertical hierarchical organization of urban space in relation to dirt and waste matter, in which the underground is equated with the lowest forms of filth. Steve Pile's discussion of 'underground cities', for example, reinforces the idea that the everyday functioning of contemporary city life relies on the support networks buried underground. The sophistication of those networks, Pile observes, provide an index of urban progress equivalent to tall or spectacular structures.[9]

Attempting to rework accounts of modernist urban sanitation in reference to appropriate theoretical frameworks provides one central challenge to those working in this field; another can be identified in a need to address cultural discourses of urban degradation, pollution and hygiene in the context of present-day urbanism. In the first chapter of this section I argue for the potentials of dirt and cleanliness as important themes in the interdisciplinary analysis of contemporary cities. First reflecting on Mary Douglas's theory of dirt, which I present as a spatial theory, I consider the existing inter-pretations, possible criticisms and further potentials of this theory in relation to urban space. Proceeding from this, I consider how the 'spaces of abjection' in the late modern city might differ in form and materiality from the urban spaces of the industrial or Fordist metropolis. This question requires a broader discussion of the usefulness of 'dirt' as a concept and analytical category. In contemporary urban visual culture and aesthetics, dirt is simultaneously celebrated as 'chic', and used as an index of socio-political breakdown, poverty and inequality. A nuanced and politically engaged approach to analysis is therefore required. Recent work by neo-Marxist urban geographers on the political ecologies of 'urban trash' and infrastructure is suggested as one useful model for future work.

The domestic themes of earlier chapters (see Section 1) surface again in Paul Watt's chapter, an investigation of notions of dirt and purity in the socio-spatial construction of the suburb, in opposition to the 'dirty' city. Drawing on the foundational work of David Sibley and his elucidation of 'landscapes of exclusion', and on the concept of 'place image', Watt explores the aspir-ations and perceptions of the inhabitants of a London suburb in terms of their understandings of the relationships between physical and social pollu-tion and cleanliness, order and disorder. First imagined as 'pure' the suburban environment soon becomes tainted through the presence of unwanted out-siders. In this account exclusionary metaphors conflate physical degradation and contamination with race and class-based prejudices. The case raises a number of themes central to contemporary public policy and debate.

In dealing with the zoning of sex offenders, Pamela Gilbert addresses a currently contentious issue in the USA, as elsewhere, framing her analysis within a broader discussion of the city as a site of sexual deviance. She explores the geographical implications of sex offence laws alongside the negative stereotyping of other 'undesirables', and their spatial segregation in, for example, stigmatized inner-city or peripheral urban areas. Drawing on media representations, Gilbert observes overlapping metaphors of physical, moral, sexual and racial dirt in the discourses of disgust surrounding the placement of sex offenders. This analysis draws on the work of Giorgio Agamben's *Homo Sacer: Sovereign Power and Bare Life* to suggest that we are dealing with a particular late modern phenomenon where the object of disgust is seen to be 'inherent in, necessary to, but always threatening to exceed and thus destroy the pure' (see page 97).

Continuing the theme of sexual pollution, Johan Andersson explores the stigmatization of gay men in relation to images of 'unhealthy' gay spaces in London around the outbreak of the AIDS crisis in the 1980s. He argues that, in reaction to negative representation and association with disease and contamination, an interior design aesthetic emerged in the new gay bars of London's Soho district that provided an exaggerated representation of hygiene and cleanliness. This argument draws on the model of Adrian Forty's account, driven by Mary Douglas's theory of dirt, of the emergence of the modernist aesthetic of hygiene in interior and product design (see page 2).

Overlaps between medical knowledge and the understanding of disease and the moral discourses of religious purification are the central focus of Dominic Janes's historical geography of the treatment of prostitutes in early Victorian London, and the establishment of a refuge for their reform in the district of Pimlico. In elucidating this case Janes draws on theories of dirt from social anthropology, and on a Foucauldian analysis of the networks of power underlying the construction of socio-spatial boundaries and the institutional technologies of cleansing. As with Gilbert and Andersson, the urban geographies of sexual pollution are here seen to result from subtle interactions between political ideologies, scientific understanding and dominant moral values.

In the final two chapters of this section, in quite different ways, Paul Dobraszczyk and David L. Pike turn our attention beneath the city streets to the hidden infrastructures that deal with waste – sewers and their cartographic and cinematic representation. Dobraszczyk reworks the conventional historical narratives attached to the development of London's sewers in the mid-nineteenth century. In doing so he draws on the evidence provided by the *Ordnance Survey of London*, and a survey of the pre-existing sewer network, both produced in the run up to the construction in the 1860s of the main drainage system, the first citywide system in the world. The analysis of the old and new sewer spaces, and their combined representation in a hybrid map, suggests contradictions in urban ideologies of improvement that may find parallels in contemporary programmes of 'regeneration' and 'renewal'.

In the concluding chapter of the section, Pike, like Dobraszczyk, is concerned with how sewer spaces are imagined and represented, but in the more recent cultural arena of cinematic representation. His extensive survey of the depiction of sewer spaces identifies recurrent tropes and reflects on their significance for our understanding of the spaces themselves, of the mythologies of monstrosity and dystopia associated with them, and of their symbolic operation in particular historical contexts. Both Dobraszczyk and Pike, in providing a cultural context in which to consider the development of urban infrastructures for dealing with dirt take us beyond the possibilities of a narrow technical or formal history of urban sanitation systems.

Chapter 5

Degradation and Regeneration: Theories of Dirt and the Contemporary City

BEN CAMPKIN

[Filth] represents a cultural location at which the human body, social hierarchy, psychological subjectivity, and material objects converge.[1]

The seductive simplicity of the observation that 'dirt is matter out of place', popularized by Mary Douglas (1921–2007), has ensured its frequent and productive recycling in a wide range of academic disciplines.[2] Few anthropological texts can have had such a notable impact outside the discipline as Douglas's *Purity and Danger: An Analysis of Concepts of Pollution and Taboo.* Indeed, most writers who have turned their attention to 'dirt' since Douglas have referred directly to her work. The ideas in *Purity and Danger* have particularly stimulated work in spatially and visually orientated disciplines – from anthropology to archaeology, architecture, architectural history, art history, geography, psychoanalysis, sociology, philosophy and beyond. The majority of the authors in this volume have drawn on this theory and they collectively demonstrate its malleability in clarifying the distinct questions and perspectives of their different disciplines. As such, Douglas's work forms a lynchpin through many different subject areas, methodological approaches and intellectual positions, which makes it difficult to comprehend that, until the late 1970s, it was considered marginal within the discipline of anthropology itself.[3]

In this chapter I present a critical rereading of Douglas's theory, reflecting on its characteristics, strengths and limitations both in general and in relation to spatial concerns. I consider the conceptual position embodied in *Purity and Danger,* and the author's methodological approach, before turning to responses to her thesis in spatial disciplines, and particularly in relation to 'post-industrial' London.[4] More recent theoretical developments are also considered, ranging from the notion of the 'abject', first developed in psycho-analytic theory, to a more recent conception of 'urban trash' by neo-Marxist geographers Eric Swyngedouw and Maria Kaïka.[5] The discussion is used as a platform from which to think through the potentials and problems of 'dirt' as a theoretical focus in analysing contemporary cities. How might such theories inform our understanding of processes of urban degradation and regener-ation? How far in contemporary British art and architecture is the notion of dirt as 'matter out of place' contested through what art historian Julian Stallabrass has described as the current 'cultural celebration of urban debasement'?[6] In present-day London, in tension with campaigns of urban sanitization and renewal, dirt is in vogue, aestheticized, valued and celebrated in visual culture. Two examples that bridge art and architecture – Adjaye/Associates' Dirty House (2001–02) and Matthew Lloyd Architects' *Clean up* (2006) – are explored in illustrating the contemporary aesthetics of dirt and cleanliness in London.

Locating 'matter out of place'

For Douglas, dirt is equivalent to shifting categories of disorder, ambiguity, anomaly and impurity. It causes anxiety by disrupting the 'normal' ordered relations through which we understand the world. It is threatening because it does not have a proper place in our classification of things. Hence she writes: 'For us dirt is a kind of compendium category for all events which blur, smudge, contradict, or otherwise confuse accepted classifications. The under-lying feeling is that a system of values which is habitually expressed in a given arrangement of things has been violated.'[7] Douglas's symbolic or semiotic understanding of dirt, leads her to articulate a theory that empha-sizes the visual and spatial characteristics attached to pollution belief systems and practices.[8] Pollution and prohibition are discussed in terms of borders and boundaries, and threats to those borders and boundaries. In prefacing the final edition of *Purity and Danger* produced in her lifetime, Douglas again places emphasis on the spatiality of her subject, writing that: 'Taboo is a spontaneous coding practice which sets up a vocabulary of spatial limits and physical and verbal signals to hedge around vulnerable relations.'[9] In elimin-ating dirt of all kinds we are involved in a perpetual spatial and visual process of arranging and rearranging the environment, 'making the world conform to an idea'.[10]

It follows, then, that there are many possible areas of spatial investigation in which Douglas's ideas on dirt may be useful, and in some cases have already proved to be so, both physical spaces and spaces of representation. At the most literal level, the arguments put forward in *Purity and Danger* are valuable in the analysis of spaces specifically identified as 'pure' or 'dirty', in either a real or symbolic sense, such as sacred spaces, medical buildings, bathrooms, or dumps, sewers and cemeteries. Ways of thinking about the ordering of space and specific buildings of different scales are also suggested – the zoning of exterior city spaces, but equally the partitioning of interior domestic spaces. The spatialized discussion of prohibition, transgression and punishment provides a platform from which to explore the role of the built fabric as an instrument in the production of, or as a reflection of, individual, social or cultural ordering systems. Related to this point, the theory of dirt put forward in *Purity and Danger*, and by extension other theories of dirt, may enable us to understand better the processes through which specific buildings and whole city districts are kept in an orderly state through, for example, symbolic cleansing by sweeping and whitewashing; the infra-structures and discourses of urban hygiene; or the social, symbolic and physical 'sanitization' processes associated with gentrification and driven by flows of capital. In this, theories of dirt and cleanliness may assist in answering a key question: how do the 'spaces of abjection' in the late modern city differ in form and materiality from those associated with the urban spaces of the industrial or Fordist metropolis?

Responses to Douglas's ideas in relation to the design and experience of space include sociologist Zygmunt Bauman's investigation of waste in contemporary society; Mark Cousins's psychoanalytic investigation of the architectural aesthetics of ugliness; Adrian Forty's exploration of the modernist aesthetics of hygiene and cleanliness in design history; the archi-tectural installations of Katherine Shonfield with Frank O'Sullivan and muf Architects; geographer David Sibley's analysis of spatial processes of margin-alization and 'landscapes of exclusion'; Michael Thompson's theory of rubbish in relation to gentrification;[11] and Patrick Wright's cultural history of the gentrifying district of Dalston in London. The combined scope of these works illustrates the potential of *Purity and Danger* as the grounding for an interdisciplinary spatial enquiry.[12] These varied accounts suggest that Douglas's theory has been especially productive as a tool for unravelling the hygienist ideologies underpinning modernist art, design and architecture; and that it has further under-exploited potential in the analysis of so-called 'post-industrial' and contemporary cultural production.

Given the closed and categorical certainty of the formula 'dirt is matter out of place', it is almost too easy to repeat it as a truism without further critical reflection or contextualization. It fits well with Douglas's rhetorical academic style, but taking it out of context goes against the logic of a structuralist argument where, as Richard Fardon has argued in reference to *Purity and Danger*, in a cumulative sequence 'any single quotation taken out of context risks missing the reversal or rethinking of a subsequent statement.'[13] So how should we properly locate this phrase and the book's arguments?

For Douglas, writing in the tradition of structuralist social anthropology, individual pollution beliefs and behaviours provide a useful index for understanding macro-level social systems. *Purity and Danger* demonstrates an interest in how culture is embedded in 'the concrete, the mundane', and at a more abstract level in the 'collective ordering of social life' through systems of classification.[14] Theories of dirt are in essence theories of order if we take Douglas's view that there is no such thing as dirt without classification.[15] This central interest in order and its spatialization parallels Douglas's contemporaries, such as Michel Foucault, whose post-strucutralist theories have played a more prominent role in recent architectural and urban studies.[16]

Rather than a grand meta-theory of dirt, however, the reader is presented with what Douglas describes as 'homely' arguments.[17] Emphatically ordinary, often domestic, metaphors are deployed to develop the book's ideas, mirroring the banal matter of dirt itself, and opening up the topic to an empathetic response in the reader based on his or her everyday experience.[18] Even so, critics such as Jonathan Culler have charged Douglas with a failure to deal adequately with ordinary, inoffensive, 'innocent' junk, junk that is not necessarily polluting or defiling. What becomes clear is that while she argues that 'classifying is a human universal', a tendency to ground the broad category of 'dirt' in the terrain of domesticity, as well as an openness to a plurality of meanings derived from a given classification system, mean that Douglas's work does not fit comfortably in the canon of structuralist anthropology in which we might otherwise place her.[19]

Problematizing a purely medical or 'naturalist' conception of beliefs about hygiene, Douglas instead places emphasis on the cultural production and social significance of what she terms 'pollution behaviours'.[20] Dirt beliefs are therefore seen to be determined through bodily sensations, through physiological and psychological processes, which are inextricably linked. Such processes appear to be intuitive ('an underlying feeling' – see page 69 above) or 'natural'. Pollutants of numerous varieties are considered – physical, bacteriological, social, moral, religious – and combinations of these. The balance of responses is shaped by the kind of dirt being dealt with on any given occasion. In Douglas's understanding, direct links are made between physical states and social conditions or morality, with one type of dirt frequently being seen to overlap another, operating on different material and metaphorical levels. Oscillating between different understandings of where thought or perception reside, this account embodies a tension between a structuralist and phenomenological perspective on dirt. However, beyond a scientific or technical preoccupation with pollution, cleanliness, cleaning or sanitation, this approach is valuable in providing a platform for thinking about the interactions between the different levels, both imaginary and environmental, at which, for example, an urban district may be ascribed as 'dirty', or stigmatized relative to more orderly city spaces.

Douglas places emphasis on the social construction of dirt, leading to the categorization of her work as a 'social theory' by Elizabeth Shove.[21] In attempting to understand the hygiene rituals of 'primitive' religions, *Purity and Danger* reflects on the establishment and maintenance of order through prohibition and taboo in contemporary Western societies. This method of comparative social anthropology, which draws on the model of Émile Durkheim, helps us to understand the relational dimension of social and individual responses to dirt, and their cultural and historical specificity.[22] In this account there is no such thing as absolute dirt – it is a matter of perception and classification. Douglas's method of comparing contemporary Western forms of pollution behaviour with those of so-called 'primitive' religions exposed an uncomfortable reality, namely, that though naturalized and presented as rational, modern Western conceptions of dirt are constructed through symbolic systems equivalent to the superstitious practices attached to 'primitive' religious rituals.[23] In this understanding, forms of behaviour associated with dirt are revealing of cultural differentiation, although all societies are seen to develop 'pollution behaviours' of one kind or another. As Sibley has written in his discussion of *Purity and Danger*, the 'argument about purification and defilement needs to be qualified in regard to time and place'.[24] Yet it is an important aspect of Douglas's work that she attempts to move beyond the conventional boundaries of her own discipline in highlighting parallels between 'primitive' and contemporary Western societies.

How then should we view *Purity and Danger* now? Douglas's conception of culture as a unified system of values across a community, shared and agreed rules, codes and ideas across a homogenous society, now appears rather dated. So, of course, does some of her terminology, such as the classification of societies alien to her own as 'primitive'. Furthermore, even if we accept that 'dirt is matter out of place', as Fardon has noted numerous writers since Douglas have observed 'that the formulation is not reversible: all matter out of place is not dirt'.[25]

William Cohen has also recently challenged the universalism inherent in Douglas's approach.[26] In the preface to the final edition of her book published in her lifetime (2002), Douglas reiterates her view that 'everyone universally finds dirt offensive', while how it is defined will depend on localized classificatory systems. Though she argues that the definition of dirt is in flux according to different cultural and historical contexts, for Douglas the idea of 'dirt' and our reactions to it are constant. Is this not itself an ahistorical and paradoxical assumption, and an assumption that obscures the changing materialities, effects and perceptions of dirt across time and space? Though challenging to our systems of categorization and value attribution, dirt clearly does have 'a place' within those systems. As Cohen writes, we need to recognize that 'contradictory ideas – about filth as both polluting and valuable – can be held at once.'[27] Furthermore, even when tidied up, put 'in place', some kinds of dirt may retain their threat. For Douglas, as Cohen writes, 'Pollution is not simply the opposite of cleanliness; it also arises out of a confusion of categories,'[28] and yet many writers who have taken up Douglas's ideas have downplayed this ambiguity in favour of a simple binary understanding of dirty/clean as though 'matter out of place' were a stable and clearly defined category in itself rather than a catch-all term.

Enjoying and aestheticizing urban dirt

In *A Journey through Ruins*, urban commentator Patrick Wright draws on Douglas's work in his discussion of the social, physical and cultural landscape of London at the close of the twentieth century. Wright reads Douglas's concept of dirt as 'the domain in which all ... differences are lost', a broad conceptual category for what lies 'outside of a culture'.[29] In this he at first seems critical of Douglas, and implicitly of other abstract 'elegant theories about dirt'.[30] 'We know about defilement on Dalston Lane too,' he writes.[31] At the same time, however, Douglas's theory drives the author's intricate narrative of Dalston's blighted environment, enabling him to connect different aspects of urban degradation in a critique of 'the end of planning, the end of reform, the end of State responsibility' under Thatcherism.[32] Wright's text introduces the polarity in contemporary debates about dirt between what Carol Wolkowitz terms 'postmodern and/or poststructural dirt ... purified through abstraction' and 'the idea of "real" dirt' (see page 15). Wright is disparaging about other artistic representations that aestheticize the contemporary urban landscape as ruin, about what he evocatively terms the 'morbid aesthetics of the second blitz'. Yet, *A Journey through Ruins* itself echoes this artistic strategy in simultaneously romanticizing blight and dereliction while providing a critique of the political and economic conditions that produced such neglect.

Douglas acknowledges that her theory of dirt may be inadequate for dealing with such aesthetic ambiguities in art, and with the role of dirt and disorder in creative processes.[33] Since *Purity and Danger*, psychoanalytic theory has provided an important arena for the development of ideas about dirt at both social and individual levels. Does the notion of the abject help to elucidate the recent predilection for urban dirt and decay in British art and architectural aesthetics? Or does this theory distance us too far from the 'real dirt' referred to by Wolkowitz and from Douglas's domestic metaphors of everyday matter?

Douglas's 'dirt' and Kristeva's 'abjection' are similarly articulated in spatial terms of boundaries and borders. However, sociologist Zygmunt Bauman's recent account of waste, also driven by Douglas's ideas on dirt, suggests how these concepts diverge when he writes that:

> We do not visit those [refuse] mountains, neither in body nor in thought, as we do not stroll through rough districts, mean streets, urban ghettoes, asylum seekers' camps and other no-go areas. We carefully avoid them (or are directed away from them) in our compulsive tourist escapades. We dispose of leftovers in the most radical and effective way: we make them invisible by not looking and unthinkable by not thinking.[34]

As has often been the case in interpretations of Douglas, this analysis is stated too categorically. Contemporary 'spaces of abjection' cannot be discussed in such clear-cut terms. Instead, a more fluid conception of urban boundaries, and of our attitudes towards dirt and 'dirty' places, is required. How do we account, for example, for the juxtaposition of different high/low class land uses side by side, for the new domestic, cultural and commercial uses of buildings and spaces formerly associated with and tainted or polluted by industry, or for the attractions of 'edgy' urban neighbourhoods?

The 'Dirty House', designed by David Adjaye (Adjaye/Associates) and built for the artists Sue Webster and Tim Noble, whose work uses recycled domestic rubbish as the main material, provides a useful example here (Figure 5.1). The name of the house, a conversion of a factory to domestic use, its exterior painted in anti-flyposting paint, suggests a self-conscious play on the contemporary aesthetic value of 'dirt', and highlights the appropriation and recycling of the formerly industrially-tainted district of Shoreditch by artists and architects.[35] Shoreditch, though certainly no 'ghetto', is now a classic example of a gentrified district where new luxury art galleries sit side by side with degraded local authority housing. While, as Bauman suggests, we may avoid certain extreme urban spaces of abjection 'in body', in contemporary cultural production we often visit them 'in thought' and through artistic representation. In the case of Shoreditch, the areas' 'edginess' and aesthetics of urban decay have provided an attraction to artists and architects alike, in turn prompting its accelerated gentrification.

Clean up, an event-based installation that formed part of the 2006 London Architecture Biennale, is another project that illustrates the complexities of

5.1 The Dirty House (2001–2002), Adjaye/Associates, Shoreditch, London.

contemporary understandings of dirt in relation to urban space. In this work, London-based architectural practice Matthew Lloyd Architects teamed up with the artist 'Moose', known for his 'clean graffiti' or 'grime writing', in which slogans are revealed from dirty urban surfaces through using the high-pressure cleaning equipment normally associated with teams of local authority street cleaners. In *Clean up* the architects set out to counter the trend for temporary sculptural design installations associated with the biennale, and instead to clean up Clerkenwell Green physically, repainting and repairing railings and benches with the intention of improving the quality of the public space. While on the day of the event the architects were joined by the local borough's professional cleaning team, it is interesting that they had to have a number of meetings to negotiate with the council to allow them to clean up the space – this was not a given public right.

While the architects painted and repaired (Figure 5.2), Moose used templates to create appropriate slogans on the surrounding urban fabric (Figure 5.3). His clean graffiti is interesting because, through method and media, it confuses the categories of 'clean' and 'dirty' in an unsettling way. Graffiti is often read as damage and as a sign of urban neglect: Moose's carefully inscribed writing, adopting the visual rhetoric of graffiti, highlights the filth around it. Given the artist's employment in other projects by large multinationals for advertising campaigns, his work seems contradictory in both celebrating urban grime and participating in corporate urban sanitization. It simultaneously highlights public space as 'public', echoing the rebellious acts of graffiti artists, often presented as

5.2 *Clean up*, Clerkenwell Green, London Architecture Biennale (2006).

destructive vandals ('they cannot complain if all we do is clean'), while also explicitly (and subliminally) communicating corporate advertising motifs on publicly owned and maintained urban infrastructures. This raises questions about dirt's actual and metaphorical meanings, as it does of the 'filthy lucre' itself.

From 'dirt' to 'urban trash': new perspectives

The abject is a concept that leaves room for the idea that we may be ambivalent about dirt. Many contemporary urban spaces demand an interpretation that accounts for the interactions between notions of material, spatial, psychological and social dirt and systems for imposing cleanliness. Responses to stigmatized public spaces – including obsessive surveillance, the patrol of boundaries, or closure, parallel the psychological process of abjection at a social level.[36] As well as accounting for a greater level of ambivalence the abject highlights with greater clarity the relationship between marginalized people and their spatial and material contexts. In contrast to the majority of interpretations of Douglas, which polarize the binary between 'dirty' and 'clean', the notion of the abject leaves more room for the idea that 'filth, under certain circumstances, might surprisingly be a good or enjoyable thing',[37] that one might desire to see and experience abject

5.3 *Clean up*, Clerkenwell Green, London Architecture Biennale (2006), detail.

spaces, and that the marginalized may exist next to the mainstream, the excluded next to the included.

In addition to Douglas's cultural anthropological perspective and to psychoanalytic theory, another key body of work that adopts an implicit or explicit neo-Marxian theoretical position on urban dirt and degradation emerges around urban dirt, waste, stigmatized spaces and their representation.[38] Julian Stallabrass exemplifies this approach in art history in his critique of the use that so-called 'Young British Artists' in contemporary Britain make of the degraded inner city.[39] In urban geography, Maria Kaïka and Eric Swyngedouw's analysis of 'urban trash' is evocative. They write that:

> No matter how sanitized and clean, both in symbolic and literary terms, our cities have become, the 'urban trash' in the form of networks, dirt, sewerage, pipes, homeless people etc. keeps lurking underneath the city, in the corners, at the outskirts, bursting out on occasion in the form of rats, disease, homelessness, garbage piles, polluted water, floods, bursting pipes.[40]

While on the one hand it might be argued that the term 'urban trash' conflates and confuses different types of dirt and urban phenomena, and that such conflation is unhelpful in analysis, there are also benefits to this approach. An intentionally loose tag, it facilitates the connection of urban infrastructure, the main focus of Swyngedouw and Kaïka's essay, with other forms of physical dirt, waste and mess, both organic (sewage) and inorganic (pipes). Moving on from pipes to homeless people, this definition also traverses matter and human beings, the city's fabric and its inhabitants. As the list develops, other forms of organic and inorganic, animate and inanimate matter are introduced. It can be argued that the process of making such connections is useful through facilitating a more nuanced understanding of the interactions between cultural, social, political, historical and economic factors in the production of spaces of abjection. Certainly, the links between such different phenomena are not fictitious. On a geographical level there are close relationships between the spatial distribution patterns of different kinds of waste matter, things or excluded people. In this sense, our perception of an urban place as 'dirty' is constructed through the combination of different, yet inextricably linked, things, people and conditions at specific locations.

Unlike Douglas, for whom 'dirt' replaces the commodity as the artefact that unlocks the meaning of a social system, neo-Marxist analyses of dirt and degradation are firmly rooted in the political, economic and historical dynamics behind the production of particular spaces.[41] For Swyngedouw and Kaïka:

> Perpetual change and an ever shifting mosaic of environmentally and socioculturally distinct urban ecologies – varying from the manufactured landscaped gardens of gated communities and high technology campuses to the ecological war zones of depressed neighbourhoods with lead-painted walls and asbestos covered ceilings, waste dumps and pollutant-infested areas – still shape the choreography of a capitalist urbanization process.[42]

The suggestion is that, in the context of the late modern city, such juxtapositions are becoming more intense and more visible. Pollutants are seen to have an historically, culturally and geographically specific 'nature', while we can usefully make meaningful connections between eighteenth-century discourses around miasmatic theory, nineteenth-century industrial and organic wastes and twenty-first century bacteriological and environmental concerns.[43]

Conclusion

With her combined interests in dirt and culture and their spatialization, Douglas paves the way for us to move beyond the possibilities of the dominant narrowly focused technical histories of urban sanitation or environmental pollution. However, while *Purity and Danger* provides a nuanced account of dirt, its subtleties have sometimes been overlooked, and the topic as a whole has been under theorized since the book's publication. Evaluating this theory in relation to more recent work on dirt requires us to unravel many contrasting conceptual and analytical frameworks across a multidisciplinary field. Ultimately, though 'dirt' can be a productive theoretical focus for the interdisciplinary analysis of contemporary cities, their representation and urban aesthetics, it is necessary to rethink 'dirt theory' beyond the structuralist foundations and universalizing tendencies of Douglas's account. In contemporary London we are faced with a cultural predilection for urban dirt, a marketable 'chic' attached to the aesthetics of neglect, decay and degradation, in an ambiguous relationship with a drive for 'regeneration', 'renewal' and gentrification. In this context theories of dirt and cleanliness can usefully intersect with theories of space and of capitalist urbanization, to elucidate the processes at work.

Acknowledgements

I am grateful to Johan Anderson, Iain Borden, Rosie Cox and Matthew Gandy for comments on draft versions of this chapter.

Chapter 6

From the Dirty City to the Spoiled Suburb

PAUL WATT

Perceptions of physical dirt and social disorder have long been central to the socio-spatial distinction between the urban and the suburban. The dirty/disorderly city is routinely juxtaposed with the pure/orderly suburb, a juxtaposition that in Anglo-American countries is entangled with class and racialized social distinctions. In this chapter, drawing on research on home-owners living in a fringe London suburb called 'Eastside', I discuss the contemporary relevance of such 'place images'. I highlight interrelationships between physical dirt and social disorder in both the city and the suburb, with dirt and disorder routinely equated with the visible public presence of certain lower-status social types such as youths and tenants as well as racialized immigrant and minority ethnic groups. Although Eastside represented a 'clean' space for its new residents in comparison with the city they had left behind, it was also far more 'spoiled' than many might prefer.

Place images of the city and the suburb

It has been suggested that residential space is, if anything, *becoming more* significant as a marker of social distinction because other traditional signifiers, notably occupation, have lost some of their previous purchase.[1] Places, such as residential areas, are constituted not only by their physical location but also by the meanings ascribed to them.[2] One useful concept for understanding such meanings is 'place images', defined by Rob Shields as 'the various discrete meanings associated with real places or regions regardless of their character in reality'.[3] As Shields argues, such images are partial and result from stereotyping or prejudices about places and their inhabitants. Place images constitute condensed versions of the stories people tell about their own and others' neighbourhoods and are formed by the discursive practices of many groups and organizations, including the mass media, government agencies and businesses, as well as residents.

Despite their simplistic nature and weak empirical veracity, place images matter. For one thing they inform decisions on moving house, as one UK Channel 4 TV programme on house buying, *Location, Location, Location*, endlessly reiterates. Historically, one of the main trends in residential mobility has been suburbanization, a move that has been influenced by the desire of the upwardly mobile to live in areas with 'people like them'.[4] The city/suburb contrast has taken the form of a series of social and spatial binaries that in Anglo-American countries involve the demonization of the urban and the valorization of the suburban.[5] The city is associated with physical and social manifestations of dirt, famously described by Mary Douglas as 'essentially disorder'.[6] Sibley has drawn on psychoanalytic theory, notably Julia Kristeva's concept of 'abjection', to highlight the relevance of the threatening potential of dirt and disorder for social geography.[7] Abjection occurs via the ultimately futile attempt to maintain a border between the self and its own impure polluting forms (of waste and excrement), forms that promote feelings of anxiety and disgust. According to Kristeva, abjection is caused by that 'which does not respect borders, positions, rules'.[8] Thus, as Sibley argues, border maintenance between the pure and the defiled constitutes a key, albeit insecure, element in those exclusionary social processes that have a spatial component: 'the consciousness of dirt and disorder is increased and we can anticipate that a feeling of abjection will be particularly strong in those environments, domestic interiors, neighbourhoods which are symbolically pure.'[9]

As Sibley points out, one such 'symbolically pure' environment that is constituted by rigid external border maintenance, including the anxious monitoring and removal of polluting impure elements ('strangers'),[10] is the North American suburb, juxtaposed by Richard Sennett with the messy diversity characteristic of cities.[11] According to Sibley, the 'purified suburb' is dominated by a 'concern with order, conformity and social homogeneity',[12] a concern that is mobilized around securing its spatial boundaries. As Sibley highlights, and as we discuss below, the appearance of 'dirt' creates abject feelings of anxiety and disgust because it signifies the presence of low status 'others', prominent in cities, who threaten the purity of suburban space. The dominant place image of suburbia, especially in Anglo-American culture, remains one of order based on social homogeneity, whiteness, heterosexual couples, political conservatism, materialism and insular self-satisfaction.[13]

In contrast, cities are messy places full of strangers and, as Zygmunt

Bauman argues, this confluence of strangers means that cities are character-ized by risk and unpredictability.[14] Recent studies of London's middle and working classes have indicated that the identification and control of risk in relation, for example, to schooling, crime and antisocial behaviour, is fundamental in terms of understanding Londoners' place images.[15] Risk can, up to a point, be measured and thereby controlled, as seen in the anxious scrutinizing of school league tables by middle-class parents.[16] Everyday life in contemporary global cities, however, is so multifaceted and complex that the calibration of risk can only be taken so far.[17] Instead, it is the spatial *signs* of risk (the syringe on the stairwell, the youths on the street corner) that mark out dirt and disorder and that guide city dwellers in their cartographies of aversion, in other words their mental maps of where *not* to live, walk, park their cars or send their children to school.

Dirt, purity and suburbanization in England

As Clapson argues, suburbia constitutes an aspirational space in which people can feel they have bettered themselves and moved 'up' as well as 'out' among similarly upwardly mobile families.[18] This aspirational aspect of suburbanization can be traced back to the English middle classes turning their backs on the city during the 1880s as they attempted to distance them-selves spatially from the 'dirty' manual working classes who worked with their hands, lived in overcrowded slum neighbourhoods and engaged in what were considered illicit sexual practices.[19] The suburbs came to be associated with bourgeois notions of social order and sexual propriety, a confluence of environmental and moral purity with class elevation. Suburbanization in England in the interwar and postwar periods was partly driven by the middle-class search for a pure space away from the polluted and polluting inner cities and their working-class denizens.[20]

The notion that suburbia represents a homogeneous and culturally sterile middle-class space has, however, come under considerable attack from those social scientists who are re-envisioning suburbia in more nuanced social and cultural terms that highlight its historical and contemporary geographical, class, ethnic and architectural diversity.[21] Prominent among these is the social historian Mark Clapson who has emphasized the significant working-class presence found in many English suburbs.[22] This presence is linked to the building of housing estates in suburban areas for workers and their families by local government (councils), a process that was begun in the interwar period but greatly enhanced in the postwar period. This suburban council housing expansion facilitated working-class out-migration, as exemplified by East Enders moving to the Greenleigh estate in Young and Willmott's classic, albeit romanticized, account of 1950s' east London.[23] The creation of such 'council estates' has proved to be one of the major ways that English suburbs are distinguishable from their North American counterparts and is highly significant for contemporary suburban place images, as we discuss below.

Postwar suburban housing, whether rented or owned, not only came with better fixtures and fittings, but also implied a subjective sense of moving *up* coterminous with moving *out*. Thus, although housing played a key role in motivating migration from English inner-city areas, it was often intertwined with more intangible factors such as the desire to improve social position by escaping 'deteriorating' disorderly areas and their dirty inhabitants: 'they wanted to put distance between themselves and those they perceived as roughs or undesirables.'[24] As Clapson argues, the move out fed upon and exaggerated status differences within the working class, notably the long-standing if imprecise distinction between 'rough' and 'respectable' workers and their families. However, this intra-class status distinction acquired racialized connotations since, as Clapson notes, those perceived to be of a lower status could include 'immigrants' whose presence acted as a spur for white Britons to leave the inner city for suburban areas.[25] Seminal urban sociological studies from the 1960s show that immigrants were routinely castigated for their 'dirty' living arrangements, including strange cooking smells and sights, multi-occupancy and rundown houses.[26]

The presence of black and Asian minority ethnic groups in English cities became associated with place images of urban decline that emanated from politicians and the mass media, as well as the lay public, images that crystallized around the 'riots' of the 1980s.[27] The 'inner city' came to constitute a racialized place image in binary contrast to the suburbs: 'the association between "black inner city" and disorder clearly depends on parallel associations between white suburbs and order.'[28] Although the city/ suburban binary in England has never had the same stark 'chocolate cities and vanilla suburbs'[29] demographic and cultural texture as found in the United States, 'white flight' contributed to working and middle-class suburbanization from the 1960s onwards, including that of Londoners moving out to Essex and Kent.[30]

The contemporary relationship of suburbia and suburbanization to racism and ethnic identities is increasingly complex.[31] In relation to that epitome of English suburbia, the Home Counties, I have previously highlighted the multifaceted nature of place images in relation to everyday leisure activities among ethnically diverse groups of young people.[32] Suburbia is becoming more multi-ethnic in character, at the same time that aggressive forms of white racism have been identified in certain suburban housing estates.[33] In the second part of this chapter I consider these issues around race and suburbanization and perceptions of dirt and disorder in relation to the London area, focusing on the example of a suburb located in the county of Essex, given the pseudonym 'Eastside'.[34]

83

The Eastside suburb

Like many English suburbs, Eastside is an architectural and social hybrid encompassing a traditional rural village, a sprawling modernist postwar council housing estate, plus a series of newer private housing developments. Londoners have moved to Eastside over several decades, first into council housing but increasingly into owner occupation. As such, Eastside represents an ideal location to consider how residential preferences link with place images and social distinctions, not only in relation to the London the Eastsiders had left behind but also in relation to their new suburban neighbourhood. The research employed both a survey and semi-structured interviews and focused on those residents, mainly homeowners, who had moved from an address within the Greater London boundary to Eastside during the previous ten-year period.[35]

The survey respondents were 'typically suburban' in the sense that they were predominantly white, middle-aged, married or cohabiting heterosexual couples. At the same time, there was also greater social diversity than this suburban stereotype might suggest, with a significant minority of divorced and single people as well as a small percentage from non-white ethnic backgrounds. In terms of social class, the survey sample can be divided into two, broadly reflecting class differences. Over half lived in a large new private estate given the name 'Woodlands', described by local estate agents as a 'prestigious' location, somewhat set apart from the rest of Eastside with a distinctive rural feel. The Woodlands estate is dominated by the managerial and professional middle classes living in detached and semi-detached houses, although a few manual workers, such as taxi drivers, were also present. The other part of the survey sample lived in several private housing developments, including flats as well as houses, given the collective name 'Newtown estates'. These are scattered both adjacent to and among the council housing estate that dominates Eastside. The Newtown residents were more working class than their Woodlands' counterparts, but even then managers and professionals still accounted for a quarter of the Newtown sample.

Nearly nine out of ten 'Eastsiders' in the survey had moved from east London. Nearly half came from Havering, the nearest east London borough to Eastside. Havering is quite dissimilar from the rest of east London because not only is it less deprived and contains some very affluent suburbs, like for example Upminster, but it remains predominantly white. Apart from Havering, the other main zone of origin was the rest of east London, namely the six boroughs of Barking and Dagenham, Hackney, Newham, Redbridge, Tower Hamlets and Waltham Forest. These six east London boroughs are characterized by concentrations of social and economic deprivation as well as large multi-ethnic populations.[36] The remaining 13 per cent of the survey respondents came from elsewhere in London.

From London to Eastside: dirt, disorder and narratives of urban decline

Interviewees were asked several questions aimed at discerning their rationale for moving from London to Eastside. Their reasons reflected a combination of 'push' factors, those prompting them to leave their previous London home, and 'pull' factors drawing them towards Eastside. Housing, in terms of relative affordability, size and quality, was extremely important, while personal issues (for example getting married or divorced) were also significant. Area also played a role for most respondents as they described wanting to live in a 'better' or 'nicer' neighbourhood, while some also wanted 'better schools' for their children. Moving to a better area was especially important for people who had moved from east London, apart from Havering.

With the exception of those from the more upmarket parts of Havering, themes of physical dirt and social disorder tended to dominate views on city living. Negative assessments of noise, smell, congestion, lack of space and the general appearance of the physical environment were prominent. For example, one area of Tower Hamlets was described by S.63 as 'dirty, smelly, just a dump'.[37] Elements of physical dirt and social disorder often went together, as seen in S.24's list of dislikes about Newham: 'The area was near to gasworks and factories, there was a stench in the air, not pleasant in the summer especially. There was high crime and vandalism, drugs on the doorstep.'

To understand the significance of urban place images and the intertwining of physical dirt with social disorder, we must introduce a temporal as well as spatial dimension into the analysis. Place images are not fixed but can change their meaning over time. The 'same' place can thus engender very different meanings depending on whether the present or the past is being described, while images of the present can gain their meaning from how the past is *remembered* to have existed. Such remembered images can be extremely powerful since they draw upon nostalgic yearnings for times gone by that can reverberate back to childhood.[38]

As I have argued in a study of council tenants in north London, one of the ways that London neighbourhoods are spoken about by long-term residents, especially the white working class, is in terms of 'narratives of urban decline'.[39] In such narratives, the 'community' of the past is said to have broken down, as signified and even caused by shifts in leisure and shopping outlets, for example the move away from street markets to supermarkets,[40] plus the unwelcome appearance of 'low-status outsiders' (problem tenants, Bengalis) in the neighbourhood. Similarly, for those Eastside interviewees who had been born and brought up in east London, the place images of their previous London neighbourhoods highlighted a lost 'community' of intense mutual interaction and shared identities. Such narratives of urban decline were prominent in accounts of working-class neighbourhoods, but also featured in relation to some middle-class areas. Nostalgic accounts of a lost, morally stable and holistic community were by no means monopolized by the elderly, as might at first be thought. Tony was in his late twenties and described his upbringing in Newham in the following crime-free terms:

> Everyone knew everyone so everyone looked after each other; there was no trouble. You didn't see the police, you didn't need the police round there, although there was quite a few of us all running round the streets, but now it just seems all the kids around there are ... they're smashing cars and nicking radios now. It was never like that when we was kids because you'd never get away with it because everyone knew who you was so ...

Given that Tony would have grown up during the 1980s and 1990s, his account was heavily nostalgic, reflecting widely-held London working-class mythologies about the 'good old days'.[41] He went on to describe how much he 'hated' the area in the current period when he went back there to visit his parents. His place images of the disorderly present (kids running amok) contrast sharply with past cleanliness and order:

> You seem to remember things all nice and shiny and clean, and you go back there now and it's ... it's like a war zone, well not a war zone, but there's trashy cars, there's houses falling apart, all the gardens are overgrown and I just don't remember it like that as a kid.

What is important here is the way that narratives centred on the breakdown of a previous moral social order ('the community') are conflated with the shift from a 'clean' to a 'dirty' environment dominated by broken cars and over-grown gardens. Tony attributed the latter to another main source of pollution for many ex-Londoners, namely tenants who, unlike homeowners, were con-sidered not to care about their property:

> Well, next door but one to my Mum and Dad, I mean every time I go back there's a different family living there and they don't care about the houses. A lot of them are falling apart now, the gardens are all overgrown. I think one of them does ... he must be some sort of mechanical thing, he can't speak English but he's got all cars around there up on his driveway and he's pulling the engines out the cars and doing stuff, because it's not meant to be a garage, there's oil all over the floor, it's terrible.

The above illustrates Douglas's notion of dirt as being 'matter out of place'.[42]

Fixing cars is not a problem *per se*, for example if it is done in a garage, but it takes on the appearance of dirt, and causes great consternation, when it is done in the driveway. As the above quotation also hints, via the reference to the non-English speaking neighbour, the discourses of dirt and disorder could take an exclusionary racist form. Several white British interviewees linked the deterioration of 'their' previous areas to the presence of minority ethnic groups loosely defined as non-Anglophone, non-white and/or non-British ('Asians', 'Bosnians', 'refugees'). For example, John had moved to Eastside from Hackney and was very clear that he had moved to a 'better area' because of the 'standard of people who live there'. He described the physical collapse of the East End where he had been brought up and how he wanted a 'litter boundary where you can say, "right, we will accept that, but nothing below that"'. Boundary maintenance was important since it would not only prevent the spread of physical dirt in the form of litter, but it would also shore up the threatened health (and thereby identity) of white British residents:

> I will go back to any tower block in Hackney or Bethnal Green, if you put a percentage of Asians in there, they will put it down, because they live differently, they spit everywhere, their cooking stuff goes everywhere. In the summer, they're infested with cockroaches. I am not being funny. White people didn't suffer with that before, but now it is a health risk, it is just the way they live.

In John's racist discourse, the previously 'healthy' (morally hygienic) white east London community was being undermined by the presence of alien others, rather than by the poverty and substandard housing prevalent in boroughs such as Hackney and Tower Hamlets. The Asian 'others' were thought to bring dirt (cockroaches, spittle) and therefore disease.[43] Avoiding such others by moving to Eastside therefore highlights the significance of white flight *vis-à-vis* Londoners' suburban migration.[44]

In the narratives of urban decline, the sense of loss could evoke strong emotions in the interviewees. What was being expressed was a sense of abjection, in Kristeva's terms, of disgust that the borders of the past neighbourhood-based community had been breached by polluting elements (youths, tenants, immigrants, Asians) and these same elements had ultimately destroyed it. The remembered lost community was a 'symbolically pure' space in Sibley's terms, even if it never really existed as such.

Blots on the suburban landscape

What did the suburban in-movers think about Eastside once they had moved there? Most were very satisfied with their housing and to a somewhat lesser extent with their neighbourhoods. Eastside was routinely described as 'quiet', 'peaceful', 'convenient' and close to the countryside, as well as 'clean' or 'cleaner', indicating the power of the suburban purity image. In fact, one-quarter of the survey respondents could think of nothing they disliked about living in the area. In many ways a benign picture can be painted of suburban order, cleanliness and tranquillity as opposed to the urban disorder, dirt and ever present risk they had left behind in London, and especially for those who had moved from east London, apart from Havering.

Despite this image of suburban purity and order, there was also evidence of either overt or more submerged disquiet. Some of this related to inade-quate infrastructure, notably the paucity of public transport and limited shopping and leisure facilities. However, much of the disquiet centred on the perceived qualities of the Eastside area and the way it contained more dirty, disorderly urban elements than many residents would have ideally liked. Rather than Eastside being uniformly uncontaminated and 'clean', it would be more accurate instead to describe it as a 'spoiled suburb'.

In both the survey and interviews, respondents frequently qualified their more positive place images about 'the area' by making a spatial distinction between their more immediate neighbourhood and the rest of Eastside. Such qualificatory statements were especially prominent among people who lived in the Woodlands estate: 'it's the [Eastside] area I don't like; Woodlands estate is quiet and peaceful' (S.104). The middle-class Woodlands residents routinely described their estate as an 'oasis', one that was located within an otherwise urban desert that had managed to replicate, albeit to a lesser degree, the inner-city dirt and disorderliness they had fled London to avoid in the first place. The blots on the Eastside suburban landscape included the council estate, the state schools, the local shops and pubs, as well as nearby travellers' sites. To a greater or lesser extent, these were stigmatized polluted places to avoid. The large council estate in particular was associated with various combinations of crime, antisocial behaviour and poverty, as well as constituting a form of physical pollution: 'the [council] housing estate in Eastside is an eyesore' (S.19). The neighbourhood shops and pubs were often described as 'tatty' and 'rough' places to avoid.

Some ex-Londoners had moved to Eastside to get a 'better' education for their children by escaping inner-city schools. While several expressed satis-faction with the education provision in their new area, others included the local schools in their list of area dislikes. Negative comments about the state schools were more pronounced among the residents of Woodlands than among their Newtown counterparts. The semi-structured interviews revealed the depth of dissatisfaction with the local schools plus the various strategies that parents engaged in both to gain information and to prevent their chil-dren going to such schools.[45] The middle-class parents living in the Woodlands estate tended to send their children outside the Eastside area, either elsewhere in Essex or to affluent suburban areas in London. One Woodlands mother (Lesley) explained her neighbour's 'disgusted' reaction to the local schools:

> Just the way the children were unruly, toilets were filthy, the class-rooms were filthy, they just didn't look like they were, you know, what you would expect in a school or what I would expect in a school anyway. I know this sounds horrible as well, but you get lots of slow children. We've got a lot of camp sites round here, so you get a lot of travellers' children going to these schools so you know then English isn't always their first language so the teachers spend a lot of time trying to help these children so your children aren't progressing.

While Lesley was very concerned not to appear 'snobbish', at the same time she expressed distaste for the 'dirty' elements associated with the local schools, both physical ('filthy classrooms') and social ('unruly children'). The local schools did not live up to her or other Woodlands parents' educational expectations, expectations bound up with a moral order that was threatened by signs of dirt. These signs also had racialized connotations in relation to those children who came from another blot on the suburban landscape, namely travellers' camp sites of which there are many in Essex. Rather than truly escaping the 'roughs and toughs' found in inner-city schools,[46] the middle-class parents simply encountered different versions of these same polluting others.

As well as pre-existing sites of dirt and disorder, the Eastside residents also expressed concern about polluting 'flows', not least the drift of ex-city dwellers ironically making the selfsame move as the interviewees. For example, Rob from Dagenham praised Eastside's cleanliness and order, but he also expressed doubts about whether this could be maintained:

> People talk about how Essex is this and that but Essex is a clean area, it's a nice area, at the moment. Whether it stays that way or not, I don't know. I know you've got a lot of yobs moving into this part of Essex, moved out of London, most of them lived on the ganglands and different bits and pieces but it's still a nice place to live at the moment, no tall high-rise flats and things.

Similarly, Barbara, who was in her sixties, commented on how moving from Newham meant that she could now mix with a 'better class' of person, and at the same time 'it doesn't feel so dirty to me here'. However, she thought that polluting urban elements were beginning to make their appearance felt in Eastside and that this was precipitating a change in the area:

89

But when we first came here, I know it's only a short while really, it's been ten years, and I've noticed the decline since. I know it sounds silly, there was a lot more green verges; now they've started to cement the roads up and even dogs [are] fouling the park. Now, we've never seen ... I've noticed that within the last year or so, there's a difference there. Whether it's because the Londoners have moved out and brought some of their dirty habits with them [laughs] I don't know, with their animals, but I've noticed that within the borough within the last couple of years.

The porous, precarious nature of the boundary separating Eastside from London reflects Kristeva's notion of abjection since there was a sense of dread and anxiety that polluting elements were slipping through. For some interviewees, these elements took a racialized form. Ewan was originally from Scotland, but prior to coming to Eastside he had lived for several years in north London in an area he described as 'rough' because of the presence of East European refugees: 'There were Romanian women peeing outside the station, Albanians, Kosovans. There were cockroaches coming up from the flat below. It *was* a nice estate, but shopping trolleys were dumped, burnt out cars, the area went downhill and it's starting to happen here, it's following us out.'

The aspirant imagination, pure and spoiled suburbs

Most of the ex-Londoners regarded their move out to Eastside positively. They had secured either a first or a better step on the property ladder and were pleased with their homes. They were somewhat less pleased with the Eastside area, although those who had moved from east London, with the exception of those from Havering, generally considered it an improvement. They had successfully left behind the dirty, disorderly city, one in which previous neighbourhood-based communities had dissolved. Abjection, feelings of anxiety and disgust, were expressed in relation to these narratives of urban decline as the pure imagined community of the past had been penetrated and overwhelmed by a gamut of polluting 'others' (like youths, tenants and immigrants). Suburban relocation had a white flight connotation for several ex-Londoners, even if this was not necessarily the only or most significant part of their overall rationale for leaving the city.

Eastside's purity, however, was partial. There were too many blots on the suburban landscape such as the council estate. The latter was the product of an earlier round of state driven housing investment, built to accommodate the postwar Fordist working class, but one that more recent home-owning newcomers felt threatened their real or aspirational sense of class exclusivity. Although a significant proportion of the Eastside interviewees were working class in occupational terms, home ownership acted as a significant marker of social distinction in consumption terms, as is typically the case in England.[47] In addition, several Eastsiders, particularly the middle-class Woodlands residents, held negative views about the local schools. Racist discourses existed around another potential blot on the landscape in the form of traveller encampments. The urban/suburban boundary was furthermore insecure because polluting urban elements, 'yobs' as well as racialized 'others' (immigrants, especially those from Africa and eastern Europe), were flowing down the Thames and seeping into Eastside. Rather than the pure suburb of the socially aspirant imagination, Eastside constituted a 'spoiled suburb', one that contained too many dirty, disorderly elements of city life. The Woodlands estate came closest to the ideal suburban place image, but its location within Eastside ultimately rendered it flawed. The feelings of abjection identified among the socially aspirant Eastsiders who had been brought up in east London are likely to persist given their uneasy suspension between two equally out of reach pure places, namely the long lost community of their youth and the affluent suburb of their imagined futures.

Given the increasing social pluralism found in many suburban areas, it may very well be that the 'symbolically pure' exclusive suburb only ever really exists in the imaginations of the upwardly mobile. Research on a wealthy New York suburb highlighted the connections its affluent residents made between dirt and the presence of racialized others including, ironically, the Latino day labourers employed to keep the suburban landscape manicured.[48] The suburban hinterlands of global cities such as London and New York are increasingly taking on the messiness characteristic of cities, thereby blurring the urban/suburban binary. While Clapson has correctly highlighted the aspirational nature of suburbia, his approach is too benign since he fails to uncover the deep exclusionary concerns underpinning the aspirant imagination.[49] A future suburban research agenda might focus on how and why particular social categories come to have 'dirty' attributes even in the 'cleanest' suburbs.

Chapter 7

Dangers Lurking Everywhere: The Sex Offender as Pollution

PAMELA K. GILBERT

The national television talk show, 'The View', selected Coral Gables as one of the sexiest suburbs in America.

The city of Coral Gables also enacted a law that restricts where people convicted of felony sex offences can live in the city. This municipality joins a number of other south Florida cities that prohibit sexual offenders and sexual predators convicted of crimes from establishing temporary or permanent residence within 2500 feet of 'any school, designated public school bus stop, daycare center, park, playground or other place where children congregate'.

As the two quotes above, taken from the same page of a glossy promotional brochure for the city of Coral Gables, suggest, sex and the city are uneasy bedfellows. Though the confusing juxtaposition of 'suburb' and 'city' suggest more desperate housewives than street edginess, the brochure makes clear that Coral Gables's 'sexiness' is based not on its beautiful people, but on its 'fine living, upscale shopping and gourmet cuisine'.[1] The entire brochure is fronted by this description of the founding of Coral Gables: George Merrick had a 'dream ... to build a City Beautiful, without blot or blemish, without ugliness or dirt'.[2] But in a beach city proud of its 'sexiness', inevitably, dirt happens.

The association of the city with sexual licence and sophistication – or perversion – is an old one in Western culture. In US history, the image of the utopian, gleaming 'city on a hill' from Matthew 5:14 has been used since Puritan John Winthrop's famous 1630 New England sermon, 'A Model of Christian Charity', to its repeated invocation in Ronald Reagan speeches, to invoke the perfectly civil, utopian civilization – a holy, indeed, sacred place. In 1974, Reagan quoted Winthrop and insisted that America had fulfilled the promise of the city of the hill: 'We are not a sick society. ... We are indeed, and we are today, the last best hope of man on earth.'[3] This image of godly and healthy American civility is often set against the image of the 'cities of the plains' defined specifically by sexual deviance and 'cleansed' by God in a cataclysmic act of destruction. Indeed, ignoring the damage to hundreds of rural communities devastated by recent storms, various right-wing evangelicals preferred to read the wreckage wrought by Hurricane Katrina as a judgement on famously sexy New Orleans.[4]

Mapping deviance: sex offender laws

Given this association, it is scarcely surprising that it is non-normative, non-reproductive sexuality that is most closely associated with disgust and boundary transgression. Sex shops, for example, are aggressively regulated through zoning and obscenity laws, as are their products. But nothing generates quite as much horror these days as sex offenders and sexual predators. From 1989 to 1999, a series of notification laws (often collectively referred to as Megan's laws, after Megan Kanka, the child rape-murder victim of a repeat offender) have dovetailed with a series of measures aimed at containing the mobility of sex offenders within high density areas to create an unprecedented apparent transparency and geographic precision in mapping the locations of the 'polluting' threat posed by such individuals. By 1999, all 50 states of the USA had passed some such legislation.[5] Such laws publicize the locations (by home address) of those who have committed crimes designated as sex offences. In turn, many cities have passed laws regulating where such offenders may live – keeping them 1000, 2000 or 2500 feet from various sites considered especially vulnerable, such as schools or daycare centres. These laws promised to map the dangers of the urban landscape and eventually to contain them. However, this transparency is misleading and reveals more about our imaginary relationship to sex, 'dirt' and the city than it does about actual dangers in the urban environment.

Steve Macek argues that the 'panic over inner-city pathology and chaos has been structured and informed by a conservative discourse that consistently blamed the victims of the urban crisis for their plight and constructed the central city as an object of middle-class fear.'[6] He traces how, over the second half of the twentieth century, US federal lending and development policies fostered suburbanization and white flight, while concentrating minorities in large urban cores. As critics such as Macek, and Peter Stallybrass and Allon White have pointed out, since at least the nineteenth century the poor of the urban core have been associated with and ultimately identified as filth, both moral and physical.[7] Physical filth has been culturally defined in the West as related to the abject materials of a transgressive physicality – 'matter out of place' – including faeces, semen and other bodily fluids. Moral filth is often related to proscribed sexual practices. In the recent US context that has taken on a particular racial cast as well.

Due to the density of population and therefore schools, churches and other proscribed areas, several cities have been forced to move their sexual offenders to nearby rural areas, where they then live in high concentrations, often unable to find jobs. Worse, the inability to settle in any viable place tends to make some offenders homeless. If they remain homeless, or find a home in a proscribed area, they often go 'off the grid', failing to report their location. Many police and district attorneys consider this problem more serious than having offenders living near a church.[8] City officials often resort to placing 'undesirable' people and property just beyond the edge of the city in poor neighborhoods, or in industrial areas. In Seattle, the attempt to zone its main industrial area as an area hospitable to strip clubs generated resistance from business owners. As editorialist Mike Peringer complains:[9]

> In Sodo alone ... [this] four square-mile area provides about 20 per cent of the city's revenue ... and 70 per cent of its goods and services. Why then are we considered the dumping ground for projects deemed unsuitable for other areas of the city? We are home to the State Secured Facility, commonly known as sex offender housing, and the new headquarters for the Department of Corrections. Now the mayor and City Council want to put the strip club zone right smack in the middle of Sodo.

The metaphor of the dumping ground and sex offenders as refuse or vermin is pervasive in public discussion. (The use of financial productivity to justify immunity from such 'dumping' is also telling.) As one newspaper reader commented on a scheme to zone offenders out of a Kansas city, 'Cities should be required to keep the filth they breed: Offenders should be required to return from whence they came.'[10] Cities are thus considered as sites of especial danger, both producing and concentrating such dangers.

Dangers lurking everywhere

Given this pervasive association, it is perhaps surprising to note that the horrifying high-profile US cases that have driven the current concern about sex offenders are not representative of those affected by the notification and zoning laws. Most of these cases, involving the abduction, rape and murder of children (Megan Kanka, Polly Klaas, Ashley Estell and Jessica Lunsford) by repeat sex offenders have been committed in small towns and rural areas. All these cases, for which laws were named, were white on white crimes.[11] Yet, in actual offender registries, blacks are much more likely to be tagged as offenders than whites. Law professor Daniel M. Filler notes that African-Americans are 'grossly over-represented' on notification lists and that in some US states African-Americans are 16 times more subject to inclusion on such state-sponsored websites than whites.[12]

Further, people are often identified as sex offenders who are not violent and not dangerous to children. For example, one young woman whose photo was used to advertise her presence as a sex offender in the small city of Gainesville, Florida was so identified on the basis of her commission of a 'crime against nature' in Louisiana, which was probably either prostitution or engagement in consensual lesbian sex.[13] Her inclusion on a list designed to alert the public to paedophiles or violent offenders is unhelpful at best. Filler observes that, although all 50 US states now have notification laws, their regulations vary wildly. Some states only give public notice in the cases of those 'convicted of serious sexual offenses and child kidnapping', whereas others include nonsexual violent offences, and several include 'regulatory sexual offenses, such as prostitution, which effectively transforms their notification laws into anti-vice schemes'.[14] Finally, although the crimes used to mobilize consent to the notification and zoning laws are appalling acts by repeat offenders, most children affected by violence, sexual or otherwise, are more at risk in their homes and from family members than from unrelated prior sex offenders. Legal scholar Mona Lynch notes, as do several commentators on this discourse, that the sex offender is always figured in legislators' discussions as male, never as a family member or intimate of his victims: the threat is represented as outside the family, which is itself the realm of the 'pure and innocent'.[15] However, only about 3 per cent of child sexual abuse and only around 6 per cent of child murders are committed by strangers.[16]

These scare tactics swell the numbers of 'sexual offenders' until a relatively rare event comes to seem an ever-present threat. In Gainesville, Florida, public schools took eight months to change the location of a bus stop when a parent discovered that the stop was at a sex offender's front lawn, because there were ten sex offenders living within a half-mile or less of that bus stop.[17] In a small edge city near Orlando, Florida, local activists were able temporarily to stall the building of a mega church they opposed for reasons to do with traffic and urban sprawl by using their sex offenders to enforce exclusive zoning in reverse, because there were two sex offenders living within 1000 feet of the proposed site, and more than 30 of them living within a mile of the proposed building.[18] Some housing developers are even advertising planned communities with explicit anti-offender zoning.[19]

Phillip Jenkins traces the history of moral panics about child molestation in the United States and finds that periodic pendulum swings between expansive views of what constitutes molestation and a sense of ubiquitous threat alternate with relatively relaxed attitudes towards many practices we today think of as criminal. He argues that fears of the sex fiend peaked after the Second World War, but then shifted back to a liberal model for the next twenty-five or so years. Now, however, we have moved back to a model under which most sex offenders are viewed with little differentiation as identical with torturers and serial killers. As he remarks, 'in each era, the prevailing opinion was supported by what appeared at the time to be convincing objective research.'[20] In the 1980s, he observes, police and law makers targeted sexual offences as top priorities, and made it easier to convict on such charges. These changes had predictable results:

> There were about 58,000 sex offenders in the nation's prisons in 1988; by 1990 that number had increased to 85,000, a 47 per cent increase in just three years, and sex offenders (however defined) composed one-sixth of all inmates in federal and state institutions. ... Although the upsurge in the numbers of known and convicted offenders resulted largely from the reorientation in law-enforcement priorities, it lent credence to claims that the sexual abuse of children was an epidemic out of control.[21]

At the time Jenkins's book, published in 2006, went to press, California offered as part of its state notification programme a CD with records of 64,000 sex offenders.[22] Texas publicly lists even its juvenile sex offenders; the youngest is ten years old.[23]

Danger and disgust

Legal scholar Mona Lynch, drawing on Mary Douglas's foundational work in *Purity and Danger*, suggests that policymaking about sex offenders is not based on reason or data, but is 'steeped in a constellation of emotional expressions of disgust, fear of contagion, and pollution avoidance, manifested in a legislative concern about boundary vulnerabilities between social spheres of the pure and the dangerous'.[24] She examines two characteristics of disgust in legislative debates on sex offenders. The first has to do with the 'highly polluting or contaminating nature of disgust elicitors', and the second deals with the 'sphere of purity that must be protected from contamination. Disgust works as a dichotomy, rather than as a continuum, so that the distinct categories of the disgusting and the pure (or non-disgusting) must not be blurred.'[25] The disgusting, she notes, is often understood as that which violates spatial boundaries, and purity can only be protected by reinforcing such boundaries, often through extreme measures. This 'boundary building', she notes, may act as a 'communalizing force'.[26]

In the debates she examines, sex offenders are described as 'dangerous contaminators of what is pure in America'. But they also are portrayed as having super- or subhuman qualities of being amorphous and ubiquitous. 'They intrude, disrespect boundaries, creep, and invade the social spheres of purity.'[27] In relation to the city, the proximity of the disgusting and the delightful has special symbolic weight. Joyce Carol Oates has posed the problem this way:

> American literature of the twentieth century suggests that the City …
> has absorbed into itself presumably opposed images of the 'sacred' and
> the 'secular'. … A result of this fusion of polar symbols is that the
> contemporary City, as an expression of human ingenuity and, indeed,
> a material expression of civilization itself, must always be read as if it
> were Utopian (that is, 'sacred') – and consequently a tragic disappoint-
> ment, a species of hell.[28]

I would like to build on Lynch's comments about the 'disgusting' or polluting nature of sex offenders and Oates's insights on the city, but also to suggest that rather than addressing 'polar opposites', which implies a significant imaginary spatial separation, we are in fact addressing a specifically late modern perception of the disgusting as inherent in, necessary to, but always threatening to exceed and thus destroy the pure. In the political sphere, Giorgio Agamben and Lauren Berlant have located such boundary-violation threats at the very heart of modern sovereignty and citizenship.[29] The sex offender is 'our' necessary Other in an era in which we figure physical violation as an apolitical and unmotivated crime against innocence, and avoid the consideration of violence at the heart of state action motivated by political or social goals.

The sacred and the unclean have always symbolically lain very close to each other; what is most pure is most subject to defilement, most in constant danger. Mary Douglas, analysing the concept of '*sacer*' or sacred, notes that in 'primitive' religions there is a two-way danger of defilement between divinity and the secular rather than a simple polar opposition between the holy and profane.[30] More recently Giorgio Agamben has analysed '*sacer*' (*homo sacer*) to trace its continuing confusion of the holy and the defiled within modernity. The *homo sacer* was traditionally defined in laws dating back to

Roman times as the man who had been banished; every hand was against him, and he was stripped of his political status as a member of the community. He could be killed without penalty, but legally he could not be murdered or sacrificed. Such a person occupies a status between human and not human, between being politically counted as living or dead. Yet, at the same time, as the term suggests, the nature of banishment was close to the sacred – the realm wherein death and life, the divine and human touched. The *homo sacer*, he argues, is the proscribed personhood that guarantees sovereignty by its ritual status. Sovereignty is what confers the power to confer the status of *homo sacer*.

Agamben traces the history of the concept in the West, leading to such modern incarnations as the Jewish death camp prisoner in the Nazi era and the non-enemy combatants held by the USA at Guantanamo Bay during the US and allied forces' wars with Afghanistan and Iraq. The *homo sacer*, he argues, is the proscribed personhood that guarantees sovereignty by its ritual status. Sovereignty needs the *homo sacer* to shore up its powers; it is the ability to designate the *homo sacer* that demonstrates the state's power and offers a logic to justify its authority. The community is bound together in its relation to the proscribed. While in no way wishing to invoke a comparison of the sex offender's moral status with the victims of the state power that Giorgio Agamben identifies, I would argue that presently, in much the way that *homo sacer* does, the 'inhuman' sexual offender structurally guarantees the coherence of sexuality and the law by being the proscribed, defiled and defiling object of disgust, fear, desire and discipline. The most popular of the spectacularly successful US *Law and Order* television shows, the *Special Victims Unit*, focuses on the commission, pursuit and punishment of urban (New York City) sex offenders, especially paedophiles. The public may be disgusted by paedophilia but it is also riveted by it – 'we' love these stories.[31] The obsession with structural containment shown in zoning laws, with geographical organization, provides a way to mobilize and also make spatially legible fears about urban concentration.

As critic Winfried Menninghaus points out in his epic study, *Disgust: The Theory and History of a Strong Sensation*, by the late eighteenth century philosophers had a carefully elaborated theory of disgust as part of their analysis of aesthetics. 'In its violent defense against the approach of something inassimilable, the unpleasant disgust-sensation evokes a particularly intense awareness of self. For nothing less is at stake in disgust than the physical or moral integrity of those who feel it.'[32] Disgust, comprised both of repulsion and fascination, is persistently associated in Western culture with death, old age, and the feminine, with proscribed sexuality, fecundity and the openings of the body. In eighteenth-century European aesthetics articulated around classical ideals of the body, Menninghaus points out, an ideal of the seamless, closed body emerged: as Herder put it, the beautiful body was like 'softly blown' glass – a continuous line without interruption.[33] Openings of the body, and their implied relation to the interior depths of corporeality, were inherently disgusting, and had to be handled artistically with the utmost care to preserve the aesthetic experience. These theories continued to be foundational for the aesthetics of the body. Late modern theories of the good and the beautiful were constructed in opposition to the disgusting, and for such twentieth-century theorists as Freud and Battaille, civilization is actually based on the disgusting – the non-excludable exclusion from polite inter-course, the organic real at the heart of social artifice. To have a body, one must have openings; material must enter and exit the body. The denial of the body's permeability and its abject products is fundamental to modern society, but of course shit happens. Managing both what happens and the denial that it does has been at the heart of urban planning for most of the late modern period.

Planning for the disgusting

As Stallybrass and White have argued, the nineteenth-century city is organized around the binaries of filth/cleanliness and the constant fear of their transgression, or contamination, driven by the engine of desire.[34] This fear 'was articulated above all through the "body" of the city, which had to be surveyed to be controlled'.[35] As I have argued elsewhere, by the mid-century, this surveillance – equated with the very essence of civilization – had become institutionalized in the mechanisms of sanitary inspection and had entered both literary and visual culture, the latter principally in the form of maps.[36] By the mid-century, the 'lower bodily strata' of both city and its inhabitants, which Stallybrass and White describe as being identified with both sewage and underclass behaviour, was increasingly expressed as both disease and anti-modernity.

The spread of maps as tools for understanding the environment and the population paralleled a spatialization of governmental knowledge of the social body. Social mapping enabled cartographers to represent what they perceived to be before them and, it was hoped, make the territory thus represented conform to an ideal. Early sanitary cartographers of disease and sewerage founded their claims to authority in part on the connection of disease to vice, using a largely sanitary model of disease produced by filth.[37] Using the rhetoric of civilization and barbarism, cleanliness and filth, they laid out the identification of health with urban improvement, and both with moral progress and civilization.

Medical mapping in the nineteenth century was increasingly related to intervention by a state that came to be seen as the proper guardian of public health and civil behaviour. The planned city seems to promise freedom, commerce, prosperity and unproblematic connection. But within that is the uncivil, dirty and dangerous to which we are exposed in the gregarious proximity of the urban space. Mapping not only spatialized the threat to civility but also articulated the city as a vulnerable body. The latest form of mapping, which seeks to contain the filthy and disgusting, is also related to moral issues and the violation of bodily and social boundaries, but in an era in which sewerage is largely manageable, attention has turned to other kinds of bodily practice. The city is divided into zones of purity and zones of danger. Sex offenders, like the polluting refuse to which they are so often compared, are dispersed throughout the city and liable to circulate freely unless carefully contained – a mobile and pervasive threat. Mapping and zoning locates that threat and offers the fantasy that their mobility can be contained, that zones of purity, associated with the figure of the child, can be sealed off.

Sex offenders and civility

One part of his discussion of the history of *homo sacer* – a category on which, according to Agamben, modern notions of sovereignty are wholly dependent – is particularly germane to our construction of sex offenders in relation to the city as a site of urbanity and civilization. To place a man under the ban, to declare him a '*homo sacer*' under various permutations of Roman and Anglo Saxon laws, is to declare him nonhuman under the law, but not an animal either – a peculiar combination of both. Agamben notes that in various legal traditions, the *homo sacer* has been defined as a wolf-man, wolf's head, or 'man without peace'.[38] This violation of animal–human boundaries sets such creatures at odds with the human community. 'What had to remain in the collective unconsciousness as a monstrous hybrid of human and animal, divided between the forest and the city – the werewolf – is therefore in its origin the figure of the man who has been banned from the city.'[39] The city here is the ancient figure of the city as a zone of civility and law, within which society was structured and from which it is ruled. This city, then, is less a particular city or settlement than the idea of a city as it was manifested in classical and medieval times. This concept of the city continues to inform the utopian side of city planning and, indeed, city life. However, its dark underside, the threat of the specifically urban predator enabled by the density and anonymity that makes civic freedom uniquely possible, has been a dominant strand in representations of the city from about the late eighteenth century onward, and in twentieth-century America has been the occasion of repeated moral panics.

Agamben argues that the Hobbesian 'state of nature' has historically been understood in law not as a period prior to the founding of the city, but a principle internal to the city, 'the exception and the threshold that constitutes and dwells within it'.[40] When civility is dissolved, the state of nature is what is left, and the whole notion of civility is based on the assumption that such a state is possible at any time. It is this that upholds the authority of the law selectively to declare a person *homo sacer* – the enemy of all, the wolf-man without peace, the man against whom every hand is raised without penalty. Although, of course, legally, the sex offender's position is not so exaggerated (except possibly in Louisiana where capital punishment is stipulated for certain sex offences), socially, this is not a wholly inaccurate depiction. Although it should go without saying, I will go on record here that I am not advocating a permissive attitude to sexual violence or coercion. But, as we have already seen, many of those described as 'sex offenders' do not fit the definition of those against whom such legislation was designed to protect.[41] Through notification laws, such offenders are set apart and stripped of legal protections available to other categories of offenders. Although not legally subject to beatings and murder, in fact that is often the result of notification publicity. Legislators and private citizens alike frequently describe offenders as filth, trash, vermin and other nonhuman objects of disgust and loathing. Their imaginary relationship to the civility of the population as well as to the dystopian urban imaginary, frames such offenders as *homines sacri*.

If sex offenders, then, operate in the social imaginary as the guarantors of our civility, who can no longer simply be expunged from the city but must remain within and of it as foci for communal loathing, then zoning restrictions against such offenders supply us with a spatial metaphor for civility and safety. The fact that their locations are mapped offers the fantasy of a city whose dangers can be made entirely legible, as well as a complementary horror story in which such dangers are liable to pop out of every apartment building. Moreover, if such mapping identifies zones of purity or civility, it is telling that schools, daycare centres and churches are what we choose to protect. (Are there really more children at church than in the mall? And, for that matter, are they not safer at church and school, where they are more likely to be accompanied by adults, than at a mall or fast food outlet? And why are children singled out more than adults?) There is nothing obvious about the spatial containment of sexual offenders. In an era of internet connections, mere proximity to a church centre is hardly the most serious threat to anyone's safety. An able bodied sex offender ought to be able to walk 2500 feet. Also, since most offenders on the database target women and female adolescents more than children, it might make more sense to keep them away from women's bookstores and gynaecological clinics than daycare centres. Although such zoning suggests that sex offences are crimes of opportunity, we do not treat other crimes of opportunity this way – forcing car thieves to live far from public parking lots, for example.

Lauren Berlant has written extensively about the infantilization of the image of the citizen in the United States, part of a general movement toward replacing political discussion in the public sphere with what Hannah Arendt called the social – the sphere of intimacy. Once politics can revolve around what Berlant calls 'intimate things', sexual practices and family values, the public sphere can effectually be emptied of political content and the American citizen represented as an 'innocent' child perpetually under siege from sexual and other threats[42] – though also potentially monstrous, violent (because violated) and perverse (because perverted). But it also means the perpetual saturation of the public sphere by precisely the sexuality that is seen as polluting to the innocence of the child. As James Kincaid has pointed out, representations of the hyper-sexualized child teeter vertiginously on the edge of this dichotomy.[43] If the sexually innocent child is the citizen *par excellence*, then the sex offender is beyond all others the threat to civility and American identity. Taking questions of the troubled city away from issues of racial tension, economic inequality, or pervasive political differences in values reflected in the international turmoil of the last several years, the sex offender brings all 'decent' Americans together in righteous indignation, and promises an easy containment of those problems, even while gesturing to the extensive propagation of the threat and need for constant watchfulness.

I would suggest then that, instead of the 'polar opposites' between purity and pollution, delight and disgust, as we see in the Coral Gables brochure cited at the beginning of this chapter, that the two produce and depend on each other occupying the same space. They are not polar opposites, but contiguous grounds whose segregation depends on constant vigilance to guarantee our own civility. Nowhere is this contiguity more obvious or vexed than in the city, where urban density and the promise of autonomy, pleasure and civility vie with the disgust that lies at the heart of the utopian, modern, clean city on a hill. To contain symbolically the threat of the disgust that *must* lie at the heart of such autonomy, pleasure and power, we create the *homo sacer*, or wolf man, the imaginary child molester. And, in the expansion and proliferation of this symbolic threat, real dangers are masked and diluted within an enormous crowd of imaginary bogeys. Their association with filth mobilizes structures of feeling associated with the city and the body that obscure the function of sex offenders in our culture while seeming to make transparent the structure of our urban communities.

Chapter 8

Hygiene Aesthetics on London's Gay Scene: The Stigma of AIDS

JOHAN ANDERSSON

In this chapter I explore how stereotypical notions of gay venues as corrupting spaces, primarily derived from cinema, were recycled in media representations of London's gay scene in the 1980s. Although not specifically about 'dirt' in a physical sense,[1] these media representations stigmatized London's gay venues as dangerous and contagious spaces associated with violent crime and sexual disease. The architectural features of gay pubs at the time, which tended to be dark spaces with discreet entrances and exteriors, came to symbolize an unhealthy and hidden subculture associated with sexual contamination. Here it will be suggested that the emergence of a new type of gay venue in the early 1990s, characterized by open-fronted façades, minimalist interior design, and natural light, can be read as a commercial response to this earlier stigmatization. In particular, the use of hygiene aesthetics and certain forms of aesthetic labour were effective attempts to rid the commercial gay scene of some of its unhealthy connotations in the midst of the AIDS crisis. Earlier work on the gay scene in Soho has focused on the new visibility of gay men in public spaces, which was primarily achieved through the entrepreneurial clustering of venues within a small territory.[2] Here, the aim is to build on these studies by examining the interior spaces of Soho's new gay scene, interpreted against the backdrop of the media portrayal of earlier gay venues.

Sexual murders and AIDS

In the British mainstream media, gay bars and clubs featured rarely until the 1980s when a number of high profile crime investigations into gay murders coincided with the AIDS crisis. Drawing on literary and cinematic notions of the gay underworld, the reporting of violent crimes associated with London's gay scene often contributed to sensationalist imaginings of gay men and the urban spaces they frequented as contaminating. From the mid-1980s onwards, AIDS also came to feature in this type of crime reporting (typically as a murder motive) and earlier notions of gay venues as dangerous and corrupting spaces took on a new significance associated with death and the spread of disease.

The association between homosexual subcultures and the criminal underworld was a prominent theme in postwar cinema. As film historian Richard Dyer has shown, in the 1940s and 1950s film noir was the only cinematic genre that featured gay and lesbian characters. The settings for film noir borrow heavily from the gangster genre and are characterized by 'desolation, brutality, threat and alienation, as caught in images of pavements glistening with rain, ill-lit streets, dingy bars and grubby rooming-houses'.[3] Although specific gay milieux rarely featured in film noir, this iconography of urban alienation in films with gay characters helped to shape the perception of the gay world as a form of twilight zone – parallel or overlapping with the criminal underworld.[4] Later, from the 1960s onwards, homosexual themes were made more explicit in a number of thrillers that revolved around gay murders. As Dyer has argued, these films 'tend to be semi-prurient, anthropological excursions into this peculiar, other, dangerous world, with endless scenes of gay bars. ... It's an imaginary, anonymous, fetishistic, sexually-driven and very violent world.'[5]

One example of this genre is Gordon Douglas's *The Detective* (1968), in which Frank Sinatra plays a police lieutenant who goes to investigate a murder in New York's gay community. After wrongly convicting the victim's psychotic flat mate (a hysterical portrait of the tormented homosexual) it unfolds that the real murderer is a self-loathing closeted man who is 'more ashamed of being a homosexual than a murderer'.[6] This theme of gay-on-gay violence was later developed in William Friedkin's controversial film *Cruising* (1980), in which Al Pacino plays the lead role of a cop who goes undercover on New York's gay scene to find a sadistic serial gay killer. Eventually, Pacino's character becomes, or recognizes that he is, gay and, as a result (the last scene of the film suggests), he too begins to kill other gay men. The implied message that the gay scene is a contagious space where previously straight men can be contaminated with homosexuality (or alternatively that homosexual self-recognition turns men into psychotic self-loathing murderers) caused an outcry after the film's release.[7] Similar ideas and images of the

104

gay world, however, appeared in British crime journalism following the police hunts and trials of three serial killers of gay men in London in the 1980s and early 1990s.

The most high profile of these cases followed the arrest in 1983 of Dennis Nielsen, who had strangled 15 young men, many of whom he had picked up in London's gay pubs. Since most of Nielsen's victims were not reported missing, there was no media coverage of the murders prior to the arrest, which happened by chance. Instead, Brian Masters's book *Killing for Company*, to which Nielsen contributed with interviews, diaries and drawings, has become the most circulated description of how the murderer used London's gay pubs to find potential victims. Despite being a balanced and unprejudiced study in many ways, negative stereotypes are nevertheless present in the descriptions of London's gay scene, which is referred to as 'arid' and 'subterranean'.[8] According to Masters, 'the majority of men who congregate in these pubs are not interested in each other except as potential sexual encounters'.[9] This negative view is shared or possibly informed by Nielsen who is quoted describing 'the soul destroying pub scene and its resulting one-night stands'.[10] Nielsen also implies that he could not cope with the separation of being left in the mornings and, as a result, began to strangle his bedfellows: 'I was afraid to wake him in case he left me. Trembling with fear I strangled his struggling body and when he was dead I took his young body back to bed with me.'[11] For Nielsen, according to Masters, the gay scene represented a 'mortifying ephemerality'[12] and, as the title of the book suggests, he was 'killing for company'. Although it would be unfair to reduce Masters's book to this simplistic argument, one aspect of his analysis implies that the promiscuous (and 'soul destroying') gay scene was part of the explanation for the murders. This proposed link between promiscuity and death anticipates some of the later reporting on violent crime on London's gay scene during the AIDS crisis.

Shortly after the Dennis Nielsen trials, the media also began to report about AIDS and gay venues. In addition to their previous association with crime, prostitution and violence (which had all been part of the press coverage around Nielsen), such venues were also stigmatized now as public health hazards harbouring incurable disease. In the well-publicized case of Michael Lupo, a London serial killer sentenced to life imprisonment in 1987 for strangling four gay men, the new threat of AIDS seemed to merge with the older threat of violent crime. Lupo was HIV-positive and the press treated his medical status as a potential murder motive: had he gone on a killing-spree as a form of revenge indiscriminately directed at other gay men? This theory was implied in a headline in *The Times*: 'Aids sufferer haunted bars in war against homosexuals'.[13] The newspaper descriptions of London's 'homosexual haunts' and the 'derelict areas' frequented by the killer (who was described as a 'gay cruiser', implying a link between promiscuity and murder) underlined the dangers of the gay world.[14] That Lupo had been arrested on a dance floor also seemed highly symbolic: even the most hedonistic space associated with a gay lifestyle was a place where death lurked in the form of HIV-infected serial killers.[15]

It is easy to recognize the precedents of these media images of homosexual serial killers from thrillers such as *The Detective* and *Cruising*, but internalized AIDS-phobia, or an irrational drive for revenge against other gay men, has replaced the internalized homophobia. These pseudo-psychological interpretations of self-loathing and revenge were popular in the media in the 1980s and early 1990s and the motives of murders involving gay men were frequently framed in terms of AIDS. 'Man killed male lover who said he had Aids' read one headline in the *Independent* in early 1990, with the article describing how the murder had taken place inside a Soho nightclub.[16] Only weeks later the same newspaper ran a story on how 'A masochistic homosexual with Aids pleaded for more as he was punched and kicked to death by three men' on Hampstead Heath.[17] Reports like these clearly contributed to the perception of London's gay geography – whether in the commercial spaces of Soho's nightclubs or on cruising grounds like Hampstead Heath – as an unhealthy and dangerous world characterized by HIV-related violence.

In the early 1990s yet another serial killer, Colin Ireland, targeted London's gay venues and it was reported that three of his victims had been HIV-positive. Once again the press painted a picture of the gay underworld as characterized by sleaze, disease and HIV-motivated murders.[18] According to some newspaper reports, Ireland was the third serial killer (after Nielsen and Lupo) to have picked up at least one of his victims in The Coleherne pub in Earl's Court in west London[19] and, in response to these reports, the chairman of London's Tory MPs demanded that The Coleherne have its licence withdrawn.[20] This gives a good illustration of how the gay scene – or in this case a particular gay pub – was seen as part of the problem and, by association, somehow guilty of the violent acts some of its customers carried out.

The idea that you could eliminate a type of crime by eliminating the space in which the victims came into contact with the perpetrators also informed the policing of AIDS in the 1980s. Occasionally, quoting licensing infringements, the Metropolitan Police would try to close down gay venues in what could be seen as attempts to minimize the spaces in which HIV-negative men mixed with those who were HIV-positive. In January 1987, for example, the *Guardian* reported that the police had raided one of London's oldest gay venues, the Vauxhall Tavern in south London:

> Police, many wearing surgical rubber gloves, raided the Vauxhall Tavern, a gay London pub, early on Saturday and arrested 11 people

for drunkenness. The raid increased fears in the gay community that Aids is leading to a campaign of harassment of homosexuals by the police. Scotland Yard was unable yesterday to give any explanation other than confirm that the raid had taken place.[21]

The 'surgical rubber gloves' paint a stark picture of how gay venues were perceived as contaminated spaces in the midst of the AIDS crisis and the heavy handed raid suggests that homosexuality in itself was seen as something contagious that needed to be policed. A year later, the *Guardian* again reported an insensitive police operation when: 'police sent an extraordinary battalion of 60 officers in to "investigate" a possible licensing infringement at The Bell, a gay pub in King's Cross'.[22] Section 28 of the Local Government Act 1988, which was introduced at the same time and prohibited local authorities from 'promoting homosexuality', was based on a similar idea as the police harassment of gay venues: if young people were prevented from coming into touch with (contagious) homosexual material, they would not be contaminated with homosexuality or with AIDS.

Although liberal newspapers like the *Guardian* took a firm stance against Section 28 and police harassment of gay venues, some of its reporting around AIDS contributed to the perception of London's gay scene as an unhealthy subculture. One feature described one of London's most established gay venues, the London Apprentice in Shoreditch in the East End, as a place where HIV was regarded as destiny or even as a 'game': '"It's like a game of Russian roulette," says Tom, gay manager of the LA. "If that's the game they want to play, you can't stop them".'[23] The author of the article then went on to suggest that there was a form of 'logic' behind this 'game': 'If Aids is trying to stop us having sex, then we must have sex to prove to ourselves that we are not defeated by it. This is the logic that brings men to the LA.'[24] And to give this morbid argument an appropriately atmospheric and melodramatic setting, the London Apprentice was described in the vocabulary of the seedy and unhealthy underworld: 'The air is heady, thick with smoke, shafts of coloured light piercing the gloom. ... Aids dangles like a flashing neon sign in the midst of the gay community.'[25]

The clichéd features of the gay underworld – 'smoke', 'gloom' and 'neon' – had by now come to be associated with AIDS. Although journalists may have over-emphasized these characteristics when they reported from the gay scene, the darkness and smoke essentially derived from the architectural features of gay venues, which were secretive, reflecting the homophobia of the time. The pubs mentioned in media representations here – the Coleherne, the Vauxhall Tavern and the London Apprentice – were, like most other gay venues in London, boarded up with discreet exteriors and entrances. The lack of natural ventilation and light, through the lack of windows and open entrances, made these venues dark and smoky spaces, but with AIDS the 'smoke' and gloom' also came to represent an unhealthy and contaminated subculture.

Hygiene aesthetics and aesthetic labour in 1990s Soho

In this climate of stigmatization, a cluster of new gay venues opened up around Old Compton Street in Soho in the early 1990s. Soho has at different points in time been identified as London's French quarter, bohemia and red-light district, but since the 1980s the area has increasingly been associated with the media industries and trendy nightlife. The concentration of several gay venues in this centrally located but relatively secluded and pedestrian friendly area was significant because it created a space in which same sex desire was expressed openly in the streets.[26] In aesthetic terms the new gay venues also looked different: in contrast to the discreet and dark gay pubs of the past, they were bright spaces marketed as 'continental bars' with open-fronted entrances.

The first new gay bars in the area were Village West One on Hanway Street and Village Soho on Wardour Street, which both opened in 1991 and were run by business partners Gordon Lewis and Gary Henshaw. Over the next few years they expanded their business with new bars and nightclubs while other entrepreneurs followed their formula of 'continental bars'. In an interview for London's weekly lifestyle magazine *Time Out*, Lewis explained that they had tried to create 'an alternative to the public house and instead have something like you'd find in Paris or Amsterdam'.[27] Similarly, Henshaw told the *Independent* that they wanted to 'pursue the continental idea' and 'get away from the British pub atmosphere in general' by serving 'cappuccinos [and] good food'.[28] This rejection of the public house in favour of 'continental bars' and coffee culture was part of a wider trend of Europeanized consumption habits in Britain at the time, but in the particular context of the gay economy these European design and consumption references can also be read as reactions to the legal and political situation in the UK. In the early 1990s the gay media, but also broadsheet national newspapers, began to highlight that British law on gay issues was increasingly out of synch with more liberal European countries and often contradicted European law. Gay and lesbian holidaymakers in cities such as Paris, Amsterdam and Berlin would also have been confronted with more open and visible gay scenes than in London. In this legal and cultural climate the public house, with its opaque exteriors, came to represent the closet and a particular form of British repression, whereas the open-fronted transparent façades of European bars signalled a more sexually liberated future.

Before opening the Village bars in London, the owners did not actually go to Europe for inspiration: instead they went north to Manchester where Britain's first open-fronted gay bar, Manto, had opened in December 1990.

8.1   Exterior, Rupert Street bar, Soho, London.

Manto, with its 30-foot plate glass windows has been referred to as a 'queer architectural statement'[29] and as a 'theatrical aesthetic' whose 'goldfish-bowl windows magnify and underline a gay presence'.[30] The Village bar owners in London consciously copied Manto's design: 'We went up to have a look at it and we copied a bit of their style. Again it was all glass – proud to be gay – and nobody hiding behind black windows.'[31] Other bar owners in Soho followed and a few years later in 1997 the open-fronted design was taken to its extreme in the bar 'Rupert Street' where the walls were glazed (see Figure 8.1): 'The blackened panes of glass have gone. The furtiveness is finished. The café bar in Rupert Street is proud to put the clientele on display through clear, curtainless windows', reported the *Financial Times*.[32] As well as making a claim on the street itself, the name Rupert Street signalled that gay life was now taking place on street level and not only in basement bars. Earlier names of gay venues in London such as Substation, Backstreet and the Fort had evoked an urban and architectural imagery of anonymous, hidden and enclosed spaces, but Rupert Street disclosed its address to everyone through its name.

The interior design equally broke with the previous tradition of dark pubs, which through the media coverage of violent crime and AIDS had become associated with a dangerous subculture. Most of Soho's new gay bars conformed to a minimalist interior design where the traditional dark colours

109

of the pub were replaced by light colours and natural light (see Figure 8.2). The walls were white – a colour Jean Baudrillard has described as 'a surgical, virginal colour which distances the body from the dangers of intimacy and tends to neutralize the drives'.[33] In addition, the wooden materials of the pub were replaced with chromed steel, zinc and glass – materials Adrian Forty has argued were welcomed in 1920s furniture design 'not just because of their associations with machines, but also because they could easily be kept clean, and, above all, could look absolutely spotless'.[34] These design trends were not merely references to Europe or Paris, but also a form of hygienic aesthetic in response to the gay scene's unhealthy underworld stigma that had become accentuated through the AIDS crisis. Before opening the first Village bars, one of the owners, Gary Henshaw, went to work in Soho's existing gay pubs – Comptons on Old Compton Street and Brief Encounters on St Martin's Lane – to see 'what they did right and what they did wrong'[35] and came to the conclusion that these venues did not seem very hygienic. Both were owned by the brewery chain Charrington and, according to Henshaw, 'They were dirty run-down places where the toilets always stank – the hidden part of a big brewery chain.'[36] At a time when gay venues were generally seen as dark and unhealthy places, the Village bars marketed themselves as clean and hygienic and this immediately had an impact in the gay press: 'The bar is always spotlessly clean, as are the toilets, and there is no lack of ashtrays,' wrote *Capital Gay* about Village West One.[37] Village Soho was promoted in a similar way in the same magazine: 'The bar is as you would expect from the people behind the Village – smart, stylish, cool and clean.'[38]

In addition to the marketed idea of cleanliness, the Village bars and their followers deployed aesthetic labour and consciously picked staff who looked healthy, clean shaven and young. Before opening Village West One, the owners interviewed 150 people and selected 14 young men with an average age of 21: 'We went for a look, we went for a young sort of fresh face, young good looking guys.'[39] If, as Lynn Hettinger has suggested, geography affects 'aesthetic labour demands',[40] Soho's own niche market promoted the classic beauty of the clean-shaven 'pretty boy'. This fresh-faced look also has to be seen as part of a wider attempt to market the new bars as 'healthy' places at a time when the gay community was coming to terms with AIDS. Trademark© – the graphic designer who produced the advertising for the Village bars – also created several iconic pictures featuring young men who conformed to this particular beauty ideal. When Henshaw, in 1993, opened his own business consultancy, he tried to capitalize on this idea of cleanliness and aesthetic labour and described it as something of his own trademark:

> I've gained a reputation for having efficient, friendly, helpful and attractive staff. It's things like that which go some way to making these

8.2 Interior, The Edge bar, Soho, London.

types of bars more successful. I really think people don't deserve dirty, scruffy bars with overflowing ashtrays and tables swimming in beer. They want to be well served in a clean and comfortable environment when they go out.[41]

Behind the management phrases, the shift from what Henshaw describes as 'dirty, scruffy bars' in favour of 'clean and comfortable environments' was symbolically important in the particular context in which it occurred. The emphasis on clean surfaces and natural light helped to shake off some of the 'dirty' and 'unhealthy' connotations the gay scene had previously had (while also creating new stereotypes of gay men drinking in the 'chi-chi bars of newly gay Soho').[42] To some extent design trends are cyclical (and more gritty counter-cultural reactions to Soho's bar scene have since emerged), but seen through the lens of AIDS and its resulting stigmatization, in this chapter I have suggested an interpretation of why the emphasis on hygiene aesthetics became so prominent in gay venues at this particular point in time. However, in addition to the marketed attempts to attract a new generation of customers by ridding the gay scene of some of its earlier stigma, the emphasis on cleanliness in Soho can also be seen to reflect a wider social shift.

Following Mary Douglas's influential book on dirt, in which she suggests that anxieties about pollution tend to occur when external or internal relationships and notions of morality in a culture are threatened, Forty has proposed an explanation for the preoccupation with hygiene in early twentieth-century design: 'If we follow her theory, we might expect the rapid social change and disintegrating social boundaries that came with the increasing political power of the working class to be behind the middle-class preoccupation with bodily, domestic and public cleanliness in the early part of this century'.[43] In a similar vein it could be argued that the early 1990s witnessed the disintegration of social boundaries and moral values in relation to sexuality as well as increased political power for gays and lesbians. These social changes occurred at a time when AIDS was still predominantly seen as a gay disease and there are well-documented examples of fears over contamination of the straight population. In that respect, Soho's hygiene aesthetics should not merely be seen as an internal gay marketing strategy, but also as a reflection of society's wider anxieties about homosexuality and AIDS at the time. Gay men were increasingly tolerated, but only in the desexualized context of the new gay economy, whose sanitized spaces seemed to protect society at large from the contamination associated with an earlier homosexual subculture.

Chapter 9

Spiritual Cleansing: Priests and Prostitutes in Early Victorian London

DOMINIC JANES

The reform of streetwalking prostitutes in Victorian London is an instance in the urban historical geography of dirt that emphasizes immaterial and spiritual as well as material and physical forms of filth. In this chapter I present a novel interpretation of Christian social policy as 'spiritual cleaning'. I analyse the process of cleansing through the use of anthropological theories of danger and pollution, rather than presenting it as the product of sentiment and religious morality, as previous work has tended to do.[1] Dirt is, of course, often physical matter that has come into inappropriate physical contact, as in mud washed from hands by a bar of soap. Dirt, however, also takes on a variety of immaterial nonphysical forms. When Shakespeare has Lady Macbeth desperately unable to wash the blood from her guilty hands, he is illustrating a relationship between physical and moral pollution. Those murdering hands can be physically but never morally clean again. This is a simple example of the geography of dirt in which pollution is unevenly spread across a symbolic physical and moral landscape.

In this chapter I want to explore some of the complex forms that dirt and cleansing can take by examining the attempted reform of prostitutes in Pimlico, a slum district in mid-nineteenth-century London. This case involves physical and nonphysical forms of dirt. The bodies of the prostitutes, which were widely understood to be rancid and contagious with disease, represented the primary physical dirt. As Lynda Nead has commented, the prostitute 'was represented as part of the refuse and dirt of the streets, the decomposing animal waste which produced atmospheric impurities and disease'.[2] However, venereal disease was imperfectly understood in the early Victorian period, and its presence and transmission were conceptualized through the filter of a Christian perspective that emphasized the sin of sex outside marriage and the threat of divine retribution. It was therefore widely believed not only that a prostitute's body was physically tainted but that her soul (and therefore her mind) was morally tainted too. Before the Contagious Diseases Acts of 1864, 1866 and 1869, which attempted to enforce medical examination of suspected prostitutes, it was the threat of moral pollution that was voiced as the most severe threat. Cleansing the early-Victorian city was, therefore, about physically cleansing the streets (removing streetwalkers) but, equally, about spiritually cleansing the prostitutes through regimes of moral reform.

Studies of comparative urban geography have stressed the importance of locating sexuality within specific spatial contexts. As Phil Hubbard argues, 'far from playing a passive backdrop to social and sexual relations, [space] plays an active role in the constitution of those relations, with the particularities of sites of sex work, whether on-street or off-street, reflecting and reproducing broader moral and social orders in a complex and sometimes contradictory manner.'[3] With this in mind I will explore a case study of attempted reform in the specific context of a Victorian slum and the reformatory that was built within it.

I will also be addressing the way in which power interacts with space by examining the production of technologies of cleansing. Christopher Otter has recently employed this Foucauldian approach in his study of slaughter houses and electricity generation in late Victorian London. He discusses technologies of cleansing as systems of control and authority that intervened in the urban environment, both physically and ideologically, to reveal and cleanse.[4] Such approaches emphasize the power of the cleansers as being primarily classificatory in determining exactly what needs to be cleansed. A number of case studies of regimes of sanitation have followed this approach, for example Warwick Anderson's study of American doctors and scientists in the colonized Philippines of the early twentieth century. Anderson writes of the 'medical production of colonial bodies and colonial space', in which the 'vulnerable, formalized bodies of the American colonists demanded sanitary quarantine'.[5] The Americans defined the locals as unclean and thereby generated a sanitary justification for their own presence. Moreover, the ultimate imperative was not purification but self-glorification; within the 'ritual frame' of the laboratory 'American scientists ... obsessively collected any specimens of Filipino feces they could lay their gloved hands on,' and such studies of the locals' shit launched meteoric medical and scientific careers.[6]

However, the case of Christian technologies of cleansing as employed in Victorian London is quite specific in the interactions between moral and physical factors in the ideologies of cleansing. The moral consensus did not consider Christian reform of prostitutes necessary, for it was not a sure route to personal advancement. In fact, many evangelical Protestants thought that prostitutes should be left to God's judgement. So the power structures that Anglo-Catholics sought to establish need to be seen, not just in the context of worldly hierarchies, but in relation to the specifically Catholic belief in the value of good works as an aid to personal salvation.

I will argue that because medical, psychological and sociological discourses and practices of sanitation have come subsequently to predominate, it is easy to forget the importance of technologies of spiritual cleansing in the evolution of the western metropolis. Moreover, the theoretical approaches that work well for the former discourses and their associated technologies of cleansing need to be rethought in the case of the latter. How then, did Christian reformers attempt to deal with early Victorian prostitution and how, thereby, were they attempting to transform urban geographies of sexual pollution? First, I shall examine the reasons for increasing concerns with dirt and pollution in general, thereby establishing the theoretical basis for my understanding of dirt as not so much a category in itself but as an aspect of boundary transgression. From there I will look at the 'refuge' established in Pimlico and its effectiveness, before summing up my reasons for regarding this specific attempt at urban sanitization as having a wider significance in the historical geographies of dirt.

Background and boundaries

There was a new craze for the moral reform of prostitutes in early Victorian England: in 1847 Charles Dickens bought a house in west London as a reformatory for fallen women, naming it Urania Cottage, and the diaries from the 1850s of the future prime minister, Mr Gladstone, record how he roamed the streets in search of prostitutes whom he might persuade to a better life. Christian moralizing was, however, nothing new, so why the sudden upsurge of activity? A key factor was a rising concern for the identification and cleansing of dirt of all kinds as part of a drive for the reform of the conditions of urban life. Cultural theorists regard this as one stage in a long process of increasing concern about filth. For instance, the French psychoanalytic theorist Dominique Laporte argues that from the sixteenth century onwards, an ongoing process of organizing and categorizing space can be identified. This process is one of separating off elements that it is considered should be apart from each other – a man from his shit, for instance, or one individual from another – as urban populations have increased and the political and economic structures of society have become progressively more elaborate.[7] Matter, such as mud, that had previously seemed simply to be part of the natural landscape, rapidly became classified as filth that needed to be cleaned from the streets. The growing size of cities and the complexity of life within them provided ample material for scientific and moral classification, which not only documented but also provided the basis for policing burgeoning social, cultural and economic diversity. Medicine and social science proceeded, therefore, to develop typologies of physical and social disease, as in Henry Mayhew's surveys of London and categorizations of the urban poor published in 1849–50 and 1861–2.[8]

In this climate, Christian reformers were increasingly influenced to action as well as rhetoric. Sin, for the reforming preacher, was what disease was for the doctor, and poverty and degradation for the social scientist. While there remained a strong body of ecclesiastical opinion that regarded social intervention as interfering in the will of God, other groups thought differently. One such group was the body of priests in the Church of England who had become influenced by the fervour of the Catholicizing Tractarian movement centred on the University of Oxford in the 1840s.

Several of their number believed in active mission in the world, particularly focused towards the urban poor. A leading figure from this group was William Bennett who worked in Knightsbridge and Pimlico in the 1840s and his successor as parish priest Robert Liddell. It was Liddell who was to found the Pimlico refuge for 'unfortunate' women.

It is crucial to realize, however, that Christian compassion in the face of sin did not amount to a radical relativistic rethinking of the nature of moral dirt and pollution. Bennett, for instance, explained in a tract addressed to his children, that impurity occurs when something 'foreign, vicious, and inferior' pollutes something superior.[9] From this viewpoint the rescue of prostitutes was a matter of rebuilding moral boundaries, purging the women of the horror within them, not of rehabilitating the horror itself. Structuralist anthropologist Mary Douglas sees society, its structures and hierarchies, as underpinned by a set of rules that depend on boundaries.[10] The French anthropologist Valerio Valeri has challenged Douglas for being insufficiently keen to 'think with the body', both physical and social, on the basis that 'it is quite likely that the unwanted invasion of the body by decay-inducing substances is the basic model of pollution everywhere.'[11] The problem is that the body wants to consume things, to take them into itself, and the challenge is how to police this so as to prevent harm. It is Douglas's model as modified by Valeri that I want to use as the structural basis of this case study. This suggests that the real sites of anxiety were the boundaries of the bodies and minds of the sanitary agents, those politicians, clergy and prominent members of society who led the campaigns for urban reform. Moreover, Valeri proposes that it is only at the theoretical level that a full separation between physical pollution and sin is maintained in Christianity.[12] The economic historian Boyd Hilton has argued that evangelical Christian ideas of the world as a place where human suffering was widespread because of God's wrath at Original Sin (Adam and Eve eating from the Tree of Knowledge in the Garden of Eden) heavily influenced early nineteenth-century England. This helps to explain why the sufferings caused by disease were widely read as being related to sin and, therefore, why morality and physicality were deeply intertwined in contemporary understandings of dirt.[13]

A 'refuge' in Pimlico

One of the greatest perils of London, according to early Victorian discourses of moral sanitation, was the profusion of prostitutes. They were widely thought of as being intrinsic to the rotten fabric of poor parts of the city, such as Pimlico; an identification explicitly brought out in the English Pre-Raphaelite painter Rossetti's watercolour *The Gate of Memory* (1857), in which a sad woman, a streetwalker with a shawl pulled about her, stands in the darkness of a city street watching urchins play – the children she will never have – while a sewer rat runs down a drain.[14] Rossetti was presenting a more sympathetic vision than many others had at the time. Gaudy garments and make-up were thought to conceal ulcers and rot. Venereal diseases were spreading so rapidly that by the 1870s they accounted for one in three sick cases in the army and one in eleven general patients in hospitals.[15] Brothels were seen as 'receptacles of pollution'.[16] Moral and physical sickness passed between the woman and the man.[17] William Tait, a Scottish surgeon who also published on the dangers of using sewage as fertilizer, aired the anxiety that contagious diseases could be spread by the guilty males to their wives.[18] The prostitute combined both miasmic and contagious models of disease. She was seen as a passive container of sickness and as playing an active role in the transference of illness. She was 'perceived both as one of the visible causes of miasma and as the invisible infection itself'.[19] According to one mid-Victorian commentator, prostitutes were 'both the pests of society and its victims ... eating the manhood and vigour of a whole generation'.[20] It was argued that, in the end, few prostitutes escaped syphilis: rather, 'the whole frame becomes a mass of living corruption'.[21]

There was a strong line of mainstream evangelical opinion that said this was God's just punishment and, therefore, nothing should be done about prostitution since those sinners deserved their fate as God cleared the streets with early deaths.[22] The Anglo-Catholics moved beyond mainstream evangelicals because the former believed that the women should not be left alone because they could not help themselves: 'an irreversible law rules our race, that of ourselves we cannot revive, when fallen. Once corrupted our nature has not power of self-restoration.' Unlike many evangelicals they believed that the Church, with its cleansing technologies of the sacraments and penitence, could and should help prostitutes in this life rather than simply praying for their future salvation.[23] The Catholic revival in the Church of England, which emerged from the 1840s, found its greatest expression in reforming missions to working-class urban districts of London. The aim of many Anglo-Catholics was to improve the moral conditions of the poor and they tended to take a very active approach to the 'cleansing of the streets' through the reform of prostitutes. Such Anglican reformers had backing from an unlikely source, the medical profession; at least as represented by the prominent doctor and author on sexual matters, William Acton, who wrote:

> Instead of, as at present, ignoring the sex passion and its con-
> sequences, the Protestant Church should boldly follow the example of
> her elder sister of Rome, and at least prepare the way for the crusade
> against vice which may succeed the vain sighs and wishes of to-day.
> Our Church can never, I am aware, exert the power which the con-
> fessional places in the hands of the Roman ecclesiastics; but I am
> convinced she might do something. I am willing to give her the
> precedence.[24]

Two other factors boosted the campaign for spiritual cleansing. First, medical treatments such as caustics up the urethra for gonorrhoea and mercury ingestion for syphilis were as unreliable as they were unpleasant. Second, such treatment was only readily available to those who could afford to pay. The new Poor Law introduced in 1834 did little more than provide prisons for the indigent. Under-funding and lack of care in the resulting state institutions hardly recommended them as an adequate solution to housing street-walkers. What good would it do a young woman to 'have been left to the foul atmosphere of a "Young Woman's Ward" in a Union Workhouse, to have every sense polluted, and every fear and thought of God stifled with impurity'.[25] In other words, such places were as overcrowded and unhealthy as slum tenements. Sermons called for something to be done about the evil, the 'bitter waters [of which] run wildly through our midst, diffusing their poison around our altars and our hearths' – and, thus, through and about the boundaries and bodies of respectable society.[26] Such evil must be contained and purged.

Activists urged that Church ministers should 'lead the wanderers back to the paths of virtue and religion' through the construction of a new generation of Christian reformatories.[27] The houses they established would have to deal with people accustomed to dwell in a 'lower region of animalized life'.[28] Clerics would need the help of the newly established Anglican nuns, the Sisters of Charity, since only very pure women could safely work with prostitutes because 'the fallen condition is one of extreme exclusion' from respectable society.[29] To protect the sisters and each other from moral reinfection, the inmates in the Anglo-Catholic penitentiaries were forbidden to talk of their sins.[30] Their verbal outlet was via confession to the priest. Meanwhile, it was seen as vital in a home for fallen women that 'their hands should be kept always busy, their minds always occupied'.[31] Moreover, it was recommended that 'pure air, refreshing walks, and the gentle labours of a garden, are almost indispensable for the recovery of health impaired by the excitements of vice'.[32] It was important that these homes be 'thoroughly industrial', since work was restorative, as well as a penalty, and helped to defray costs.[33]

One such community was established in the then slum district of Pimlico west of Victoria station in central London.[34] The Anglo-Catholic parish priest, Robert Liddell, was the successor of William Bennett whose opinions on purity and impurity I referred to above. In February 1854, Liddell gave an account of the Pimlico 'refuge' in Commercial Road to the Church Penitentiary Association, which had been formed in 1851.[35] A house with a garden was leased in 1852. Some 12 people lived in subdivided rooms. There was a day room and a small chapel, the stained glass of which showed three scenes in the life of Mary Magdalene. Liddell commented that 'this contributes greatly to mark both the sacred character of the chamber thus set apart from all common uses, and the object of the institution itself, which is to bring back penitents to Christ'.[36]

The aim was first to cleanse the streets, then to cleanse the women. The strategy was to create a series of enforced boundaries, keeping the women from walking the streets, excluding polluted or polluting words from the penitential community, and eventually eliminating even polluted thoughts. It was understood that although women volunteered to enter, sometimes due to remorse and sometimes due to poverty and desperation, their willpower could and should not be counted on. Since the life of an entrant 'has been one of disorder, and their whole system, bodily and mental, has been disordered by it', so the regime must be strictly controlling of both body and mind: hence the rigid daily routine:[37]

6.30	rise
7.30	prayer
8.00	breakfast in silence
8.30	devotional reading and catechizing
10.00	household duties
11.00	needlework and knitting, silence while one reads aloud

1.00	dinner and exercise in the garden
2.30	'occupations in class-room'
3.00	service in chapel
4.00	needlework
5.00	tea and relaxation
6.30	work
7.30	class reading and instruction
8.30	prayers and silence
9.00	supper
10.00	bed and strict silence.[38]

This amounted to training in feminine obedience as preparation for a future life as a servant or wife. As a reward for good behaviour, inmates were allowed to attend divine service at the local church of St Barnabas on Sundays.

Of those admitted, some went on to other houses, while others were successfully 'reformed' and went into domestic service, although there were not so many of these. A few discharged themselves such as 'M. A. F.' who, on 15 February 1854, after a year in the house, left of her own accord, 'a wretched bad case'.[39] Thus, as a technology of cleansing, the penitentiary appears to have had only moderate success. Although many other Church penitentiaries were established they did not succeed in developing into a mainstream instrument of urban moral and physical sanitation. This fact notwithstanding, the final section of this chapter will outline why their example is significant in wider studies of dirt and its geographies.

Conclusions

So, was this 'refuge' simply an unimpressive variant on the more typical institutions of the penal system? Women were, after all, taken in from the streets and held in a special building until it was deemed safe to let them out. However, the hospital is a better comparison (but not the mental hospital since inmates could not discharge themselves from there). Their stay was understood as representing a period of spiritual medication in which the Sisters of Mercy acted as holy nurses. But in one major way, this reformatory, like others being established across the country at the time, was conceptually more radical. The basis for this radicalism lay in the Gospels. Liddell pointed out that Christ offered his healing touch to the leper, though the latter was unclean. Therefore, Liddell drew the conclusion that no instance of 'physical or spiritual evil was *so bad* as to be *beyond the reach* of his compassion' (original italics).[40] He drew a direct analogy by saying that prostitutes were 'cast out from the sanctity of home … condemned by their miserable calling to cry out like the leper of old, – "Unclean, Unclean!"'[41] He continued by saying that 'mere separation from evil haunts and practices would not reclaim

120

them – mere seclusion would depress them; and prison-like severity would actually harden them.'[42] They must be purified by the presence of holiness: it is by 'this close contact with holy minds that penitents are led to aspire after better things'.[43] As in the story of Mary Magdalene, in which a biblical 'fallen woman' became a Roman Catholic saint, a greater spiritual repentance could come from a greater fall.

The implications of this are dramatic: this was not a prison and the inmates were not automatically inferior. In a prison the gaolers are not held to be criminals, the prisoners are; while in a hospital the patients are sick and the staff are those who are held to be well. By contrast, in the penitentiary the fact of original sin (which subsisted since the expulsion from the Garden of Eden) meant that everyone was seen as spiritually sick, even the staff. Moreover, the prostitutes' clients were also exhorted in church sermons to acknowledge their own spiritual malaise. There was another difference: medicine always recognized certain cases as incurable. The Anglo-Catholic system made no such recognition. These two factors did not, as we have seen, overturn the perceived importance of boundaries and prohibitions or remove the notion of the prostitute as polluter of the city's streets. However, the Anglo-Catholic system did create a sense of dirt as being something that was relative rather than absolute. And, since everyone could be redeemed there was value in everyone. The implication in this system of cleansing institutions was that society should think carefully before throwing away human rubbish. It is a technology of recycling more than of disposal.

Moreover, this system takes a position of positive emotional engagement with the dirty and the diseased. William Miller comments that: 'Disgust is very ambivalent about life itself, particularly human life. Life soup, *human* life soup, lies at the core of the disgusting. And that makes disgust unavoidably misanthropic in its cast. Disgust recoils at what we are and what we do, both the voluntary and the involuntary.'[44] Prison officers and doctors are meant, as 'professionals', to be able to cope with levels of corruption the ordinary person would find disgusting. However, Liddell, the founder of this penitentiary in Pimlico, was thinking about transcending disgust with the help of God's grace. The remarkable nature of this desire should be seen in the context of a wider moral climate in which, as my earlier quote from Lynda Nead highlighted, Victorian prostitutes were 'represented as part of the refuse and dirt of the streets, the decomposing animal waste which produced atmospheric impurities and disease'.[45] Just as the removal and disposal of human and animal shit was a key element of sanitary policy in Victorian London, so there were repeated calls to emphasize the removal of the streetwalkers and the irrevocably damaged nature of those women. As one writer put it, 'we deem it a duty urgently incumbent on the magistrate, to purge our streets of these obscene and dangerous perambulators.'[46] In other words, it was all too easy to confuse the diseased with the disease and to reinforce the boundaries of Victorian patriarchy by making a scapegoat of the prostitutes and preserving the social boundaries that sheltered their clients. Christian reformers perceived that the disease lay ultimately in desires rather than in the resulting physical acts. In this they emphasized a need to link the physical and the nonphysical (or, as they thought of it, the 'worldly' and the 'spiritual').

I mentioned earlier Rossetti's *Gate of Memory* (1857) with its juxtaposition of a prostitute and a drain. *Found* (begun 1854) is an unfinished work by Rossetti that depicts a young man's encounter with the woman he used to love who has become a streetwalker. In the sketches made in the early 1850s for this painting a rose is shown lying on the grill of a road drain in the foreground.[47] This is the metaphorical counterpart of the woman 'found' slumped on the ground against a wall. These two paintings provide a vivid reminder of the spatial dynamics of the nineteenth-century city. The depths of both the city and the body were associated with corruption.[48] In her work on space and embodiment, feminist philosopher Elizabeth Grosz has commented that we should see the city and the body as interrelated, and understand each as analogues, or 'assemblages of parts' that dynamically influence each other.[49] There is, in her analyses, both a continuum of built and bodily forms and of related ideas and imaginings concerning them. Both the geographies of sexual dirt and the means taken to clean them are, from such a viewpoint, composed of evolving landscapes of people, things and ideas. It is in the context of such a landscape of contested social meanings that we can begin to appreciate some of the ways in which notions of spiritual cleansing provided an important challenge to contemporary materialistic notions of the prostitute as the intrinsic embodiment of urban filth.

Chapter 10

Mapping Sewer Spaces in mid-Victorian London

PAUL DOBRASZCZYK

Sewers are paradoxically both signifiers of rational modernity and reliquaries of archaic fears: the literal and metaphorical bowels of the city, everyday yet alien spaces. The primary way of visualizing sewers is through maps, where, along with other types of subterranean infrastructure, they are translated from their normally invisible subterranean topography and made visible as lines, usually coloured red, superimposed onto the spaces beneath which they lie, such as roads, paths and buildings. So commonplace are such images that we invariably take for granted their apparently 'neutral' status: they serve a purely practical purpose and seem to provide us with an objective mirror of 'nature'. Yet, recent cartographical analysis, particularly the later work of John Brian Harley, has shown that maps are far from neutral images: they embody particular ways of viewing the world.[1] For Harley and others all maps select and present information according to their own systems of priority and, as a consequence, present only partial views, which construct – or imagine – rather than simply describe objects of knowledge.

In this chapter I focus on three types of map produced in London from 1848 to 1851 under the direction of Edwin Chadwick, which were closely related to the future improvement of the city's sanitary infrastructure: first, the Ordnance Survey of London, which mapped London's above-ground topography; second, maps produced as a result of a concurrent subterranean survey of existing sewers; and third, a 'hybrid' map that attempted to combine the results of both surveys. These maps laid the conceptual and practical foundations for the world's first citywide sewage network, the main

123

drainage system eventually constructed in the 1860s. Focusing for the first time on the interrelation between these three maps, I will bring out the contradictions inherent in the conceptualization of these new sewer spaces – contradictions overlooked in the existing literature on the subject.[2] Whereas the Ordnance Survey promoted a clear 'ideology of improvement' that sought to remake London's sewers anew, the subterranean survey uncovered the actual sewers of the city, revealing them to be monstrous, deformed and dirty spaces that needed to be cleansed through the implementation of the new vision. Yet, Edwin Chadwick eventually mapped these old dilapidated spaces as overlays onto the Ordnance Survey plan, which was, in effect, an attempt to combine two conflicting types of sewer space. When such apparent opposites – new and old, and clean and dirty – are brought together within an ideology that stresses their polarity, they inevitably throw up contradictions that upset this ideology and serve to bring out the more complex reality it conceals.

The Ordnance Survey and sanitary cartography

In mid-nineteenth century London, maps played an important role in the visual culture of the city. The development of lithography from the 1820s onwards enabled maps to be produced and marketed more cheaply than ever before; by 1851 a proliferation of maps, with a wide variety of different functions, formed a vital and accessible genre of urban representation.[3] This period also saw a rise in the importance of scientific rigour in relation to mapping, which 'strove for accuracy and clarity in depicting the urban landscape'.[4] Such a change was, in part, propelled by the emergence of the Ordnance Survey, whose origins lay in the machinations of military strategy.[5] In the decades up to 1850, the Ordnance Survey had risen to a position of cartographic dominance over civil surveyors with the production of series of maps of Great Britain. Coupled with its emphasis on military planning, the Ordnance Survey also employed new surveying techniques, culminating in the first trigonometric survey begun in 1791. With the promotion of a new scientific basis for mapmaking, the work of the Ordnance Survey became a model for those who sought to imbue other disciplines with a similar methodology.

Perhaps the most important of these in relation to sanitary reform was Edwin Chadwick (1800–90), the most obsessive cataloguer of dirt and disease in the mid-nineteenth century. Chadwick's *Report on the Sanitary Conditions of the Labouring Population of Great Britain* (1842) charted in immense detail the relationship between poor sanitation and the incidence of disease, employing a wide range of statistical data and eyewitness evidence that claimed to have a scientific basis. Sanitary cartography, developed in the later 1840s, formed not only a perfect visual complement to Chadwick's verbal report, but also a means of depicting proposed sanitary improvements.

Chadwick quickly recognized the potential of these specialist maps to strengthen his case for the wholesale sanitary reform of London, and it was during his involvement with the Metropolitan Commission of Sewers that he did this most forcefully.[6] Convened in December 1847, following recommendations made by a royal commission that had investigated sanitary problems in London,[7] the Metropolitan Commission of Sewers was a new, centralized governing body for the city's sanitation, superseding the eight separate sewer commissions that had managed London's sewers since Henry VIII's Sewers Act in 1531.[8] From the outset the main charge of the new commission was to design and construct a unified drainage network for London. The report of the 1847 royal commission had built up a picture of a metropolitan sanitary system on the verge of collapse, a primary cause of disease, governed by a multitude of conflicting interests and constructed piecemeal from information gleaned from local, parochial surveys.[9] The creation of the new Commission of Sewers was intended as a first step towards the improvement of London's sanitary infrastructure and the abolition of such existing defects.[10]

At the very first meeting of the commission on 6 December 1847, Chadwick outlined his intentions for a new survey of London, requesting an application to be directed immediately to the Board of Ordnance to survey London at the unprecedented scale of five-feet to one-mile.[11] Chadwick viewed the creation of a large-scale accurate plan of the built-up area of London as an essential prerequisite to planning a citywide sewer system.[12] As early as 1842, he had proposed that the Board of Ordnance should carry out such a survey, making a strong case against the use of civil surveyors, whom he regarded as lacking the competence and discipline of the Ordnance Survey's soldiers. For Chadwick, the new mapping of London was to have a scientific and disinterested basis, epitomized, in his view, by the Ordnance Survey.

The survey commenced on 26 January 1848 with the construction of observation posts in preparation for the triangulation of the city.[13] A contingent of 250 men from the corps of Royal Sappers and Miners – engaged at that time on large-scale surveys of towns in northern England – was brought to London to begin work.[14] Observation towers were constructed on top of Westminster Abbey and St Paul's Cathedral, on the summits of Primrose and other hills, on towers, steeples and roofs of churches, and on the terraces of public buildings. The appearance of soldiers on the streets of London and the prominence of the observation posts attracted a great deal of public attention and, in some cases, alarm: some feared that the city was to be imminently invaded. The accounts in the *Illustrated London News* reassured the public and also emphasized the pressing need for the survey:

> One would have thought that there had been surveys enough already; and so there have. The cost of many complete surveys has hitherto

been expended in piecemeal irresponsible work, in which no public confidence could be placed ... and we trust that no narrow, interested views will be allowed to interfere with the same course of proceeding as to the great works of improvement of which this survey is the base.[15]

The notion of seeing London as a unified metropolitan area, governed by scientific and objective principles, runs through much of the press coverage of the survey.[16] What is consistently emphasized is the need for a new conception of the city – one that is not based on local vested interests, but rather unified and disinterested, seeing the city as a whole, undivided by the old parochial boundaries. Existing forms of local government in London produced a profusion of boundaries: some 300 different bodies governed the city in the late 1840s, administering parishes and innumerable districts within those parishes.[17] The Ordnance Survey, as an external and supposed 'neutral' military organization, ignored the confusion of jurisdictions created as a result of these many governing authorities; instead, it mapped London as a city without boundaries, even if this did not reflect the administrative reality at the time.

Contesting views

The references to 'narrow, interested views' in the *Illustrated London News* account were indirect attacks on London's civil surveyors, who opposed the new survey. Organized into the Association of Surveyors and led by the prominent London mapmaker, James Wyld (1812–87), they argued that the new survey of London was unnecessary; instead, they proposed to carry out their own survey, making use of existing plans at a far more reasonable cost, with Wyld producing the map.[18] Chadwick was quick to respond: on 28 March 1848, the commission met Wyld to discuss his proposed plan. Henry Austin (c.1811–61) – consulting engineer to the commission – took the opportunity to defend the need for a new survey of London. He admitted the existence of accurate large-scale survey plans of parish areas, many of which were produced as a result of the Parochial Assessment Act of 1836,[19] but stated that: 'the attempt to connect these different surveys into a whole would be utterly futile, ending only in failure. ... They have been executed totally independent of each other, under different arrangement and different systems, and they never could be fitted accurately together.'[20]

With a primary emphasis on accuracy, Austin reiterated the need for any new maps of London to form an integrated whole, which he saw as missing from the older maps, such as those made by the Holborn and Finsbury Sewer Commission (Figure 10.1): maps directly inherited by the Metropolitan Commission of Sewers when it was formed in 1847. There is a profusion of descriptive information represented on such maps: individual streets and

10.1   Extract from a map made by the Holborn and Finsbury
Sewer Commission (1846).

buildings, copied from older topographic maps, form the base plan, and
overlaid are many other descriptive features including sewers, unidenti-
fied boundaries and waterways. All of this detailed information was
specific to the area of jurisdiction of the old Holborn and Finsbury
Commission and abruptly ends at the boundary of the district controlled
by the Westminster Commission, which would have produced its own local

127

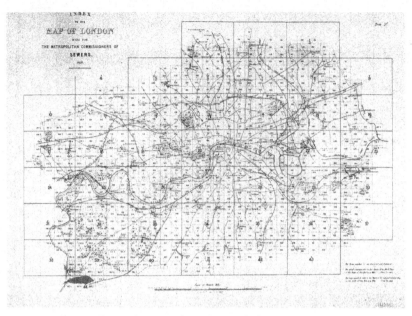

10.2 Index to the map of London made for the Metropolitan
Commissioners of Sewers (1850).

maps according to its particular needs. Austin saw such isolated surveys as
directly opposed to the notion of applying an accurate and consistent method
of surveying to the city as a whole: that is, one necessary to make it possible
to design a citywide sewerage system. As such, it was not only mapmaking
procedures that were challenged by Austin and the Commission, but also the
entire existing political and administrative framework of the city.

The Metropolitan Commission of Sewers received parliamentary validation
for the completion of the new survey with the passing of the Metropolitan
Sewers Act in September 1848.[21] Subsequently, the survey was completed very
quickly: the ground survey was finished by March 1849 with the measurement
of road levels – information also shown on the completed maps – completed
by May. By November 1849, 79 sheets of the five foot survey had been
engraved onto copper; by July 1850, the engraving of the 901 sheets that made
up the complete survey was almost complete. The extraordinary speed of the
survey, which was faster than even the original cost estimate had anticipated,
resulted in an extra ten copies of the sheets being made (in addition to the
ten already ordered) as well as the preparation of index plans at 12 inches to
the mile, comprising 44 sheets and a general index plan on a single sheet.

The view from above

The general index plan (Figure 10.2) outlines the arrangements of both the

128

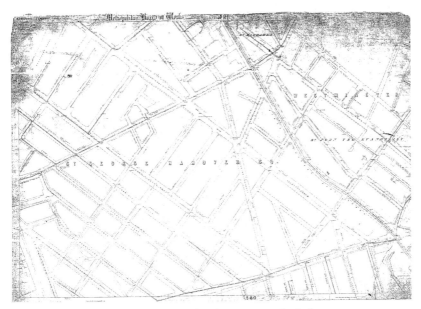

10.3   Sheet 553 of the five-feet to one-mile Ordnance
Survey of London (c.1849).

five feet to one mile sheets (Figure 10.3), and the 12 inches to one mile index
sheets (Figure 10.4). The internal coherence of the individual sheets, at both
scales, is emphasized in the general index plan (Figure 10.2); its grid-like
form shows that the multitudinous sheets of the survey are definitely not
pieced together in the manner of older plans; rather, they have their own
internal structural unity – all the sheets are shown to fit exactly together
within the overarching framework of both the 12-inch (larger rectangles) and
the five-foot sheets (smaller rectangles). This visual unity reflects the
conception of the city propagated by the Metropolitan Commission of Sewers
discussed previously: London was conceived of, and now represented as, a
unified city.

Both the five-foot (Figure 10.3) and 12-inch sheets (Figure 10.4) present
a clear promotion of this new image of the city. The existing parish
boundaries of London are replaced only by the edges of the individual sheets,
which fit together exactly to form a grid. The features depicted on both maps
reveal other structural links: dots and numbers, scattered over the entire
surface of the sheets (Figure 10.4) mark the positions at which road levels
were carefully measured, and small arrows indicate the location of the
permanent benchmarks which allowed a correlation between this aerial view
and observations at ground-level. These levels and benchmarks systematically
linked all the sheets together and also provided a foundation for calculating

129

10.4 Extract from Sheet 27 of the 12-inch Ordnance Survey
index plan (1848–51).

the gradients necessary for building a citywide sewer system. In short, the
urban region became stylized and comprehensible, in preparation for a future
intervention – that is, the construction of a unified sewer system, made
possible by the features depicted on these maps.

As abstract and totalizing images, these maps embody what David L. Pike
has described as 'the view from above' London – that is, panoramic views of
the city, seen in both city maps and gigantic painted panoramas of the city,

such as that displayed in the Colosseum after its opening in 1829.[22] The vantage point for the Colosseum panorama was the dome on top of St Paul's Cathedral, which enabled observers to encompass the entire cityscape while still being able to pick out the smallest details.[23] The Ordnance Survey, by establishing St Paul's as its central triangulation point, closely conforms to the typology of the panorama, albeit in a format that is stripped down, abstracted and without perspective, visualizing only roads and waterways. Chadwick had clearly stated the reason for this: he wanted depicted only those features that were directly connected with the construction of a unified sewer system. The map can therefore be considered as a marking out of the territory the commission needed to construct this system. Roads and waterways are marked as accurately as possible, with variations in road width carefully measured and drawn, so that sewers could be accurately planned to run beneath them. This claimed territory also framed a space of potentiality: the spaces represented would be 'colonized' by the authority of the commission as they began to plan and engineer a citywide sewer system. Consequently, the Ordnance Survey maps can be read as highly subjective and 'interested' representations of the city, even if their producers claimed to have an objective interest in applying a universal, scientific method, as opposed to the subjectivity and narrowness of their opponents. Behind this claim of transparency from Chadwick and the commission lies an implied ideology of improvement: that is, the desire to transform the city into a clean, unified and rational site that they govern.

The view from below

When Chadwick had originally outlined his plan for the proposed Ordnance Survey in January 1848, he also recommended that a subterranean survey be carried out of the built-up area of the city.[24] The subterranean survey had a very different goal from that of the Ordnance Survey: its eventual aim would be to produce maps depicting the fine details of the existing drainage, whether under the streets or in individual houses. Chadwick viewed the control of the old sewer spaces, with all their problems, as essential to the future success of any new system. This literal descent into the 'bowels' of the city conforms to another common representational trope in Victorian London: the 'view from below'. Unlike the view from above, which placed the city's substratum at a safe and clean distance, the view from below positively revelled in the dirt and chaos of subterranean spaces: in effect, a modern variant on the descent into the underworld seen in ancient mythologies.[25] However, for those who carried out the subterranean survey there was to be no such abandonment: it was to have the same scientific basis as the Ordnance Survey, as rigorous and panoramic as its counterpart from above. The maps and reports produced as a result of the subterranean survey were

131

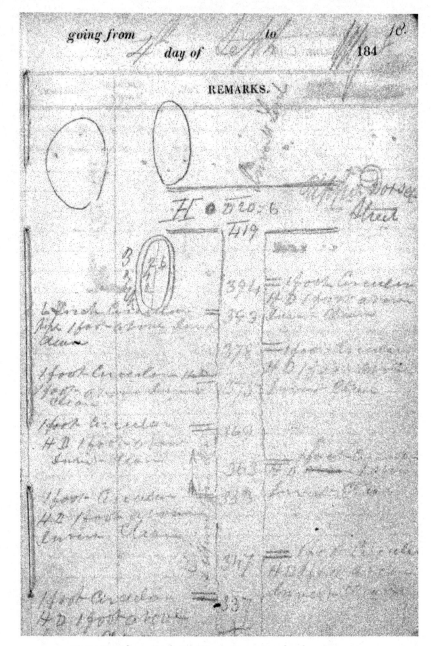

10.5 Page from Book 45, Westminster Levels, showing sewer
information collected by the surveyor T. Bevan (1848).

attempts to articulate a coherent relationship between the old and the new, between the view from above and the view from below.

On 13 April 1848 it was agreed that personnel from the Board of Ordnance – two levellers, two labourers, four other staff and two marksmen – be employed to assist with work on the subterranean survey, directed by the chief surveyor of the Metropolitan Commission of Sewers, Joseph Smith.[26] With such a tiny workforce – 250 men were used for the Ordnance Survey – the subterranean survey became a long and drawn-out process; in 1855, seven years later, it was still unfinished.[27] The surveying methods employed were similar to those used in both surveys; however, they were applied in a very different working environment. Where the surveyors of the Ordnance Survey could build observation towers to view the entire city, the subterranean surveyors had to negotiate dark and claustrophobic spaces; where the public admired the military surveyors' gleaming uniforms, those beneath the ground were hidden from public view and surrounded by filth.

The surveying of a sewer began with the determination of an access point, which was usually a manhole on the surface of a road or footway. Levellers would then descend into the sewer and lamps would be lit so that a theodolite could be used in the shadowy space to measure its level beneath the ground. The work was often dangerous, for many of the sewers contained deposits of foul matter several feet deep. Indeed, some of the men only narrowly escaped death by drowning or from explosions caused by sewer gases.[28] The levellers produced highly detailed but crude drawings in notebooks outlining the levels, dimensions and conditions of the sewers examined (Figure 10.5).[29] Representing a single page from one of these notebooks, Figure 10.5 depicts part of the sewer in Lillington Street where it joined another in Upper Dorset Street, Westminster, both streets seen on the centre-right of sheet 553 of the five-feet scale map (Figure 10.3).[30]

The reproduced drawing highlights the level of detail surveyed: the width of the sewer under Lillington Street is shown in the centre of the drawing with levels indicated in many places along its length. The rest of the sewer in Lillington Street is represented on the other pages of this notebook, with each page joining up precisely with the next. Every junction of the sewer is noted and represented: even the individual one-foot circular drains leading from the houses flanking the road to the main sewer are given a full description indicating their size, shape, and condition (here, described as 'clean'). The level of each junction above the invert (base) of the main sewer is shown, as is the cross-sectional shape of the sewer (seen just above the centre-left of the page), sketched roughly but precisely measured. Such voluminous records reflect Chadwick's intention to gain a comprehensive and minutely detailed picture of London's existing sewers.

Monstrous spaces

In August and September 1848, Joseph Smith and Henry Austin presented written reports and tables outlining the progress of the survey. These reports present an unremittingly bleak picture of London's existing sewers. Smith employs a vocabulary that gives emphasis to this picture: the recurring adjectives used are 'dilapidated', 'decayed', 'dangerous', 'defective', 'frightful', 'crushed', and 'rotten'. Austin's accounts emphasize the dangerous nature of the task of examining these sewers. Regarding the sewers in south London, he states:

> The smell is usually of the most horrible description, the air being so foul that explosion and choke damp are very frequent. On the 12th January we were very nearly losing a whole party by choke damp, the last man being dragged out on his back (through two feet of black foetid deposit) in a state of insensibility.[31]

In another incident, an explosion in the Kennington Road sewer, men working had 'the skin peeled off their faces and their hair singed'.[32] Such a monstrous disfigurement contrasts graphically with the clean orderliness of the above-ground surveyors, noted in the press coverage of the Ordnance Survey. The dangerous nature of the subterranean survey is closely related to the poor condition of the sewers, which are often depicted as irregular or badly-shaped spaces blocked by excrement. Some were also in an advanced state of decay and dilapidation: Austin describes the sewer in Cumberland Street as 'all washed away, the side walls and arch falling in; if the sewer gives way the houses will follow';[33] another sewer in Westmoreland Street and Woodstock Street 'is totally decayed throughout the entire length. It is not safe, even for a day.'[34]

These reports give an added interpretation to the information collated by the surveyors in their notebooks, relaying a sense of the heroic in the carrying out of the subterranean survey; they chart with an unflinching eye (and nose) these unknown and dangerous spaces beneath the city in all their horror. However, the notebooks, free of any descriptive language, contain a series of interconnected drawings and tables, carefully pieced together from multitudinous sections – in effect a rationalized and ordered view from below. Such differing representations highlighted the problem of how to bring together the view from above and the view from below; how to represent the old, which by definition stood in the way of the new, in a way that conformed to the 'objective' methods employed in the Ordnance Survey. In their disconnected and dirty state, the old sewers defied the new vision of the city depicting in the Ordnance Survey plans a unified series of inter-connecting spaces. Smith and Austin censure the existing sewer spaces with appropriate and interrelated language, translating the surveyors' rigorous and scientific work into a condemnatory picture and potent testament to the urgent need for a new unified system of sewers. However, by employing such 'loaded' language, they eschew the sense of objectivity that Chadwick claimed the Ordnance Survey embodied.

Conflation

In 1850, the Metropolitan Commission of Sewers mapped the information collected in the subterranean survey (Figure 10.6). This extract shows sewer lines (coloured red in the original) hand-drawn onto sheet 27 of the 12 inch to one mile Ordnance Survey index map (Figure 10.4).[35] In this map, the representation of the old sewers – seen in Austin and Smith's reports and the surveyor's notebook – is dramatically transformed: gone is the detailed information so rigorously collated by the surveyors; and gone is the sense of these sewers as disconnected and disjointed spaces – characteristics that dominated Austin and Smith's reports. Depicted instead is an obvious network of sewers seen over a wide area with major sewers, such as the King's Scholars Pond Sewer (shown at the top left of the sheet), given visual prominence by large-scale labelling. The interrelation of the existing sewers is stressed rather than specific indicators of their condition. Additional information is also overlaid onto the base plan: parish boundaries (black dashed lines); the names of some of the individual parishes (St John the Evangel[ist] at the top centre and right-hand side); and waterways (coloured blue in the original). These features, omitted from the skeleton plan (Figure 10.4), serve to introduce descriptive elements that highlight the existing topographical features and boundaries of the city. In short, they transform the skeletal plan into something quite different. If the original intentions of the subterranean survey – to gain 'a true picture ... of the existing drainage beneath the surface' – are diluted by this map then the structural unity of the Ordnance Survey is also undermined by the superimposition of a representation of the old on top of a potential new. In short, this map is no longer a unified view of the city, but an uneasy combination of opposing elements: old and new; clean and dirty; divisions and unity.

This combination map also represents an attempt to combine the two views of the city described above: the view from above and the view from below. With this conflation a new play of meaning is put in motion: the view from below, with its old, dirty and decaying sewer spaces and confusion of administrative boundaries disturbs the abstract unity of the Ordnance Survey plans – the view from above. Rather, this map suggests an incomplete and more complex meaning. The depiction of the old sewers, built under the control of the old sewer commissions, and the reintroduction of the existing parish boundaries that determined the limits

10.6   Extract from sheet 27 of the 12-inch Ordnance Survey index plan showing sewer overlays (c.1850).

of this control, undermine the structural unity seen in the Ordnance Survey plans. The city can no longer be seen as a seamless whole; instead, the existing and the old impede the assertion of such a 'totalizing' view, bringing out the contradictions at the heart of Chadwick's ideology of improvement. The scientific rationale of the Ordnance Survey, which mirrored Chadwick's new vision of the city, could not quite incorporate the old spaces into its dominating framework. For a moment, the two coexisted in a state of unresolved tension.

The observations made in this chapter prompt a wider questioning of ideologies of improvement: one that goes far beyond the particularities of Chadwick's vision for London's sewers. Central to any conception of improvement is the articulation of a relation between old and new; notions of improvement, whether sanitary or otherwise, tend to present this relation in simplistic terms: that is, the old – represented as retrogressive and dirty – is forced to give way to the new – invariably cast as progressive and cleansing. However, even in seemingly insignificant representations (in this case sewer maps), slippages can be detected within these ideologies that, in themselves, suggest the existence of a more nuanced set of relations between old and new that might yet still be uncovered. London's sewer spaces were, for Chadwick, a paradoxical site, where the desire to 'see' and control the old and the dirty conflicted with his vision for a clean and ordered future. From Chadwick's day to our own, sewers have stubbornly resisted assimilation into rationalizing ideologies; indeed, as David L. Pike powerfully illustrates (see Chapter 11), they still run wild in our urban imaginings.

Chapter 11

The Cinematic Sewer

DAVID L. PIKE

Some day a real rain will come and wash all this scum off the streets.
(Travis Bickle in *Taxi Driver*, 1976)

Drainage systems serve the essential practical function of evacuating the waste products of massive urban populations and of draining city streets to prevent flooding. As conceptual spaces, however, their function is less clear cut, combining modern visions of sanitation with archaic fantasies of the monsters that breed in the waste tunnels of society. From its origins in ancient Rome to its apogee in nineteenth-century Europe, urban drainage has been closely associated with the definition and division of the urban population between what is pure and what is filthy, what is useful and what is to be discarded.[1] More than other subterranean spaces in the modern city such as the subway or the tunnel, the sewer also possesses an artistic pedigree, from the seminal social allegory of Jean Valjean's odyssey through the *égouts* of Paris in Hugo's *Les Misérables* (1862) and the photographic documentation of Nadar to Baudelaire's exploration of the *bas-fonds* with a vocabulary of waste in *Les Fleurs du mal* (1857) to Ben Jonson's scatological poetical journey down the polluted River Fleet, 'On the Famous Voyage' (*c*.1610). The same pedigree is evident in cinematic depictions of the sewer, such as the oft-cited but seldom analysed existential postwar dramas *The Third Man* (1949) and *Kanal* (1957), and, more recently, Emir Kusturica's controversial political allegory *Underground* (1995). If the material sewer provides a physical and conceptual place for all things dirty, the cinematic sewer has for over a century provided an influential set of visual images and associations for representing that place.[2]

Underground spaces in general can be characterized by the contradictory associations they elicit due to the coexistence of qualities attributed to the spaces of modern infrastructure – controlled, ordered, quotidian and banal – and of qualities attributed to the archaic underground and the mythic underworld – shelter, riches, hidden knowledge, atavism, danger, death. The further complexity of the representation of these spaces arises from the fact that we are not accustomed to articulating these different qualities simultaneously; indeed, the ways we categorize space vertically militate against our doing so. Different subterranean spaces, like subways, sewers, tunnels, cellars and the underworld, articulate the contradictions of underground space in different ways; consequently, each space tends to appear in different generic contexts and to be employed to different thematic ends. The subway, or underground railway, embodies the quotidian qualities of the underground; it is nearly always associated with work, daily routine and the 'average' citizen. In contrast, the sewer carries in its waters the atavistic and organic elements of the city, its waste, its filth, its repressions, its dirty secrets. The subway is an extension of everyday life in its banality, its excitements, or its horrors; the sewer is a transformative experience, a descent to the underworld from which one returns, if at all, a changed individual.

Depending on the physical identity of the individual, and depending on the degree to which that individual is confined to the sewer or merely journeying through it, the cinematic sewer ranges from social allegory and political satire to the sheer horror of the monster movie. As we shall see below, when human characters find themselves in the sewers, we have *Les Misérables*, *The Third Man*, and *Kanal*; we also have the satirical mudslinging already evident in Jonson. These sewer dwellers all have at least a trace of the monstrous in them, either in the unjust label applied by society or in the amorality of a sewer rat like black marketeer Harry Lime in *The Third Man*. Recognizably human or humanized characters such as the titular Erik in *The Phantom of the Opera* or the Teenage Mutant Ninja Turtles occupy a middle ground. Vaguely sympathetic but deadly and alien monsters such as the eponymous victim of chemical dumping in *Alligator* (1980) or the mutant progeny spawned in Japan by atomic and other scientific experimentation during the 1950s have lost all physical traces of humanity, although their victim status and brute force allow them a certain autonomy as protagonist. Even irredeemable monsters such as most mutated American monsters in the Hollywood 1950s, or the giant cockroaches in Guillermo del Toro's *Mimic* (1997), the 'cannibalistic humanoid underground dwellers' of *CHUD* (1984), or the brutally feral killer of *Creep* (2005) will occur in a narrative framework that places blame for their existence on the abuses of the world above. I will begin the tour of the cinematic sewer that follows in terms of the primary urban generators of these monsters: Paris and New York. I will then examine two prevalent nonspecific metaphors of the sewer space: the militarized sewer, in which political opposition is translated into a spatial division, and the global sewer, in which the sewer becomes an image to reflect multinational rather than local conflicts.

Les égouts de Paris

The sewers of Paris have long been received as an urban spectacle – public tours were conducted throughout the late nineteenth century and the Musée des Egouts is a popular tourist attraction today.[3] So it is no surprise that in their first appearance on screen, in *La Course aux Potirons* (*The Pumpkin Chase*, 1907), variously attributed to Louis Feuillade and Émile Cohl, a stop-action animated short in which pumpkins roll out of control through the streets of Paris and in and out of the sewers, the drainage system is an integral part of the cityscape rather than a world apart. The sewers were also an important component of Feuillade's serial thrillers *Fantômas* (1913–14) and *Les Vampires* (1915). As in *La Course aux Potirons*, the subterranean spaces were a sign of the integrated but heterogeneous cityscape of Paris; however, in the thrillers, this mixed space is a token of the terrifying control of the criminal gangs rather than a phantasmagoric free-for-all. This was how modernist Paris inflected the spatial metaphorics it had inherited from the nineteenth century; rather than a world divided by class, it depicted a world in which subterranean forces – either of chaos or of crime – dominated the city. The opposite approach would prove more enduring, as in Parisian Alice Guy and her New York-based production company's popular feature *The Sewer* (1912), a suspense thriller in which in one scene the hero is attacked by genuine sewer rats brought in for the production by an animal wrangler.[4] Rather than the instability of spatial divisions, Guy's sewers are resolutely a world apart, albeit one that temporarily threatens those who enter it.

Both images of the sewer derive from the enormously influential spatial metaphor that occupies the climax of the 1862 novel *Les Misérables*, where Hugo had translated the conflicted class relations of nineteenth-century Paris onto a city divided between above- and below ground (Figure 11.1). Hugo conceived of Paris as a living organism, a 'Leviathan' that would feed on the rich produce of the surrounding country, digesting what was of immediate value and excreting through its sewers as fertilizer to be returned to that countryside what it could not make immediately useful. Through Jean Valjean's descent into the sewers and eventual redemption through them, Hugo assimilated France's poor into this natural cycle of consumption, digestion and excretion.[5] Sewer representations indigenous to Paris tended to accept the metaphor, depicting a city of diverse spaces in which both above-

11.1 Jean Valjean seeks escape and redemption through the sewer, *Les Misérables* (1978) directed by Glenn Jordan.

and underground offer qualities and defects. When there are monsters, they tend to be intelligent and charismatic, if often also rebellious and anti-authoritarian. When Paris is represented from without, as in English and American adaptations of *Les Misérables* and *The Phantom of the Opera*, the division tends to be more strictly defined, the sewer more alien and the transformation of the journey more radical.

The first of the nearly fifty whole or partial adaptations of Hugo's novels was made by Alice Guy in 1907; an American version followed in 1909 and a four-part French serial in 1913. The earliest version I have seen is the 1935 Hollywood adaptation by Richard Boleslawski, which contains an atmospheric and highly organic sewer scene shot in high-contrast black-and-white by *Citizen Kane* cinematographer Gregg Toland. There is a lot of liquid, tendrils hang from roof, and flotsam clogs up the water; Jean Valjean (Fredric March) escapes by wading in up to his eyes in the slime, a feat Inspector Javert (Charles Laughton), pursuing on his own, is unable to match. Productions tend (of necessity, given the familiarity of the story) to stick to the basic dynamics of the scene, but the representation alters depending on the generic context of the film. A 1978 version made for British television, for example, provides a resolutely material but also existential sewer, with Jean Valjean and Marius emerging from the depths covered in brown clots, their clothing heavily stained. The sewer dominates the denouement, as Jean

141

Valjean and Javert have their final confrontation within a drainage tunnel – its filth colouring the long arc of their antagonism. By contrast, the star-studded 1998 Hollywood version depicted the collector sewer in which Valjean almost drowns as a raging river, stressing the religious imagery of rebirth, and having Javert catch his quarry as he emerges from below. Finally, in the context of the long-running West End musical, the sewer is a purely metaphorical space of crisscrossed lighting and dry ice, a lightly tinted under-class and underworld out of the *Threepenny Opera* or *Guys and Dolls*, with its candy-coloured drainage pipes framing a crucial round of craps. As Corpse-picker Thénardier sings, 'here among the sewer rats' on the broken barricades – all the spaces of Paris are reduced to spectacle.

In addition to their own adaptations of Hugo's classic novel, French films have often played on its sympathetic depiction of otherness through the sewers. Jacques Becker's taut masterpiece *Le Trou* (1960) plays on these dynamics, as five men escape a Paris prison through a tunnel into the sewers. Jean-Pierre Mocky's 1985 film *Le Pactole* (*The Gold Mine*) is in many ways a modern update of Hugo's novel, as a sympathetic hero is pursued by an obsessed detective. Seizing a unique opportunity to escape his mundane life, Yves Beaulieu makes off with a supermarket's daily receipts, escaping through the sewers, fleeing with his wife, and eventually living happily ever after. The sewer thus signifies the transformation of their life, including criminal acts, but without dooming them or marking them as monstrous.

Unique to Paris, the type of underground community that in other settings will usually live in the subway, in tunnels, or in a futuristic sub-terranean city is able to inhabit the sewers without being assimilated either to the model of vermin (sewer rats) or monster (sewer alligators or mutants). In Jean-Pierre Jeunet and Marc Caro's dystopian black comedy *Délicatessen* (1990), above-ground Paris, represented by a single apartment house, is terrorized by a brutish butcher who provides human flesh to the hungry tenants of his building. In this loose allegory of the German occupation, the role of the 'resistance' is played by sewer-dwelling vegetarians. Bumbling and endearingly goofy, their uniforms resemble plastic bags and they communi-cate in a parody of resistance slang and heroic codes. Their sewer dwelling identifies them as alien to the world above, but in the vision of *Délicatessen*, being alien is preferable to being normal.

Monsters in the sewers of New York

Our tour continues in New York, where if you are an endearingly goofy sewer dweller, you must also by necessity be a mutant in a children's fantasy, as in the four eponymous Teenage Mutant Ninja Turtles, transformed by toxic 'ooze', who fight crime from their subterranean hideout.[6] This alienness adapted the class-based vertical metaphorics of Victorian Paris and London

142

11.2 Exploring the dark heart of the modern American city in *Alligator* (1980) directed by Lewis Teague.

into a division based on race.[7] The sewer representation in New York derived primarily from two earlier images: the legend of giant alligators living in the sewers popularized by Thomas Pynchon's novel, *V* (1963) and the horror movie *Alligator* (1980), and the fictional depiction by Richard Wright in *The Man Who Lived Underground* (1944) and Ralph Ellison in *Invisible Man* (1952) of blackness in America as a subterranean condition. This image was compounded by the identification of the thousands of homeless New Yorkers living beneath the city as African-American. Although representations of the so-called 'mole people' surfaced in all manner of underground spaces, in particular the subways and tunnels in which they actually lived, it was in images of the sewer that their representation merged with those of the mutated monsters.

Alligator, directed by Lewis Teague from a script by John Sayles, infuses a Pynchonesque vision of the sewers with an acute social consciousness (Figure 11.2). Transplanting the New York myth to a nameless American city that mostly looks and sounds like Chicago (but was filmed in the sewers of Los Angeles), Sayles's script expands the New York paradigm into a tongue-in-cheek microcosm of American society. Dubbed Ramón by the girl who buys him on vacation at a Florida alligator farm, the baby is flushed down the toilet by her father but never forgotten by the daughter, who grows up into Marisa Kendall (Robin Riker), a 'world-famous'

143

herpetologist. The initial object of her affections does not fare so well, feeding on toxic waste. Chased out of his nest by the obsessed heroics of suspended police detective David Madison (Robert Forster), Ramón bursts through the sidewalk of the local ghetto, and, in Sayles's words, 'the alligator eats its way through the whole socio-economic system.'[8] Ramón is never sentimentalized to the degree of misunderstood monsters such as King Kong or Godzilla, but the revolutionary impulse he embodies is taken as seriously as the genre around it: he is neither attractive nor legal, but his brand of blind, underground justice is brutally effective. Consequently, the wholly predictable false resolution – Ramón is destroyed but the last shot shows yet another baby alligator flushed down the drain to land in the same underground stomping grounds – is simultaneously and inextricably a genre contrivance to leave open the possibility of *Alligator 2* and a straightforward enunciation of the inevitable repetition of the social processes that gave rise to the first Ramón.

During the 1980s, Ramón's offspring came home to nest in the New York underground and his Midwestern-style class warfare looked more like straight racial strife the closer it got to Manhattan. *Escape from New York* (1981), *CHUD* (1984), *Underground Terror* (1988), *Ghostbusters 2* (1989), *Teenage Mutant Ninja Turtles* (1990) and *Mimic* (1997) all imagined a non- or partially human life form inhabiting the sewers beneath New York; other films, such as *Batman Returns* (1992), which rooted the penguin's villainy in having been flushed into the sewers of Gotham City as a baby, played on the same spatial mythology.[9] Most extreme, as as well making the most extensive use of actual tunnel locations, is *CHUD*. The initials are supposed to stand for cannibalistic humanoid underground dwellers, big shambling rubber outfits with glowing yellow eyes and very large teeth that make short work of their downtown victims. As it turns out, the same four letters are also stencilled on the crates of toxic waste being dumped by the city in the tunnels, standing for 'Contaminated Hazard Urban Disposal'. The underlying message, we may assume, is that the powers-that-be regard the (underground) homeless as urban disposal; like Ramón, they return transformed to wreak havoc on the surface world that begot them. There are several differences from the mutant alligator, however, the first being that the CHUDs are wholly unsympathetic, undiscriminating and evil vehicles of death. By contrast, the movie's nondeformed 'undergrounders' are uniformly Caucasian; as opposed to the mutant CHUDs, they are also distinguished as homeless cosmetically rather than physically, by virtue of a bit of charcoal smeared over their faces.

The symbolic topography established by the use of the underground space combines progressive environmental ideology with some dubious racial politics. As in *Alligator,* the villains are the officials who sacrifice the welfare

144

of the city to their own greed and misdeeds. Because there remains a dwindling colony of 'good' undergrounders, subjects photographed by Cooper, the ones transformed into CHUDs belong to the category of those who have turned bad. Conversely, the survivors, whom we meet on our first descent into the tunnels in the company of Cooper, inhabit an open, arched space; their association with a positive underground is reinforced by their names of Victor and Hugo, one of the filmmakers' several self-conscious gestures to past influences. The sociological division between temporary and permanent homelessness, between lesser and greater separation from aboveground values, is thus troped along racial lines. The goodness of the white victims is reinforced by their high-culture resonance (*Les Misérables*), while their minimal makeup suggests the possibility of simple retrieval to 'normal' society. The 'blackness' of the CHUDs, in contrast, is biologically permanent, for their very humanity is put into question by it. Moreover, they resonate with the popular culture of *The Time Machine*'s Morlocks, and are shown to have no chance of returning to the world above. There are in fact no easy racial or ethnic splits in homelessness in general or among underground dwellers in particular; however, the power of cultural representations of these groups seems to derive from a symbolic vertical hierarchy reduced, precisely, to racial lines.

The cold war sewer

The prelude to the racially charged monsters of the New York sewer came in the 1950s, when the armed forces were constantly being mobilized to deal with the destructive rampage of irradiated monsters bent on destroying the world's great cities. To be sure, not all these creatures emerged directly from the sewers, but the spatial association was usually there, as in the undersea origin of the prehistoric monster Godzilla, disturbed off the Japanese coast by the detonation of American nuclear weapons. Released the same year as *Godzilla* opened in Japan, *Them!* (1954) was a big hit for Warner Brothers and, consequently, one of the first of many movies featuring monsters mutated by nuclear explosions. The giant ants in *Them!* do not originate in the sewers; rather, they are introduced in their natural habitat, living in a large-scale version of desert ant tunnels, explored and torched by the scientist Harold Medford (Edmund Glenn), his daughter Pat (Joan Weldon), and Sergeant Ben Peterson (James Whitmore), but too late to prevent the queen from escaping to found a new colony in the storm drain tunnels of Los Angeles (Figure 11.3). The National Guard is called out, and in an efficient and deadly operation they quickly eliminate a threat that, we are told, if it had spread, would have meant the end of life as we know it. The cold war subtext is patently clear – at least in hindsight – and the realism of the location shooting of the operation highlights the military nature of the space

145

11.3 Cold war style mobilization in the storm drains of Los Angeles, *Them!*
(1954) directed by Gordon Douglas.

of the sewer. As the chosen den of creatures by nature alien to it, the sewer must be cordoned off and cleaned out to make safe the world that lies just above it and painfully vulnerable.

The same tunnels and the same military subtext had appeared five years earlier in the film noir *He Walked by Night* (1949). Roy Morgan (Richard Basehart) is a nearly catatonic underground man who murders wordlessly and without remorse, living a solitary life in anonymous Los Angeles, and devoting himself day and night to carrying out some unspecified, unmotivated, vaguely political 'plan'. Morgan's use of the storm drain tunnels beneath Los Angeles identifies him as a creature rather than a man – the trademark shot shows him escaping the police by slithering through a sidewalk drain opening – a creature so incomprehensible as only to be dealt with by hunting him down and shooting him dead. Harry Lime, too, is tracked down and killed by the military in *The Third Man*, but his character is far too charismatic for the polarizations of postwar America; his past and the loyalty of his friends humanize him even as the sewer space and his black market activities mark him firmly as a rat. The moral ambivalence of Graham Greene's script and Carol Reed's direction, however, solidifies this identity only in the final chase, where Harry is trapped in the sewers through which he had been wont to move so freely. Here too, the efficiency of the military once it identifies Harry's heretofore hidden location reminds us of the

146

ongoing mentality of wartime, but our sympathies are too split among the different characters to establish the simple equation that occurs in the Los Angeles tunnels.

Such ambiguity is equally apparent in Andrzej Wajda's *Kanal* (1956), the tale of the extinction of the Polish Home Army during the Warsaw Uprising, lost in the sewer tunnels as it tries to find its way belowground to the remaining pocket of partisans. The analogue to Harry Lime is Daisy, who navigates the sewers between the surrounded partisans and the other spaces of resistance; she is not morally compromised, but instead is physically marked by her task. 'You stink of the sewer', are the first words her lover, Jacek, says to her. She survives the final odyssey through the tunnels, only to be trapped with the dying Jacek at a drainage opening into the open air, but blocked by an iron grate; a poet loses his way mentally, and wanders the tunnels playing a sorrowful tune on his ocarina and reciting Dante; the leader of the group finds his way to what he believes to be the desired exit, emerges into the light, and is immediately taken prisoner by the Germans. The historical underpinnings are joined to an existential tone common to the 1950s underworld, especially in narratives of communist resistance: there was simply no way out.

Although familiar from Hugo, the sympathetic portrayal of sewer dwellers is unusual in militarized sewer settings; this unusual identification would seem to follow from the fact that we are getting the point of view of the other side of the cold war. At the same time, the despair of the characters befits the stance of a filmmaker who would become prominently identified with glasnost. Just as Greene and Reed took a jaundiced view toward Western *realpolitik* in *The Third Man*, so Wajda's film is a far cry from celebrating the resistance or overestimating its effect. Trapped by the drainage grate, Daisy looks longingly across the Vistula River, the camera fixed on a point everyone in the Polish audience would have known was where the Red Army had camped for two months in 1944, waiting patiently for the Germans to annihilate the Poles before crossing the river to take control of an emptied city (Figure 11.4).

The global sewer

There are two ways in which the sewer has come to function as a metaphor for global, or multinational, rather than specific urban space.[10] The first and older model is the satire. Although often local in its references, scatological satire is global in its attack on contemporary culture. In the cult black comedy *The Magic Christian* (1969) by Joseph McGrath, Peter Sellers plays a London billionaire whose demonstration of the axiom that money can buy anything reaches its logical conclusion in a scene in which scores of people dive into a pool filled with faeces to retrieve the paper bills he tosses into it.

147

11.4 Trapped between a rock and a hard place: the end of the Warsaw Uprising, *Kanal* (1957) directed by Andrzej Wajda.

The Québécois movie *Elvis Gratton XXX* (2003) applies the time-honored equation between money and filth to the modern media. The eponymous star goes from owner of a modest sewage cleaning company, Télé-égout (Tele-sewer), to a media mogul, mouthing catchy slogans along the way: 'Shit's a gold mine, we eat it.' 'Sewers and TV are all that unite us.' 'The press is a shit pump in action. Prime it and it runs on its own.' Elvis meets his inevitable fate as intravenous injections of his own media products swell his body until it explodes in a shower of brown matter. Rather than a spatialization of social conflict and stratification, scatological satire portrays a world united by its inability to clean up its own waste.

The more contemporary form of global space uses the sewers precisely to mirror the contrasts and conflicts of globalization. The core of *Underground* (1995), Emir Kusturica's sprawling allegory of postwar Yugoslavia, is an extended sequence in which the partisan fighters hide out underground, while their erstwhile leader maintains for decades the illusion that they are still at war, exploiting them as a black market munitions factory. The resistance had long used the sewer tunnels to battle the German occupation; however, the phantasmagoric final segment of the film, when the hapless underworlders have finally discovered the deception, opens up the scope of the film into an allegory of the new European community, a network of vast

148

11.5   Berlin-Athens: the Belgrade sewers open up into an illicit tunnel network
evidently spanning Europe, *Underground* (1995) directed by Emir Kusturica.

sewer and drainage tunnels crisscrossing the continent for a new generation
of Harry Limes to travel at will (Figure 11.5). Aboveground, economic
refugees die daily trying to cross the boundaries of fortress Europe; hidden
from view, illegal business has no trouble at all.

The Wachowski brothers' blockbuster sci-fi epic, *The Matrix* (1999), took
this premise even further, positing a rebel movement inhabiting the only
remaining material spaces of a world that putatively exists only in
cyberspace. The rebels travel through the vast sewage network that seams the
planet's interior, plugging in and out of the matrix with their own hacking
programmes, waiting for a Messiah, the foretold One who will have the
ability to see through and thus to manipulate the complexity of the Matrix's
programme for what it is, a stream of encoded numbers, a pattern of meaning
rather than a material reality. This seductive vision of a world divided is
familiar to the genre of dystopian science fiction, although usually the sewer
space is muted in favor of a general underworld, nocturnal, and noir atmosphere, present only associatively in such phenomena as the omnipresent rain
of *Blade Runner* or the sticky and viscous organic matter in the deep subterranean passages of the *Alien* series.

Although its visual and metaphorical potential has spawned a great
number of cinematic representations and a handful of masterpieces, the
cinematic sewer, by the very nature of this potential, will never find its way
as a spatial punctuation in an aboveground setting in a wide range of
cinematic genres, as occurs frequently with the subway, the tunnel, and the
cellar. Rather, it always occupies the navel point of the film, its centre of

gravity, and, even if limited in actual screen time as in *The Third Man*, its literal and metaphorical filth inevitably seeps out to contaminate every space with which it comes into contact.

Section 3

COUNTRY: CONSTRUCTING RURAL DIRT

Introduction

ROSIE COX

The last section of this book contains four chapters that examine relationships between notions of dirt and purity and constructions of the rural. Dirt in rural areas has been largely overlooked in the existing literature on filth and abjection. While imaginings of the rural as pure and healthy have always been central to debates on urban decay, little attention has been paid to the realities of rural life, and the traditions of writing on urban sanitation, squalor and decay have no counterpart in rural studies. The countryside does not, however, have a simple relationship with dirt. The countryside has repeatedly been conceived of as a space of moral purity and uncorrupted by the worldliness of city life. It is also imagined as being physically clean and healthy, a place to go to for fresh air and clean water. However, rural life is also traditionally based on real dirt – on mud, manure and human sweat. The grand sanitizing projects that have attempted to clean and 'civilize' the city – paving, street sweeping and mains sewerage – are largely absent from rural areas even in the most developed countries, leading to city dwellers' stereotypical representations of the countryside as dirty in the sense of being uncivilized and wild.

The chapters in this section suggest that imaginings of rural life, and its products, involve the mapping of dirt and cleanliness onto 'the rural' and 'the urban' in unexpected ways. In a range of contexts the positive connotations of traditional rural life can be seen to be embodied in and read from rural dirt. When cleanliness is associated with modernity and capitalism, dirt can take on positive attributes, representing time-honoured ways of life, closer and more equitable social relationships. The consistency of such associations endures despite the geographical spread of the objects of study in the following chapters, from Thailand to the UK and USA. Three of the authors use the example of foods – the produce of rural environments – to explore the ways in which dirt moves between people and places, constructing and reflecting relationships between them. In *Purity and Danger*, Mary Douglas discusses food hygiene in relation to religion and risk; these emerging geographies of food and environmental hygiene add new knowledge to the field and insist that we re-examine notions of purity and danger in relation to contemporary practices, cultures and anxieties – particularly those linked to health and class status.

Together, the chapters in this section demonstrate that dirt is not always a threat to be avoided but can be sought out and embraced. Their authors show clearly that dirt is not necessarily 'matter out of place' in the country, but is rather an integral part of how the countryside is constructed, in the imaginations of both rural communities and urban dwellers.

The first chapter provides a link with the urban studies in section two, examining how dirt and cleanliness play a part in rural migrants' experiences of Bangkok. Here, Alyson Brody argues that the association of modernity with urbanism and cleanliness has been a major part of the Thai government's development agenda. Perceptions of hygiene and dirt operate metaphorically to suggest the civilized and developed, and their opposites. Brody shows how the realities of this dichotomy are lived out every day by a group of cleaners working in a gleaming Bangkok shopping mall. She contrasts the constraints of their lives at the mall, where they work to produce the spotless surfaces that represent modernity to urban middle-class consumers, with the greater freedom and quality of rural life that they return to when they have the opportunity to do so.

Following this, Gareth Enticott shows how, in a completely different part of the world, dirt and impurity can similarly represent community and belonging. Enticott examines the consumption of unpasteurized milk in a village in rural Devon in the UK, tracing how the consumption or not of this 'dirty' food can signal belonging or exclusion in a small community. To do this Enticott argues for a new exploration of theoretical impurity and the adoption of hybrid theoretical approaches, such as actor-network theory (ANT), which, he argues, offer new ways to explore how relations between dirt, impurity and people affect rural community identities.

Continuing with the theme of dirty foods, in the next chapter, as part of a research group with Lewis Holloway, Laura Venn, Moya Kneafsey, Elizabeth Dowler and Helena Tuomainen, I discuss the attitudes of consumers to the produce they receive direct from growers through vegetable box schemes and farm shops. We argue that for these consumers the dirt visible on food represents a whole range of positive relationships and characteristics and can be seen as part of a moral framework within which foods are chosen and consumed. Dirt testifies to foods' provenance in a particular place, grown by a particular type of person, and signals its proximity to nature. Conversely the 'hyperclean' produce sold in supermarkets are viewed as immoral and 'contaminated' through negative associations such as unknown provenance, contact with chemicals, aesthetic uniformity resulting from the methods of production and distribution associated with globalization, and the bland taste of standardized food varieties.

Dangerously dirty food – beef contaminated with 'mad cow disease' – is the subject of the last chapter. Bruce Scholten uses Mary Douglas's discussion of food rites and Deborah Lupton's analysis of risk to understand reactions to the BSE scare. Drawing on empirical research in the UK and USA he examines the responses of different groups to the risk posed by eating beef. While perceived distance from the risk explained some people's nonchalant reactions, especially in the USA, there were others who actively embraced the threat of contaminated food, celebrating the cheapness of beef at 'BSE barbeques'. For the participants in Scholten's research, the emergence of mad cow disease indicated complex and uncomfortable relations between rural food producers, 'sniping' urbanites and the unknown powers of agribusiness. Both producers and consumers found themselves affected by the actions of agribusinesses of which they had little previous awareness.

Chapter 12

Dirt and Development: Alternative Modernities in Thailand

ALYSON BRODY

In the centre of Bangkok is an imposing shopping mall surrounded by gardens and rising up as a black, marble-clad dedication to consumerism and a progressive Thailand. Next to the mall sprawls a large slum community, the occupants of which include a significant proportion of the migrants who flood to Bangkok from the rural northeast and north looking for economic opportunity in the overcrowded metropolis. The spaces are seemingly discrete, totally separate in character and function. Inside the mall is a gleaming, almost sanitized calm, where people move as if half asleep. In the community space next door there is a sensual overload – smells of cooking and of fetid drains; people talking and laughing loudly; children crying. Relations between the two spaces, however, are porous – many of those living in the community also work in the mall, and many community-dwellers sell souvenirs to the coach loads of tourists arriving at the mall. But the physical separation is visible in the shape of the tall corrugated iron walls that enclose the community and effectively hide it from outside view.

This chapter is about boundaries – not only physical, manmade walls, but conceptual boundaries that mark out perceptions of behaviour, lifestyles and levels of development. I argue that boundaries are constructed around narratives of dirt, cleanliness, order and disorder, but the ways in which the narratives are interpreted and applied depends on the person applying them.

At the same time, the narratives reveal a great deal about experiences and understandings of rapid development in Thailand. In many ways the notion of cleanliness within the context of rapid Thai development marks the boundaries between what is considered civilized and what is not, while perceptions of hygiene and dirt have become metaphors for a wider concept of 'progress'.

The locus for the chapter is the shopping mall introduced above, but more specifically I focus on the cleaners employed to maintain the building. I discuss some of the ways in which notions of progress are translated through material effects that attempt to produce and control bodies in space and time. Specifically, I note how uniformity, docility, dirt and cleanliness play an important role in constructing meanings of the modern workforce, and in marking perceived differences between 'undisciplined' rural and 'disciplined' urban, professional work and lifestyles.

I also explore the cleaners' responses to these structures and the everyday forms of resistance that shore up a collective sense of identity. I present ways in which the women sought to reclaim themselves against the threat of uniformity and control. I map indirect forms of agency forged through everyday strategies, or what Scott terms 'everyday resistance',[1] where the women challenged aspects of the working routine, rather than aiming formal complaints at representatives of the cleaning company that employed them. I suggest that these strategies were part of a subtle critique of the rigid labour practices and standardization that characterize 'company culture' within the industrializing, globalizing Thai economy.

Setting the context: rural/urban migration in Thailand

For anyone spending a certain amount of time in Bangkok, it soon becomes clear that many of the crowded city's residents and/or workers are from 'upcountry' (*tang jangwat*). At *Songkran*, the Thai new year, Bangkok is noticeably quieter because its migrants return to their villages for the annual celebrations. Migration is not only a contemporary Thai phenomenon. From the mid-nineteenth century up to the 1980s there was intense movement within rural areas as an effect of a pioneering 'frontier' peasant culture.[2] Rural–urban migration has been a feature of Thai industrialization since the 1950s, when influxes of capital aimed at developing the economy were ploughed into new industries and businesses and demand for an urban workforce consequently increased. In the past 30 years the number of people migrating for work in urban centres has escalated because of the rapid growth of opportunities in manufacturing, construction and service industries. Bangkok, as the core of Thailand's accelerated modernization and as Thailand's administrative heart, has always attracted the largest number of migrants. Over two million people came to the city from rural areas in the 1980s and

COUNTRY

'possibly a further million entered the urban work-force on a temporary basis'.[3] Although many of the migrants are from northern Thailand, the largest percentage has always been from the northeast, known as Isan. The poorest region of Thailand, Isan also has the least forgiving climate and soil conditions, which mean that farmers are usually restricted to a single rice harvest per year. A common pattern has been for rural Isan people to migrate to Bangkok between planting and harvesting as a way of supplementing their income.

Women have accounted for almost half of these most recent migrants to Bangkok, mainly because of many companies' preference for young female employees who are often considered cheaper to employ and more submissive than men.[4] While existing literature on female migrants has tended to focus on the highly emotive topic of the sex industry, which is conservatively estimated to employ 175,000 women from rural areas,[5] there are other sectors, like the garment manufacturing and service industries, that have received less attention yet employ many migrant women. In particular, people employed in the Thai janitorial sector have remained largely invisible and voiceless in the existing literature on labour and migration,[6] despite the sector being a major employer of rural migrants into Bangkok. This is partly a function of the way in which rural–urban migration has become synonymous with the moral degradation and implicit danger associated with moving to a Western-influenced urban setting, but it is also an effect of the invisible, undervalued nature of domestic work.

New urban landscapes and mall culture

David Harvey has noted the significance of space in shaping contemporary urban experiences. He argues that control over space is the prerogative of the powerful and that the significance of space lies in the possibilities of communicating and reinforcing social hierarchies and authority through 'spatial organization and symbolism'.[7] Harvey's comments are useful in finding a perspective on the city of Bangkok, where uses of space, struggles over space and lack of space are implicit features of urbanization. The count-less newly erected, modern 'glittering towers' convey messages of affluence and progress. A defining space of the contemporary urban experience in Bangkok is the shopping mall. The mall satisfies a national obsession with shopping, which until recently was largely carried out in open markets and Chinese-owned shops in formal and informal spaces of towns and cities, while the promise of air-conditioned comfort adds the patina of luxury that modernity represents to many. As Wilson points out, however, malls are more than just shopping centres. In the space-restricted, hot, polluted city, they serve as all-encompassing leisure spaces, places where families and young couples alike can spend the day eating in restaurants, drinking coffee, seeing movies and even going ice-skating or bowling.[8]

The mall, where the cleaners who participated in my study worked, was located in a prime spot in the centre of Bangkok. Built on eight floors, it encompassed two large department stores, both with their own supermarkets; international clothes stores, many of them designer labels; Thai souvenir and handicraft shops appealing to tourists; home furnishing shops; a multiplex cinema; restaurants and bars; and an ice rink. It was frequented by middle-class Thais as well as tourists, who were often brought directly to the mall by their hotels.

Employment of the cleaners

The cleaners were employed by a company the shopping mall contracted. The company had an office in the basement of the mall, but the mall administration oversaw and monitored the operations. During the period of my research 150 cleaners were employed at the mall, of which only 20 were men. The workers were aged between 18 and 57. The majority of the women were from Isan, but there were also migrants from northern Thailand and a few women from the Bangkok area. The longest period spent working at the mall was five years and the shortest was one month, but this was difficult to gauge because the women sometimes worked for a short time, returned to their villages and then reapplied to the company at a later date. Many of the women had learnt about the company through friends or family, and came directly from their villages rather than getting the work after a period in Bangkok doing other work, although some had previous experience of working in the city.

I spent a great deal of time with women working in the mall and became close to some of them. A key component of my research methodology was to collect detailed life histories from a number of the women. I conducted a small-scale survey within the mall and spoke informally to the women at work and in their spare time. I also accompanied some of the women on visits to their home villages. A constant process of participant observation formed the backbone of my overall methodology.

Discipline and order in the mall

As Foucault makes clear, discipline is not simply an act of external supervision.[9] Obedience is exacted as much through implicit technologies of control over bodies as through direct observation. Thus, he views power as a creative force – a mode through which behaviour is naturalized. Below, I present some of the rules and practices that circumscribed space and bodies at the mall. I will go on to reflect on how these embodied realities drew on and reinforced particular 'civilizing' narratives that are axiomatic to understandings of development in Thailand.

Organizing space and time: a day in the life of a cleaner

The cleaners worked a 12 and a half hour day, with three breaks, including an hour for lunch. They were stationed differently within the mall; some were responsible for the open spaces, while others were assigned the duty of maintaining the toilets.

Every morning they would line up, with the supervisors in front and rows of cleaners facing them. The head supervisor and sometimes a representative from the shopping mall management addressed the cleaners. While at work upstairs, the cleaners assigned to the toilets could not move from their stations. Those in the main body of the mall kept to a specific area but were chastised if they were not seen to be working constantly. If I stopped to talk to any of the cleaners, a supervisor would inevitably arrive and send them off in another direction with their mops. Most notably, in the gregarious, sociable atmosphere of the mall, where customers and shop assistants talked and laughed, the cleaners worked alone and silently. As noted below, the rules stated that they were not allowed to chat with other cleaners and they were discouraged from talking to shoppers unless approached for some reason. The silence of the cleaners in the public spaces was notable in a country where the exchange of banter is a constant backdrop and an important aspect of social identity. Thus, the cleaners' presence was strategically managed to produce the illusion of invisibility: the cleaners were there, but you did not see them unless you were aware of them.

The area where the cleaners assembled in the morning and went for their breaks was an eloquent expression of status differences within the mall, as well as of the ordered working environment. In contrast to the clean, sparkling public spaces of the mall, the cleaners' common area was a dimly lit airless space without windows in which there was a pervasive smell of rotting garbage. The space had been partitioned to create an office on one side. On the wall outside the office a list of 20 rules was enshrined. These included:

- it is forbidden to bring any kind of bag to the work area;
- it is forbidden to eat food or snacks, or smoke while working;
- cleaning staff must not misbehave. They must behave as befits a cleaner;
- do not behave badly in front of your superiors;
- do not chatter with each other, joke around or shout while you are working;
- do not use or take the company's goods or products for your own use; and
- do not sleep while working.

Locating underlying narratives of change in the mall

While I do not wish to present an overly symbolic interpretation of these daily activities and the spaces in which they took place, I would argue that particular social codes were implicit in the fabric of the work environment created within the mall. At one level, a dominant discourse of extracting labour efficiently within a modern, commercial framework informed the organization of space and labourers within the mall. In *Discipline and Punish*, Foucault eloquently describes the rigours of a modern system built on the potential of bodies that perpetuates itself by controlling all that is naturally disorderly, unstructured and random about those bodies. In factories, as in the mall, 'time, space and movement' are standardized to make 'possible the meticulous control of the operations of the body, which [assure] the constant subjection of its forces and [impose] upon them a relation of docility–utility'.[10]

Intrinsically Thai ideas about developmental hierarchies tempered the overriding discourse of modern labour relations. An interview with Daw, the chief supervisor – who was from Bangkok – illuminated some of the deeper logic underlying techniques of discipline within the mall. In particular, when I asked why the rules were necessary, she told me:

> We need [rules] because things are so different for people from the provinces (*tang jangwat*). They don't do things in the usual way (*tham mai bokatit*). They don't have bosses. 'Upcountry' they are their own bosses. Here there are supervisors, senior people. It's not our house; they employ us to come and work here, so we need rules. Many things are forbidden ... like stealing. Some people who come from upcountry don't know ... they see something and take it. And it's forbidden to eat food upstairs because it doesn't look good in front of the customers.

Daw's words have particular relevance within a wider discourse of Thai development. Thailand is a nation that has been in a constant process of self-definition since the beginning of the twentieth century. It has moved through phases of national affirmation that have an important tenet in common – the desire not only to be 'civilized' (*sivilai*) but to be *seen as* civilized, as an adjunct to the achievement of economic growth.[11] Over the years, what it means to be civilized has gone through various incarnations. During the fading years of French and British colonial rule in the countries surrounding Thailand, civilization in this never colonized country meant demonstrating how Westernized Thais were able to be. From the 1950s, the ideal of progress has been subsumed under the term 'development' (*gan pattana*), entailing the restructuring of the agricultural sector and industrialization of the economy. More recently development has been equated with globalization, a desire to launch Thailand as an internationally respected player in industry, finance and technology.

The creation of order and discipline are central to this notion of 'proper' behaviour. For example, the influential writer Phya Anuman Rajadhon, whose work has been widely read in schools and other institutions, explains that civilization is based on rules for behaviour, especially 'qualities of neatness and order'.[12] These aspirations have been embodied in the nature of development programmes aimed at rural Thailand. Boonmathaya's research among villagers who have participated in such programmes revealed that, in one northeastern village, 'Government officials cooperated with the village school teachers to train children to speak politely by using the Central Thai language and [to greet] the elders in a polite manner by bowing ... their torso and heads as low as possible and walk[ing] lightly.'[13] These policies and discourses serve to frame rural Thailand in ways that echo Pigg's observations about the generic Nepalese village that has been constructed ideologically through layers of overlapping, mutually reinforcing narrative, a process that represents 'the village' as 'a space of backwardness'.[14] In the next section I will emphasize how notions of dirt and cleanliness play an important role in establishing and maintaining these perceived differences between rural 'not yet civilized' and urban 'civilized' spaces and practices.

Dirt, order and the establishment of boundaries

The elimination of dirt is integral to the narratives of order outlined above. Where disorder is behaviour out of place that betrays a lack of development, dirt is a tangible, visible substance that marks the perversion of boundaries – evoking associations with base elements and conditions not fit for humans. Thus, as Mary Douglas famously pointed out, the idea of dirt and cleanliness helps to create boundaries within which people can feel safe and in control of their environment. 'Dirt offends against order. Eliminating it is not a negative movement, but a positive effort to organize the environment.'[15] The symbolic power of cleanliness emerged publicly in early 2000 as part of a scandal involving a Thai pop star. The young woman had referred to Lao women as 'dirty' during a television broadcast that was also shown in Laos. There was an outcry from the Lao women's union, but no apology was given. It was clear that the furore had not simply been caused by the singer's naïve comments, but was triggered by deeper prejudices in her assumptions about the relatively 'undeveloped' status of Laos compared with Thailand. These discourses were made obvious to me during the fieldwork for this chapter in my conversations with middle-class urban Thais who were always concerned, when I spent time in the Thai countryside, that it would be 'very dirty'. At the same time, ways in which Thais use language strengthen particular associations; the words 'dirty' (sokoprok), 'smelly' (men) and ugly (tulee) are often said with absolute disgust while their counterparts: 'clean' (sa-at), 'good odour' (hom) and beautiful (suwai) are used to express an extremely favourable reaction. The pervasiveness of dirt as an organizing principle and a sign

162

of progress is not, of course, restricted to Thailand. Hoy, for example, historicizes the pursuit of hygiene in the United States, linking it to a process of Americanization for immigrants from Europe and Africa, who were seen as being in need of education about hygiene.[16]

I would suggest, therefore, that the visible management of dirt was key to the projection of a degree of modernity in the space of the shopping mall. Given the highly evocative conceptions of dirt and cleanliness outlined above, it is not surprising that the employment of an army of cleaners is an integral aspect of urban shopping mall culture. The ongoing task of hygiene maintenance, however perfunctory, helps to create and sustain the illusion of order around which urban 'civilization' and wealth are predicated.

Working with dirt: labour hierarchies in the mall

Thai society is extremely hierarchical, with respect and deference paid to older relatives and colleagues. In the workplace this attention to social place is reflected in the epithet 'phi' (older sibling) being accorded to someone of higher status and 'nong' (younger sibling) to someone who is considered lower in the social pecking order. For example, in a restaurant, it is customary to refer to waiting staff in a restaurant as nong, regardless of their age. These distinctions were deployed within the mall in ways that were made very clear to me on my first day of conducting research there. The assumption of many supervisors had been that I would eat my lunch with them inside the office, separate from the cleaners. My announcement that I wanted to eat with the cleaners to get to know them elicited raised eyebrows and some consternation: 'You want to eat with the children (dek dek)?' one supervisor quizzed me, referring to the cleaners who were eating their lunch in the common area outside.

A clear distinction between the groups was the types of work in which they engaged and the opportunities for public display – for being part of the mall's active, visible meanings – that the post of supervisor offered. Within the dominant, middle-class conception of moral worth and sophistication physical labour is connected with a lack of progress, coarseness, and backwardness, particularly when it involves working in dirty conditions.[17] I observed that while the mall was a public space, during its opening hours the supervisors avoided physical cleaning work. Their time was occupied with walking around the mall monitoring the ongoing work. They would also spend a considerable amount of time putting on make-up and painting their long fingernails, which were clearly not designed for dirty, physical labour. What was interesting was that these women were from similar backgrounds as the cleaners, often with similar qualifications; they did not earn much more than the cleaners and most of them also lived in the slum. Such attitudes are not unique to Thailand and, in fact, exist in many parts of

Southeast Asia. For example, Sen talks about the use of maids in Indonesia for the dirty, labour-intensive aspects of cooking that are conducted in a concealed 'back kitchen' while the lady of the house prepares food for her guests in the spotless more public front kitchen, part of a social and spatial organizational structure designed to demonstrate her skills as a hostess.[18]

Pride, pragmatism: the cleaners' perception of work, self and home

Above I have described some of the ways in which discipline was an implicit manifestation of labour practices in the mall. In this section I will begin to explore how the cleaners reclaimed themselves in the face of this structure, uniformity and low social status attached to their work.

Bourdieu has argued that the social worlds in which people grow up and move are taken for granted because everything in them refers back to that world, and thus awareness is constrained from reflecting on itself; he refers to this phenomenon as *doxa*.[19] According to his argument, the capacity to see these worlds objectively – in terms of one possibility among many – requires 'a break with primary knowledge', which could occur through movement away from a particular environment and entry into another. Using Bourdieu's analysis, I would like to argue that the process of migration and of working within a system where rules were imposed through hierarchical structures enabled the cleaners to view their rural lives and livelihoods through new eyes, to recognize that the fabric of their lives that they had taken for granted was a 'way of life' worth valuing and, in many cases, worth returning to. At the same time they were able to reflect objectively on the practices that defined their working lives in Bangkok, and on the urban ideals that framed them. The women expressed their attitudes to the rules both verbally and by subverting them in tacit ways. The small liberties they sought may seem unremarkable, but I would argue that their culmination was significant. Following Scott, they may be termed 'everyday forms of resistance', or, in my own terminology, 'everyday politics'.[20]

First, I discerned what might be termed 'working-class consciousness', particularly from the Isan women, who often stressed to me the centrality of being strong and capable of hard work as part of their expression of an Isan identity. The ability to 'withstand hardship' (*oton wai*) was a recurring theme in my conversations with the women, and comparisons would often be made with the 'weak' and 'lazy' Bangkok people, who did not know the meaning of hard work and were more concerned about outward appearances. These observations were couched in the knowledge that working with dirt, particularly human waste, did not bestow high status on the women in the larger social picture, but that there was pride to be derived from doing the job well and providing a service. This perspective was succinctly expressed in the life story of Tuk, an Isan cleaner in her late twenties who was a single mother and supported a child and her elderly mother, both of whom were living in rural Isan. She indicated that some of the women with whom she had worked were ashamed to be cleaning toilets for a living. These women's fickle attitudes became a foil for Tuk's own attitudes to work, and for the strength of character she saw as integral to her own survival and success. She told me:

> Bangkok people think we're from upcountry and we don't have any knowledge, and they like to look down on us people who do low-level work. But I don't care. Those who care can't put up with (*oton*) the work, and they leave, but I don't like it when other people look down on themselves and say: 'why do I have to do this kind of work?' If I hear someone talking like that, I ask: 'Do you think you're so high class that you can't do this work?'

Another recurring theme in conversations with the women was the 'freedom' (*khwan issara*) of rural life. Although the women made it clear that tending to rice fields and other crops was hard work, requiring physical endurance, what they missed was the unstructured time, the lack of a rigidly fixed routine and the sense of autonomy they felt. For example, Gulap, a 30 year-old cleaner from the north of Thailand, often made nostalgic references to the life she had left, even when she knew that to return would mean grinding poverty. On one occasion, when she had returned from a visit to her home village, she told me she was finding it hard being back in Bangkok and talked about a period when she had been at home, following a stint in a Bangkok factory:

I stayed at home for two years.

Was it fun?

I felt free. I felt *sabai jai* (comfortable/at ease), but I didn't have any money. I wanted to stay there for a long time, but I had no money.

What do you mean by 'free'?

I mean that whatever you want to do, you can. You have freedom. I was really *sabai jai* (at home) [during her recent visit]. I wanted to go into the rice fields and be with nature. I didn't want to go back to Bangkok at all. I went to work in the fields every day. When I came home I relaxed. Some days we had a rest or went for a trip by motorbike.

An alternative Thailand

Although I have talked about the role of nostalgia above, I am not claiming that the cleaners idealized rural life, or that I am doing the same. Instead, I suggest that the women were seeing through the strictures of a system that demanded more of them than their labour – it also required them to succumb to a rationale of development they did not fully accept. Their actions quietly endorsed an alternative vision for Thailand's future, reinforced through popular culture. For example, Thai folk singers such as Ad Carabao have a huge following in urban as well as rural areas in Thailand. Many of their songs are critical of rapid development and of the economic and political corruption that accompanies it, celebrating simpler rural values and the Thai farmer's connection to the land and his family. The songs provide the soundtrack to more directly political expressions of this alternative vision; social movements such as the Thai Assembly of the Poor – an expansive network with a large contingency in Isan – campaign for a development process that is responsive to the needs of rural communities, especially the rural poor.

Conclusion

These women migrants, who are part of a vast building maintenance industry, have remained invisible and voiceless in the existing literature on Thai labour and migration. The labour practices the women encountered in the mall reveal much about the assumptions underpinning processes of modernization in Thailand, as well as reinforcing certain organizational principles of a more generic modern 'company culture'.

In particular, I have highlighted the importance of notions of dirt and cleanliness in providing a notional boundary between 'civilized' and 'uncivilized' people and spaces. Cleanliness is a metaphor for a Bangkok-centric vision of a new Thailand, marking a break with the perceived dirt and associated disorder of 'uncivilized' rural existences. The cleaners employed to dispose of the dirt are part of the mall's subtext, necessarily visible in terms of the function they serve, but erased as individuals through the deployment of particular strategic rules and processes of 'atomization' that keep them working in separate, allocated spaces. Against this threat of diminishment, however, the cleaners 'reclaimed' a sense of their own importance in the mall's public script through the pride, or at least conscientiousness, in the jobs in which they were expected to be in direct contact with dirt and bodily waste.

At the same time, by not allowing themselves to be defined by what they did and where they worked, they were able to put their work and the mall into perspective. This is partly because, by working in a system that treated them as ubiquitous, they became able to see their rural lives objectively, as a 'way of life' that shaped their values and goals. Their presence in Bangkok was an acknowledgement that it is increasingly unsustainable to rely on rural livelihoods alone. Yet, personal knowledge of these alternative working patterns enabled them to objectify practices within the mall and to forge 'everyday forms of resistance'.[21] These expressions of sociality and alternative relationships carved out of an otherwise humourless regime were, I suggest, more than a means for the women to survive the tedium of their long days. They also marked a degree of contempt for the rigid structures imposed not only to manage a large workforce but also to fit their behaviour into a mould they considered superficial and emanating from an alien set of values.

This critical view of Bangkok-led ideals of modernity finds resonances in what I have referred to elsewhere as an 'unofficial' narrative.[22] This narrative is expressed through popular culture and social movements that call for an alternative vision of development for Thailand that is rooted in equality, respect for nature and the celebration of rural values and people. It is a narrative that places less emphasis on the cosmetic, external qualities that are often part of the 'official' projections of modernity I have discussed above. It is instead more concerned with earthy values such as honesty, hard work, love for one's family and love for the land, which it sees as fundamental to human well-being and national pride.

As far as I know, these critical reflections on the cleaners' working environment in the mall were never translated into open complaints. Instead, the women quietly subvert the structured, disciplined work regimes in ways that could be framed as 'everyday politics' or, following Scott, 'everyday forms of resistance'. For example, they appropriated spaces within the mall for sociality *khwam sanuk* (fun), aspects associated with rural work. Although the cleaners were not supposed to chat together during working hours, the toilet areas and some of the larger storage cupboards, situated away from the main shopping areas of the mall and from the eyes of the supervisors, often provided an arena where gossip could be exchanged. Flirtations were also played out in these spaces. When surveillance of the cleaners was increased during a period when the company was being assessed for an international ISO 9001 2000 standard, some of these small freedoms were undermined, creating an atmosphere of discontent and resentment.

Chapter 13

Dirty Foods, Healthy Communities?

GARETH ENTICOTT

How important are notions of impurity to rural spaces and societies? Suggestions that impurity is somehow central to rural England may appear counter-intuitive: thinking about what processes surrounded the construction of the English countryside at the turn of the twentieth century usually leads to studies of the 'purification of space' through practices of gentrification and middle-class counter-urbanization.[1] In these rural contexts, the 'other' is either well hidden or unwelcome: ethnic minorities, the poor and even agriculture are matters out of place.[2]

In this chapter I argue that forms of impurity can be vital to the construction of rural space. I explore how impurity can sometimes be central to rural community identity and how rural space is theorized. To do this, I draw on discussions of theoretical hybridity that reposition nature–society relations within social theory. Theoretical tools such as actor-network theory (ANT) provide an alternative theoretical framework with which to challenge the 'forces of purification' within the disciplinary boundaries of the social and natural sciences. Symmetrical perspectives like ANT embrace the significance of what we might call the theoretical impurities – or what Bruno Latour calls the 'missing masses'[3] – that are traditionally filtered out from dualistic accounts.

My first aim in this chapter is to explore theoretical impurity. The second is to examine the contribution that such hybrid approaches make to the understanding of constructions of rurality. In particular, the focus here is on what ANT can tell us about how relations between dirt, impurity and people impact on rural community identities. According to Ruth Liepins,[4] such a step potentially allows for a reinvigoration of rural community studies – a methodological and theoretical paradigm that has fallen from favour within rural sociology.[5] Liepins also claims that ANT has potentially much to offer in regenerating understandings of rural community. So far, however, few attempts to analyse the rural community symmetrically have been realized.[6]

I begin this chapter by revisiting the bases of ANT and its advancement of hybridity, in opposition to theoretically pure alternatives. I then turn to examine what a focus on hybridity can tell us (and equally what it does not explain) about the construction of rural community identities. Here, we explore the role of what John Law[7] calls 'heterogeneous materials', particularly those that have been labelled dirty and impure, yet remain important for rural identities. One of these is unpasteurized milk and the range of natures and bacteria within it. Since the early twentieth century, pasteurization has been a key weapon in fighting the adulteration and infection of milk with various bacteria and zoonoses, thereby creating an image of milk as 'nature's perfect food'.[8] Yet, by the end of the century, a significant number of (predominantly rural) people continued to consume and defend their right to consume unpasteurized milk, despite its association with deadly bacteria, E.coli and salmonella.[9] By examining the consumption of unpasteurized milk in one English village, in this chapter I explore the importance of hybridity and impurity for rural communities.

From purity to hybridity

In recent years, various writers have sought to challenge the dualistic nature of theoretical perspectives. At stake is the division between the natural sciences dealing with natural processes; and the social sciences discussing all things that are cultural. These distinctions are grounded in attempts to legitimize, protect and justify the existence of different disciplines.[10] Yet, such dualisms can be damaging: Peter Dickens argues that these divisions of labour are a key factor underlying the inability to understand adequately and relate to the natural world.[11] Efforts to maintain these divisions – in effect maintain the purity of theoretical traditions – inevitably lead to a fractured, incomplete view of the world where knowledge is in some respects incapable of understanding the complex interconnections and relations that compose the world.[12] Increasingly, though, there is agreement that to do worthwhile sociological research dualistic oppositions above all between culture (or society) and nature have to be rejected.[13] This is by no means an easy task – as Ted Benton states, 'the really difficult problems only start here.'[14]

A popular tool with which to transcend these dualisms has been actor-network theory (ANT). Bruno Latour, John Law and Michel Callon – the architects of ANT – situate ANT in the belief that 'there is no thinkable life without the participation – in all its meanings of the word – of nonhumans, and especially machines and artefacts.'[15] They argue that 'entities take their form and acquire their attributes as a result of their relations with other entities.'[16] According to ANT, identities are effects or outcomes of intricately woven together networks of relations.[17] The identities formed by these networks therefore 'perform' the categories they constitute. As part of this relational approach, ANT extends agency to all entities within networks. Latour argues that action comprises 'not what people do' but 'what is accomplished along with others'.[18] Actors then need to be viewed heterogeneously – they can be social, natural or technological – and can only act because they are enmeshed within networks, creating 'hybrid collectifs'.[19]

Latour's essential point is therefore that heterogeneous material from either side of these dualisms co-constructed categories within the world. Boundaries like the 'social' or 'natural' are never pure divisions, but are located somewhere between the two. As Latour points out: 'yes society exists for real, but no it is not socially constructed. Even in this, the most primitive concept of all social theory, nonhumans proliferate making it impossible to recognize a "pure" society.'[20] Thus, neither society nor nature can offer an explanatory description, for they are not pure categories. Yet, as Latour repeatedly argues, binary modes of social theory have consistently denied the significance of this hybridity: not only are these binaries heterogeneous effects, but the very process of dividing the world up into these categories proliferates the binding up of humans and nonhumans into further hybrid networks.[21]

Within this hybrid world, the task of the researcher is to engage with the complexity of these hybrid networks to assess how those combinations are made and held together.[22] Following ANT, impurity becomes emergent from those heterogeneous subjects and objects that are woven together in networks. Within rural studies, it is not hard to think of the range of heterogeneous actors that are implicated in the construction of rural community, but that also pose constant threats to orderings of rural identity. For example, 'hybrid events' such as the BSE and foot and mouth crises reveal how new alignments of the social, natural and technological have become mixed into new relationships.[23] The 2001 UK foot and mouth outbreak can be broken down into a series of heterogeneous linkages between 'viral agents, climatic conditions, styles of farming, systems of transportation and market requirements'.[24] In these new relations the 'exchange of properties' between actors spiralled out of control causing unforeseen and terrible consequences: they reconfigured the spaces of the rural community into new heterogeneous topologies, making the activities it previously specified impossible and others necessary.

Hybridity and the extensive self

The symmetrical position Latour advocated is not without controversy.[25] Critics point to ANT's failure to acknowledge that humans possess intentions resulting from language-based forms of reflection.[26] Nature and other nonhumans on the other hand, do not possess these capacities and it is intentional agency that mobilizes actors to construct networks and order specific nonhumans in the first place.[27] Ian Hacking[28] demonstrates this point by arguing that humans are different from nonhumans because they are aware of classifications made about them. Like ANT, Hacking sees heterogeneous frameworks representing social and material infrastructures as responsible for creating identities and classifications. These material and social infrastructures make substantial differences to the way people behave in the way they prescribe behaviour, but also in the ways humans reflectively interact with these infrastructures, a possibility not afforded to nonhumans. Hacking therefore distinguishes between 'interactive kinds' – classifications and identities that 'interact with things of that kind, namely people ... who can become aware of how they are classified and modify their behaviour accordingly' – and 'indifferent kinds', which refer to classifications that do not interact with the things (nonhumans and heterogeneous materials) they are classifying because they are not aware of them.

This reworking of ANT suggests that attention is directed to how humans use heterogeneity for their own reflective purposes. This is demonstrated through Karin Knorr-Cetina's notion of 'objectualization'.[29] Knorr-Cetina argues that individualization has led to desocialization in which new identities are forged by forming relations with objects. These 'object worlds', or object-centred environments, 'situate and stabilize selves, define individual identity just as much as communities or families used to, and which promote forms of sociality ... that feed on and supplement the human forms of sociality studied by social scientists'. In this way, 'a strong thesis of objectualization would imply that objects displace human beings as relationship partners and embedding environments, or that they increasingly mediate human relationships making the latter dependent on the former.'

While Knorr-Cetina echoes ANT's concern for the study of heterogeneous relationships, her notion of an object world nevertheless emphasizes that humans construct these object relations for their own social purposes. Jonathan Murdoch[30] extends this analysis by arguing that the countryside could be seen as an object world in which the self is formed extensively through linkages with heterogeneous rural objects such as green fields, traditional buildings and animals. This concept of the 'extensive self' suggests that the self is (always) geographically spread across heterogeneous objects, but that these relations serve to 'centre' the self. The significant aspect of these relationships is not that they are heterogeneous, but that they 'function to stabilize social modes of being [and] ... somehow work to "express" particular forms of social identity such as class, ethnicity or gender'.[31] Moreover, while forms of heterogeneity may reinforce traditional social states of selfhood, 'to talk of hybridity detracts from a full appreciation of the social self and the role it plays in holding heterogeneous relationships together'.[32] By way of example, Murdoch points to Michael Bell's analysis of the rural community of 'Childerley'.[33] Here, Bell shows how existing and new residents of the village forge relations with rural objects, natures and people. In doing so, they create 'extensive selves' across these objects, thereby stabilizing the 'morally good' identity of the 'country person'. These identities and object relations result from interactions with those other less desirable identities, namely those 'morally ambiguous' identities associated with class and urban living.

This journey from theoretical purity to hybridity highlights the complexity of such a task. But it also raises other questions. First, if hybridity leads back to a consideration of a socially constructed extensive self, what other extensive selves are there within the countryside? While some versions may be comprised by distinct patterns of heterogeneity, the countryside is highly differentiated.[34] It should be no surprise therefore, to find other extensive selves aligned to different interpretations of selfhood, attempting to secure themselves in different patterns of heterogeneous relations, each with their unique characteristics. In this way, by tracing these different sets of heterogeneity, we might also learn how the countryside becomes differentiated. Within these sets of heterogeneity, we might also be able to see how concepts such as impurity come to be defined and renegotiated by the actors implicated within them.

Second, if different sets of heterogeneity are implicated within the extensive self, to what extent might we consider heterogeneous actors and relations other than humans shaping and influencing these modes of selfhood? In developing the concept of the extensive self, Murdoch relies on Bell's analysis of Childerley and portrays a set of heterogeneous relations revolving around a nature that is purified, socialized and disciplined. In this countryside there appears to be little ambivalence or resistance to this extensive self. Yet, in other patterns of heterogeneity, there might be greater opportunity for nonhuman agency to challenge and reconfigure these extensive selves, and in effect articulate a more ecological geographical or community self. These other extensive selves may find their relational identities challenged by a range of other forms of wild and impure nature, acting intentionally or 'transformatively'.[35] Indeed, the inherent characteristics of these forms of nature and heterogeneous materials may be fundamental to their enrolment within these networks. Thus, given the potential range of extensive selves, it might be expected to find different ecologies of heterogeneity 'on a continuum, extending from those situations where "social" (or "interactive") factors are paramount to those where "natural" (or "indifferent") factors are decisive'.[36]

Hybridity, community and unpasteurized milk

To answer these questions, let us turn to a case study of the consumption of a so-called impure food in one rural community. 'Ash Dean' is a small village in rural northwest Devon.[37] It is perhaps no different from a number of other villages in the area in that it still has an agricultural focus but an increasing number of retirement and lifestyle counter-urbanizers are living alongside its longstanding local residents. In this sense, it is symbolic of the 'contested' countryside.[38] The actions of one of the village farmers, however, mark Ash Dean out as different. Dairy farmer Michael Goswell sells his milk to residents; or rather, his wife takes bottles of milk round to residents every morning in her Land Rover.

This is an unusual attempt at farm diversification, for the milk is unpasteurized and bottled straight from Michael Goswell's bulk tank in his dairy. This is a difficult job. It requires all manner of extra forms to fill in and bacterial tests to ensure that the milk passes public hygiene regulations. Indeed, as Michael Goswell pointed out, it was largely more hassle than its worth. If he had to, he would give it up, but for his wife it was a way of staying in touch with friends throughout the village and catching up on village gossip. Pasteurizing the milk, though, would be far too costly: the milk round was a labour of love and not an economic endeavour.

Not all the residents have the milk, but a substantial number do, mainly the families who have lived in the village since before anyone can remember. There are newcomers to the village who drink the milk, but there are also longstanding residents who do not consume it. Everyone though is aware of the risks, or at least the risks defined by public health agencies. For a start, the milk arrives in a bottle, which suggests potential hazards. Yet, the warnings of dangerous bacteria within the milk fail to put off the villagers.

Instead, these risks are renegotiated through a range of lay understandings of risk, bacteria and health. While the milk might contain E.coli, villagers point to their consumption of it over many years without any adverse reaction. The lack of local evidence reassures them that there is no dangerous bacteria in the milk and reaffirms their consumption habits. Indeed, to make their point villagers point to the longevity of the village's most senior residents, reflecting ideas of 'candidacy'[39] from medical sociology.

Contests over the impurity of unpasteurized milk also derive from a distinct culture of nature. The scientific view of unpasteurized milk presents a purified view of nature – something that needs to be made inert, and completely free of the bacteria, germs and microbes associated with E.coli

173

and salmonella, before it is safe to consume. Pasteurization achieves this by sterilizing the milk and leaving it 'pure'. Villagers, however, take issue with this view of purity. For them, pasteurization removes germs and bacteria whether they are harmful to health or not, resulting in a product stripped of natural life. Unpasteurized milk is viewed differently through a culture of nature, which embraces nature as alive and possessing its own transformative agency that can positively benefit human health. This culture of nature therefore revolves the benefits of all forms of nature, both good and bad. People should subject themselves to these effects by immersing themselves in nature by whatever means possible. However, for nature to improve health, then one needs to be exposed to nature in its entirety – both its positive and negative features – and it is only by experiencing both of these can one hope to benefit from nature. For these rural consumers then, 'clean' and 'pure' foods are to be regarded with suspicion and seen as hazardous. Those with impurities on the other hand are welcomed and regarded as healthy. For example:

I had to go into hospital a while back. When I was in there I asked them when I would be able to start drinking raw milk again. Anyway, they looked at me and said 'Raw milk – what do you mean when? Never! Never!' But they just don't understand do they? All these health regulations are stupid because now you are getting to a point where no one is getting any germs in food so they do not have the antibodies to fight off infection.

This belief that 'germs are good' is also embedded in ideas of what it means to be rural and local. A prevailing rural discourse is that 'rural people', through their daily contact with nature, have the most appropriate expertise for deciding what judgements to make about nature.[40] At the same time, possessing this experienced knowledge of nature is essential to claiming a true rural identity. Such a view is evident in the rejection of the impurity of unpasteurized milk. For a start, engaging with living nature is part of being rural. Rural people have to put up with both the positive and negative aspects of living with nature. However, these negativities need not be purified or hidden away. Rather, it is the process of living alongside them that allows a rural identity to co-evolve:

In the country you've got to be prepared to get on, get muddy, dirty and that – because that's what it's like … wellies on and in the mud – that's a proper country person for you.

You have to put your old clothes on and get out and get in the muck –

if it's gotta be done, it's gotta be done. ... If you lived on a farm – you know, you get a bit of hay come in the kitchen and a bit of straw in under the door – you know you just live with it, but these townies are rushing around picking it up every time – they would get the Hoover out.

The same is true in relation to the consumption of Michael Goswell's milk. Its visible consumption, for example by buying it from the village milk round, offers the opportunity to demonstrate one's rural status by conferring a rural identity. By drinking unpasteurized milk, consumers reveal that they know nature and all its facets. In doing so, consumers become rural, but by connecting rural identity with particular ways of knowing nature, the appreciation of impurity also marks out a life worth living, based on a different set of rationalities.[41]

It is not only a rural identity that is acquired through the consumption of unpasteurized milk, but also a local/community identity. Trust and the security provided by local social relations are central to these relationships. In this way, unpasteurized milk is an important actor in constituting and binding the community together and its consumption stakes out a claim to community membership. For example, the provision of the milk round by the Goswells is embedded in a concern to 'check up' on the elderly residents to ensure they are well, share gossip and keep in regular contact with other villagers. This concern is shared by the villagers, who display immense loyalty to the Goswells, declaring that they would never go anywhere else to get their milk. This loyalty to community social relations is equally a loyalty to the (im)purity of unpasteurized milk. In fact, so strong are these loyalties that residents will develop alternative forms of behaviour to claim community membership through unpasteurized milk. One elderly local lady, whose doctor forbade her to consume the milk because of her ill health, boiled the milk to allow her to continue buying it. By contrast, one parent who had moved into the village was concerned about the health implications but bought it anyway:

I have Michael's milk. And I know when people have young children – when I moved into the village they tended to have tummy bugs quite a lot and you worry with young children where it's coming from – whether it's the water, the milk, the food. But you wouldn't stop the milk because you might sort of supplement it with milk from elsewhere and not give it to your children, but you probably wouldn't say so – you certainly wouldn't stop it.

There are threats, though, to these heterogeneous relations. The arrival of new villagers with different attitudes to nature and (im)purity threaten both the continued sale of the milk and the community itself. These new residents might initially be prepared to try it to break into the local community, but more often than not, the milk is deemed too risky, even if it does mean community membership is compromised: 'When we first got here we thought we'd try it, but then our two children went down with these nasty tummy bugs so we stopped it straight away and haven't had it since.'

These different attitudes lead to a fragmentation of community identities, defining the limits of community membership and the status of insiders/ outsiders. Villagers who do not drink the milk are seen as outsiders and newcomers, as people who see nature through a purified lens and who cannot therefore be considered rural. Their reluctance to join in with this community of food highlights what to consumers appears as an anti-community ethic and they are blamed for the declining provision of village services and sales of unpasteurized milk. Perceptions of (im)purity provide the key to a divided community, controlling membership of communities and rendering claims to a rural identity elusive.

Conclusion: the importance of impurity for rurality

These accounts of the consumption of unpasteurized milk in Ash Dean tell a number of different stories. First, they demonstrate the range of hetero-geneity at play in the construction of rural space. The Goswells' milk round constructs a network of heterogeneous subjects and objects that give character to the space in which they are embedded, through for example the establishment of norms of behaviour. In this way, the heterogeneous relation-ships found within Ash Dean reflect the practice of rural differentiation.

Second, tracing the heterogeneous networks that construct the rural extensive self demonstrates the renegotiation of concepts such as impurity. In Ash Dean, impurity comes not to be defined by official discourses of health and safety, but by the local community. In this way, the consumption of unpasteurized milk reveals how these hybrid forms of nature are central to the creation of an extensive self. Unlike the purified middle-class construc-tions of the countryside, the extensive selves in Ash Dean are qualitatively different. The relations villagers form with unpasteurized milk allow them to access and construct a distinct community and rural identity. To engage with the (im)pure heterogeneity associated with unpasteurized milk is to become a local or rural person. This attempt to 'centre the self' on a rural identity is also related to a mistrust of scientific discourses of risk and resentment of those incomers whose decision not to participate in these community rituals erodes community identities. As a result, the construction of the extensive self and its relations to the heterogeneous objects and subjects of rurality reflects other forms of rural activism and defensive localism.[42]

Finally, these accounts highlight the configuration of an extensive self that is both socially ordered and embedded in social (rural) modes of selfhood. In Hacking's terms, it is an interactive achievement – villagers have sought links with specific rural objects because they are aware of what it means to be rural and, importantly, want to achieve that status. However, what is important to villagers is that the relationships they make with nature are somehow precarious. Thus, while unpasteurized milk centres rural identities, it does so because of a culture of nature that values its own transformative agency. Residents talk, for example, about the transformative agency of unpasteurized milk and how the consumption of impurity can positively transform human health. Engaging with the challenges of nature, its agencies and its (im)purities is part and parcel of this rural identity. In this sense, it is not only a sense of security that this extensive self provides. In some senses, the insecurity afforded by nature's agencies and (im)purities seems to be an important factor in these relationships. Thus, while no one is eager to see these relationships fall apart, that nature has the potential to transform them is not lost on anyone. Living with the uncertainty of nature and its transformative agency is therefore what is so central to the Ash Dean extensive self. While social desires shape the selection of rural heterogeneity, the agencies of these heterogeneous subjects and objects are crucial in characterizing the extensive self. It is here, then, that we can see the co-production of rural community identity.

In this chapter I have therefore sought to show how impurity can be central to notions of rurality and community. To appreciate the importance of impurity, though, it was necessary to journey through dualistic theory to the theoretical terrain of ANT to bring to life the 'missing masses'. In following these heterogeneous materials into the extensive self, we have seen how impurity is constructed within heterogeneous relations and how some impure rural objects and subjects are vital to the construction of rural identity and rural community. Relationships with impurity come to co-produce rurality, at least in Ash Dean. Of course, this is only one heterogeneous extensive self, but it marks out a distinct difference to others, such as Murdoch's analysis of Bell's 'Childerley'. There are likely to be others too, in which different heterogeneous ecologies construct and secure multiple rural community identities. Tracking the relationships made with heterogeneous subjects and objects across rural space might therefore be crucial to understanding the differentiation of the English countryside.

Chapter 14

Dirty Vegetables: Connecting Consumers to the Growing of their Food

LEWIS HOLLOWAY, LAURA VENN,
ROSIE COX, MOYA KNEAFSEY,
ELIZABETH DOWLER, HELENA TUOMAINEN

For most people in Britain, the USA and other parts of the global North today, food seems simply to 'appear' in supermarkets rather than come out of the ground or have some other 'natural' origin. The appearance of this food is strictly regulated, even for fresh fruit, vegetables and meat: signs of the organic origins of food (for example soil, blood) are banished and blemishes are not tolerated. There has been much recent academic interest, however, in so-called 'alternative food networks' (AFN), in which consumers get at least some of their food directly from growers or producers. Such food, in contrast to supermarket food, often *does* retain the evidence of its production. In this chapter we discuss how participants in AFN feel about their food. We explore the ambiguous relationships that can exist between these food consumers and food that, unlike the hyper-clean products associated with contemporary supermarkets, bears the traces of the environment within which it was produced – in particular, the soil or dirt in which vegetables are grown.

In outline what we want to suggest is the following. First, drawing on geographer David Sibley's work,[1] we recognize that food is often psychologically problematic; it is something that transgresses boundaries between the self and the outside. Second, dirt often signifies defilement, something from which people feel a desire to distance themselves.[2] Beyond its material presence, dirt has 'wider existential significance',[3] standing for an external threat to a sense of a coherent, bounded and defensible identity. It follows that supposedly 'dirty' substances present on food, for example evidence of soil, manure or blood, can be doubly psychologically problematic. We must eat, yet in the modern era increasingly feel revulsion at this evidence of the origins of food. Supermarket consumers have increasingly got used to food that is heavily packaged – individually plastic wrapped cucumbers or swedes, for example, or bloodless and anonymous pieces of meat. Thus, supermarkets have increasingly distanced food consumers from the earthy, dirty environmental conditions in which their food is produced. Yet, in response to a growing sense of unease with supermarket-dominated food supply systems, for many consumers there is, conversely, a desire actually to connect with the people, processes and places associated with their food, and for some this has meant buying into 'alternative' food networks where food is sourced in ways that do less to conceal its origins, and where the dirt on food might attest to its production under what are regarded as more natural conditions, even though such dirt might still be experienced as a challenge to self-identity. So, in the AFN we have been studying, the relationships with dirt on food are in many cases actually affirmative of a set of positive differences between such food and 'conventionally'-sourced food, while the unnatural, sanitized appearance of wrapped, processed foods becomes a cause for suspicion. It is this that we want to explore in a little more detail in this chapter.

Much has been made of the increased separation of consumers and producers in modern food systems, which are characterized by industrialized agriculture and the retailing of heavily processed foodstuffs through supermarkets.[4] Nevertheless, and perhaps as a result, there has been increasing interest in 'alternative' modes of food provision, which aim to 'reconnect' consumers, producers and food. Recent academic interest in AFN has spawned a large literature concerned with attempts to define and conceptualize the term,[5] relate it to themes such as rural development and agricultural sustainability[6] and, from various theoretical perspectives, to explore specific case studies or types of AFN.[7] In summary, these 'alternatives' seek to construct more sustainable, open and trusting relationships between food producers and consumers, often deploying strategies for the 'direct marketing' of food from producers to consumers, using mechanisms such as box delivery schemes, farmers markets, or community supported agriculture (in which, for example, consumers subscribe an annual payment to the farmer in return for a share of the farm's produce). These relationships are usually associated with particular geographical locations and ethical frameworks that address a range of concerns including, for example, food transport, the use of agro-chemicals, human health, animal welfare, unfair trading practices and labour exploitation. A crucial feature that distinguishes these relationships from those of conventional food production and consumption is that there is an element of 'close connection' between producers, consumers and food. This suggests some degree of consumer engagement with the production of food, ranging from direct knowledge of the producer, production methods or place of production, to actual participation in the growing of food.

This chapter is part of a larger research project[8] that is examining the types of relationships operating between producers and consumers in these 'alternative' and 'reconnected' food networks and the ways in which these are discursively, practically and materially constructed. Here we focus on food anxiety in relation to the concepts of food 'dirtiness' and 'cleanliness' in some of the comparisons our research subjects made between their experiences of food from alternative and conventional (supermarket) food networks.

Food anxieties in a risky world: distance and separation

Food anxieties are a persistent phenomenon associated with long-term processes of modernization. The historian Erica Rappaport[9] usefully reminds us that anxieties about adulteration date back to at least the mid-Victorian era, and the fictional and journalistic writings of authors such as William Cobbett in the early nineteenth century and Upton Sinclair in the early twentieth[10] evidence a wide social concern with the effects of industrializing food systems on both food quality and safety and the social and economic conditions of those involved in food growing and processing. Burnett discusses the history of food adulteration at length, and clearly makes links between the risk of adulteration and the distancing of consumers and producers:

> The root causes of adulteration are to be found in the changes which took place in this period of rapid industrialization and urbanization, a period when an ever-increasing proportion of the population was becoming dependent on commercial services for the supply of its food and, as capitalism and specialization advanced, further and further removed from the ultimate food-producers.[11]

Burnett defines food adulteration as the use of cheaper and nutritionally inferior substitutes to replace the proper constituents of food, the removal of essential ingredients, or the adding of foreign substances to impart fictitious flavour, appearance or strength. Such practices are enabled by an industrialized, distanced food system in which consumers literally do not know where their food has come from or how it has been made.

Adulteration is, however, only one element of food anxiety. The French sociologist Claude Fischler, for example, has argued that the very act of eating is itself infused with anxiety and suspicion because it is linked with the process of 'incorporation'.[12] Food crosses the barrier between the 'outside' world and the 'inside' world of the body. In this process we incorporate all or some of the food's properties: 'we become what we eat. Incorporation is the basis of identity.'[13] Consequently, it is vital to identify foods in both the literal and figurative sense, for 'if we do not know what we eat, how can we know what we are?'[14] For Fischler, much of the anxiety surrounding food consumption is directly related to the ways in which food supply systems are currently structured. Writing about the contemporary United Kingdom, Felicity Lawrence, in her best-selling *Not on the Label,* argues that 'paradoxically, as we have become more affluent as a nation, we have also become more anxious about our food and how it is produced.'[15] Compared with pre-industrialized food systems, modern production processes are highly complex and the ways in which food is grown and processed have become ever more opaque to the consumer. In addition to some of the more obvious concerns about the effects of highly processed and modified foods on human health, there is also evidence of a range of different socio-ethical and environmental anxieties and, perhaps most significantly, a perceived distancing of consumers from the people, processes and places associated with their food.

The contemporary food chain is a mass market, mechanized, specialized industry that sees raw materials produced, processed and distributed nationally and internationally, and delivered to consumers all within a complex framework of hygiene, safety and food microbiology legislation, but often with all signs that the produce once came from a specific environment being destroyed in the process. This process is not limited purely to processed foods; increasingly selections of fresh vegetables and fruit have been submitted to the industrial cleaning and preparation facilities of large food factories, removing any visible traces of dirt (seen as an impurity in the conventional market) as produce is washed, scrubbed, peeled, sliced, diced and packaged ready for the pan with no preparation required at all and even 'unprepared' fruit and vegetables are washed, sorted and selected on the basis of colour, regularity and size, again reducing the 'naturalness' of their appearance.

Yet, for some there is a demand for food from sources that can be identified as more localized, more natural and where there can be a greater degree of knowledge of how food is actually grown. Hence, as Fischler contends, 'the growing demand for symbols of nature could be interpreted in terms of a response to, a reaction against, the increasingly serious problem we have in *identifying* our food.'[16] He believes a shift is taking place in what Western culture perceives to belong to the categories of purity and pollution. Whereas traditionally raw foodstuffs had to be 'civilized' or 'tamed' through processing in order to become fit for consumption, this 'industrial purification' appears no longer to guarantee symbolic purity. Instead, it breeds 'symbolic danger' in the form of chemicals or trace elements. As a consequence, people start preferring 'natural' or 'organic' food.

Gareth Enticott, in recent ethnographic research (see Chapter 13, this volume) pursues the theme of consumer preferences for 'natural' and 'local' food.[17] While much research has identified this trend, Enticott's work is particularly useful in identifying important nuances in the construction of food qualities. Enticott argues that the 'natural' qualities of food are not fixed but open to negotiation and that consumers may draw on different 'cultures of nature' when making food choices. For example, they may turn to foods containing 'impure', 'raw' natures such as unpasteurized cheese:

> Such a culture of nature would appreciate nature's 'raw' and 'impure' qualities, for example, those microbes, bacteria and chemicals usually expelled. Whilst these impurities scientifically represent a health risk, consumers adopting this culture of nature do not construct them in this way, instead associating risks with industrialized production systems and purified natures.[18]

Enticott's case study on the consumption of unpasteurized milk also demonstrates the significance of spatial and ethical contexts for the negotiation of consumption decisions. He reveals that it is

> strongly linked to the demonstration of a rural identity which rejects the alternative way of living implicated in scientific definitions of risk and which evolves from distinct (rural) moral behaviours. These moralities emphasize particular relations with nature and the belief that all natures including 'germs' are beneficial ... and relying on local knowledges such as previous experience to inform consumption decisions.[19]

Thus, some consumers challenge scientific discourses of food safety and purity. Previous experience of consuming unpasteurized milk and the evidence presented by the longevity and good health of elderly people who have always done so reassures consumers that the product is safe and indeed has health-giving properties.

In some cases, then, it would appear that an association between food and what might otherwise be regarded as 'impurities' can, given a certain outlook on nature, be regarded in a far more positive manner. We turn now to consider our 'alternative food networks' as instances of this phenomenon of a turn to the natural in a relatively small sector of food consumption practices, and focus on relationships with 'natural dirt', which is often present on the foods obtained from such networks.

Consumers and 'dirty food'

An initial review revealed a wealth of unconventional food networks in the UK.[20] The research focused on schemes with a direct link between food producers and consumers, and involved interviewing producers and consumers in six AFN case studies to determine how relationships between them are being reconstructed through participation in such networks.[21] For the remainder of this chapter we present insights into the perceptions of participants in some of these alternative food networks of how food is produced and draw attention to how consumers perceive dirt on their food and relate this to particular notions of food quality. We focus here mainly on schemes that supply fruit and vegetables, though other schemes also involve meat and dairy products. In depth interviews were conducted with participants in the different schemes, and we draw here on the ways in which they described their relationships with food that arrives in a more 'natural', dirty state. Interviewees were selected to illustrate a range of social groups, but were not intended to be representative of a wider population. We thus do not indicate speakers' personal characteristics, for we do not want to suggest causal associations between a speaker's gender or age and their comments.

Two complementary themes emerged from discussions with consumers about 'dirty' food. First, that in the cases of these alternative food networks, the dirt that comes with their 'alternative' foods has a series of positive rather than negative associations. And second, that in contrast food that is too cleanly packaged and presented has a set of negative associations.

The positive associations of dirty food

It was clear that, for many of our consumers, the dirt on their food had quite positive connotations. Most straightforwardly, such dirt implied that food is fresh. For example, when it was suggested in interview that the soil on food was an inconvenience, one participant in EarthShare, a community supported agriculture (CSA) scheme in Scotland, responded: 'Oh no that's a positive thing for me ... you know they came out of the soil just this afternoon, you know, that's nice I like that. And you can't beat the freshness.' Similarly, evidence of the physical environments in which food has been grown can be regarded as positive within a particular culture of nature that sees such evidence as marking food that is very different from supermarket food, and

14.1 Dirty vegetables from a Waterland box.

that represents an ethically 'better' way to consume. A couple who get an organic box discussed their fruit and vegetables as follows:

Interviewee 1: You get carrots with dirt still on them ... and it's wonderful, but you get veg that looks veg shaped. ... We've had a couple of apples that they've had worm holes in them. Let me think, this is natural, cut that bit off, stew the rest, it's not a problem. ... A lot of people want it prepackaged.
Interviewee 2: A lot of people wouldn't take apples with worm holes in them, it's the 'ick' factor.
Interviewee 1: You cut in half, you throw that half away, well if you're in the country still just throw it on the ground, it'll rot down and there's not a problem, and eat the bit that's OK.

For these respondents, the contrast between supermarket-driven relation-ships with nature and the relationships with nature that are part of their participation in AFN are clear: where evidence of the natural processes of growing food is erased in supermarkets, food from AFN that is dirty, imperfectly shaped and with evidence of what might conventionally be seen as the polluting presence of insects and other fauna, a set of positive associations between good food and a sort of earthy, rural naturalness is drawn, for example in seeing the production and rotting of food as part of a natural cycle. At the same time, notions of quality are redefined in different ways from those apparent in supermarkets. Rather than perfectly clean and wrapped, identically sized and coloured vegetables and fruits, quality in AFN is defined in terms of the pleasure taken in the taste and more variable appearance of the food. In other words, this food might be understood better in terms of a sensual, pleasurable experience rather than in terms of the anxiety of ingestion.

For example, one farm shop customer commented that:

> Well it used to be that celery was always filthy when you bought it, you used to have to bring it home and really clean it, it was so dirty, it was covered in mud whereas now you think 'Well, has it been in the ground?' don't you? Really. Yes, it is, it's true, dirty celery … and for a while you used to be able to buy dirty celery or this clean stuff and everyone used to say, 'oh the dirty celery tastes better'.

These comments suggest that what seems to be desired from participation in AFN is a knowledge of food and the conditions under which it is produced, which we might also understand as a sense of connectedness to the site and processes of food production that are literally carried to the consumer through the food and the 'dirty' traces of nature that adhere to it.

This desire for connectedness is present, for example, in the following comments, the first from an active participant in EarthShare CSA who actually contributes their time to doing some of the work in the field, the second from someone who purchases from a farm shop.

> It's organic stuff, it's good stuff, you know it's … local produce you know … I'm really surprised at myself coming out with that because it's like, a few years ago I think I was more a person that, you know I wanted things easier but I think … now that I have more the time and space you know to, to really be into the vegetables and you know really work, because it is part of, part of, real part of my life now. So yeah it's really good to feel the earth, you know.

> Because it is back to basics that yeah in my childhood my parents grew most of the vegetables so that was home grown with the mud on and that's what we get now again, home grown with the mud on although we don't grow them ourselves. So it's basically back to the old fashioned, healthy involved way of food growing, delivering and consuming.

As these excerpts suggest, participants in alternative food networks engage in particular discourses about nature, where soil or dirt on their food is seen not as a threatening impurity but as a guarantee of freshness, naturalness and wholesomeness. Soil clinging to food acts as a direct connection with the land, and with the people and processes engaged in growing it.

The negative associations of clean food

In contrast to the significance of dirt as a signifier of freshness, health, naturalness and connectedness, the effect of 'distancing' between food production and the food consumer, which is what supermarkets achieve, was something that made our consumers suspicious of much supermarket food. For the following farm shop consumer, for example, the apparent hyper-cleanliness of supermarket vegetables was associated with a feeling about the food being unnatural and unhealthy.

> I mean I don't mind a bit of dirt on my carrots. I mean there's something a bit sort of unhealthy looking about these carrots that are washed completely clean, they're sweating in polythene. ... I don't like buying pre-packaged vegetables at all. They look very neat and tidy and clean but I don't like it. I would rather just buy them as they come out of the ground.

We might note too in this quote the metaphorical allusion to the bodily residue of sweat, as an abject impurity that ironically makes these seemingly hyperclean packaged commodities appear dirty again. The same respondent later suggested that we, as consumers, had all become 'silly' in our demands for cleaned, packaged produce.

In a similar reference, but to a meat product this time, two more farm shop consumers discussed in rather queasy terms the repulsive whiteness of supermarket chicken:

Interviewee 1: But these chickens were so white that I sort of poked it and ...
Interviewee 2: and they looked different ... different consistency when you touched them.

In this context the 'unnatural' whiteness and strange consistency of the meat is associated with suspicion of the industrialized agricultural processes that produce such foods, as well as with a sensual repulsion at its appearance and texture.

From our discussions about food with consumers, forms of impurity or pollution other than soil seemed to be prominent contributors to the anxieties they expressed about their food. While soil, as a visible pollutant, was generally seen in positive terms, as shown above, invisible dirt or contaminants were much more problematic, and were directly associated with foods sourced from more conventional supermarket outlets. Indeed, it was the anxieties surrounding these conventional foods that led the consumers to the alternative sources they used. For example, one farm shop consumer said that 'I don't want chemicals and crap in my food,' and contrasted this with the hand-making of food sold in the farm shop. Again, it is worth mentioning the metaphorical use of another bodily waste, 'crap', which is used here to emphasize the anxiety felt about industrially processed food.

Others expressed more widely the sense of anxiety that came from conventionally processed foods, showing how that anxiety could be associated with not knowing who had handled the food, where it came from, or where it had been. One farm shop consumer thus said that they washed all their fruit and vegetables, even pre-washed supermarket salad and vegetables, because 'I mean if nothing else it's been handled and may have little things landing in it. It's bound to because it's, you know, it's been in the world. So I wash it.' Similarly, another commented:

> The bagged lettuce and things when I heard that there were more germs inside one of those bags because of the fact that they're not washed in clean water and you don't know who's actually putting them into the bags and whether the people putting them into the bags who were being paid to do it had washed their hands.

So here the potential for pollution of food by unknown people and unknown processes 'out in the world', as the earlier comment suggested, is responsible for a sense of food anxiety, which is responded to by washing produce in an attempt to remove what is clearly felt to be the possibility or probability of a polluting presence. The fact that supermarket food is presented as sanitized, as cleaned and wrapped in plastic, then, far from allaying fears produces new sets of anxieties. As one final comment here suggests, it is 'the dirt you can't see you worry about'.

Conclusions

When we started our investigations into these aspects of consumers' relationships with their food we anticipated that there would be ambiguity in the discussions of the presence of soil and other evidence of growing conditions, which seemed to characterize food from the alternative sources in which we were interested. However, in fact we find that despite some minor irritation that food has to be scrubbed clean of attached soil, consumers who purchase food from AFN overwhelmingly see such dirt as attesting to certain key characteristics of the food: its 'naturalness', healthiness and wholesomeness, and the sense they get from it of connection to the people, places and processes involved in growing the food.

In contrast, the hyperclean appearance and packaged nature of the food from more conventional sources is regarded with suspicion. These standards of quality, which supermarkets have been able to define and which are reliant on the sanitized presentation of highly standardized food products, are seemingly being rejected by at least some consumers who favour an alternative set of quality indicators, such as taste, and a more or less direct sense of connectivity with the process of food production.

More broadly then, we might suggest that there is, implicitly, a moral framework or moral geography present in our consumers' discussion of their foods. In this framework, food that is 'dirty' is regarded not just as providing a better sensual eating experience, but as embodying 'better' moral principles. These include, for example, a perception that organic production is better than conventional farming, that local production is better than food chains that transport products over great distances, that food that is in some way 'closer' to nature and displays evidence of that closeness is better than food that is cleaned and wrapped, and that direct connections with the producers of food are better than food that comes from anonymous sources. Ironically, then, for some consumers, hyperclean supermarket food is contaminated by negative moral associations, and by the unknown-ness and invisibility of its provenance. In these cases, then, the increasingly sophisticated attempts by conventional retailers to mark foods with symbols of quality assurance[22] might be seen as simply something else that actually distances food from consumers, by establishing yet more centres of judgement and control, which are located in further anonymous places, while the actual traces of dirt that cling to foods from alternative sources act as more direct guarantees for these consumers of the quality and provenance of their foods.

Chapter 15

Dirty Cows: Perceptions of BSE/vCJD

BRUCE A. SCHOLTEN

When the UK government lifted the veil of secrecy from the dairy industry in 1996, admitting a link between mad cow disease and a fatal neural disease in humans, it opened intensive, globalizing food systems to unprecedented scrutiny. Mad cow disease, or bovine spongiform encephalopathy (BSE) in cows, appears as a variant of Creutzfeldt-Jakob disease (CJD) in people. They are examples of transmissible spongiform encephalopathies (TSEs), which many scientists believe are related to scrapie in sheep, and kuru and Alzheimer's disease in people.[1]

In this chapter I highlight consumer attitudes and behaviour to BSE revealed in fieldwork in Seattle, in the USA, and Newcastle upon Tyne, in the UK.[2] To understand responses to BSE I use the claim by Mary Douglas and others that risk perceptions are socially constructed. My data show that perceptions of BSE as a dangerous risk vary between countries and within subgroups, but there is no simple relationship between imagining meat as 'dirty' and avoiding that meat. In fact, it seems that for some people risky food could be just another thrill.[3]

Occasionally, cartoons depict BSE victims with brains like Swiss cheese. The metaphor is visually apposite, but the symptoms of this fatal disease are not amusing. Once animal or human victims show mobility impairment, restlessness and paranoia, they usually die within a year. In his review of the UK government's 5112-page *BSE Inquiry*, Hugh Pennington, professor (emeritus) of medical microbiology at the University of Aberdeen, relates the case of a young woman who showed signs of vCJD in 1996, although she had been vegetarian since 1985 when she was 13.[4] Diagnoses of depression, anorexia and agoraphobia finally gave way to the conclusion that she indeed suffered from BSE/vCJD. Her father said: 'the most harrowing thing was sometimes in bed at night ... she howled like a sick injured animal.'

Although some scientists believe that BSE resulted from a natural mutation, many suspect that blame for the spread of the disease from bovines to humans lies in imprudent changes to long-established methods of animal rendering before recycling in other animals' feed, during the early Thatcher administration. Bovine anatomy precludes attacking and eating other animals, so meat was absent from cows' diets until humans began rendering carcasses into cattle feed about 200 years ago. Because the practice reduced waste and boosted yield, it was considered to be prudently efficient and became routine in countries that included Germany, the USA and the UK until 1996. Unfortunately, it seems that TSEs leapt species a few years after the UK introduced a cheaper but unsafe method of flash heating carcasses.[5] Pennington writes: 'There is no doubt at all that BSE is an English disease: it started in England and has claimed most of its cattle victims there. But it is not a parochial matter: its scientific, medical and political repercussions are global and general.'

In the decade after 1996, the UK lost overseas beef markets worth about £4 billion annually (then about US$ 7 billion). In the years since the Christmas 2003 discovery of one mad cow in a rural abattoir east of Seattle, Washington State lost about $4.4 billion in associated costs.[6] Although fewer than 160 people had died of the disease in Britain by February 2006, and only 28 in other countries, great uncertainty remains about it.[7]

Most ominous are signs that its incubation period could be triple the 11 years of the UK woman recorded above. Prion scientist John Collinge and colleagues who studied kuru in New Guinea found cases of that TSE with incubation periods of over 50 years.[8] If kuru is related to BSE/vCJD, the portents bode ill for future outbreaks. Unlike foot and mouth disease, it cannot be passed in the air. But, the fact that ingestion of infected tissue can pass the contagion pinpoints blame on humans who masterminded this very process in intensive agriculture. Blood transfusions from BSE hosts have led to deaths among sufferers of haemophilia in France and of US tennis player Arthur Ashe. Although meat, bone meal and blood were banned from cattle feed in most countries after 1996, *USA Today* reported in 2003 that the country continued to recycle cows' blood in feed for cows and other animals.[9] For such reasons Sarah Whatmore calls mad cow disease an archetypal food scare due to the 'intensive feeding regime of the industrial cow'. She writes:

> The practice provoked revulsion and disbelief in equal measure among
> an unsuspecting public. What kind of rationality was it that could

make sense of such routine cannibalism? The rationalities both exposed and overshadowed by the spectre of the disease were those of cost-cutting and profit-margins in a corporate animal feed industry careless of the offensive detail of how their products were derived, and of balance sheets and productivity gains for farmers accustomed to gauging their husbandry in terms of the metabolic conversion of inputs into outputs. At once 'man-made' and 'pathogenous', the hybrid potency of the disease resonated with gut apprehensions of the corporeal kinship and fleshy currency between cows and people.[10]

Contamination is carried by agents called prions – a new form of infectious dirt. Prions are neither bacterium nor virus, and cannot easily be killed by chemicals, heat or radiation because they have no DNA. Professor Stanley Prusiner won the 1997 Nobel Prize for identifying these protein molecules, which in their pathogenic form cause adjacent protein molecules to loop in a pattern that induces the Swiss cheese effect, hampering brain function and mobility until death. There is no cure for BSE and, because it can be passed from mother to calf, hundreds of thousands of cows have been destroyed in the UK and other countries. Prions' mysterious resistance to what Douglas terms cleaning or purification, indicates that the surest path to purification of animals and humans is in exalting food ways unbesmirched by BSE – alternative food networks promoting sustainable methods such as organic food. Organic beef can be trusted as free of BSE prions because organic agriculture has no place for unnatural chemical inputs – not to mention meat – in cows' diets.

Douglas, dirt and dirty foods

Any doubt that anthropologist Mary Douglas's 1966 analysis of concepts of pollution and taboo can illuminate BSE is answered in her preface to the 2002 edition. She recounts how the book went from sleeper to classic, as the emphasis in the 1960s on 'unsatisfied claims to [human] freedom'[11] shifted to angst in the 1970s on the dangers of pollution in air, water, oceans and food, caused by 'monstrous technological developments'[12] made possible only in the last century. Douglas writes that in response to these new threats, 'A new academic discipline emerged – risk analysis – to which *Purity and Danger* seemed to be relevant in a more general way than I had ever imagined.'[13]

BSE corresponds easily to Douglas's lexicon of cleanliness and contamination. In the new preface she explicitly states that 'dirt is dangerous'.[14] Douglas calls her book a 'treatise on the idea of dirt and contagion' inspired by her bout with measles in the 1950s, while writing a monograph on the food rules of the Lele in Africa. She develops themes on how taboos condition 'local consensus on how their world is organized'.[15] This includes a discussion of Old Testament dietary laws allowing the Israelites to eat cows, goats and sheep, but making pigs taboo. Taboos may seem arbitrary to outsiders, but are explained in terms of their practical effect in relieving 'cognitive discomfort caused by ambiguity' in daily life.[16] Douglas explains that 'dirt makes a bridge between our own contemporary culture and cultures where behaviour that blurs the great classifications of the universe is taboo. We denounce it by calling it dirty and dangerous; they taboo it.'[17]

This describes a historic shift in seeing the pathologies of diseases, such as measles or BSE, in terms of medical and hygiene practices rather than religion and taboo. Douglas further observes that 'when the controllers of opinion want a different way of life, the taboos will lose credibility and their selected view of the universe will be revised.'[18] Certainly, the winners in war, politics and business can influence societal frames of reference. Yet, I argue that the shift to hygiene from taboo is neither complete nor irreversible.[19] Evidence for my claim comes from bio-ethic issues (such as the early 2007 request by UK scientists for government permission to test hybrid animal/human embryos)[20] that get as much attention from religionists as scientists – and a related observation of Douglas that 'political affiliation is the best indicator of attitudes to risk'.[21]

A number of recent food scares and debates can be understood in terms of disputes over the changing boundaries of what is thought of as being pure enough to eat. On the agribusiness side of such debates, in seeking progress and profit researchers challenge time-honoured distinctions between species, and even kingdoms, via genetic modification (GM). In one case scientists combined fish and plant genes.[22] In the case of BSE, agribusiness lobbied regulators to approve new methods of purifying meat and bone meal (MBM). For centuries sheep were fed to cows safely, but the government BSE Inquiry (2000) found that bovine cannibalism was unsafe. Lord Phillips suggested that BSE stemmed from a mutation in the 1970s, and while its origins might 'never be known', it was 'probably coincidence' that it went epizootic after rendering rules changed. Although some scientists conjecture that BSE in cattle may be the result of such spontaneous mutation, others believe that the deregulation of animal rendering and purification rules before recycling in cattle feed, during the deregulatory zeal of the early Thatcher administration, 1979 to 1984, cannot be ignored.

In resistance to agribusiness are those who condemn such practices as dirty, promiscuous mixing that is bound to spread contagion. People on this side of the debate do not necessarily reject scientific method. They generally subscribe to theories of hygiene in lieu of taboos, but are critical of what they see as blinkered scientific reductionism by agribusiness. These people might echo the precepts of Leviticus, of which Douglas writes that 'hybrids and other contaminations are abominated' to such an extent that the Israelites are warned 'You shall not let your cattle breed with a different kind.'[23] This warning, wherein holiness requires that 'different classes of things should not be confused' could well include the feeding of other animals to ruminant herbivores.

Consumers, BSE and responses to risk

Douglas remarks that, 'Dangers are manifold and omnipresent. Action would be paralysed if individuals attended to them all; anxiety has to be selective.'[24] In 1986 sociologist Ulrich Beck included anthropogenic effects on the biogenetics of food in his influential *Risk Society* thesis.[25] This was concomitant with the identification of BSE in cows, a decade before the UK government implicated human agency in BSE/vCJD. Anthony Giddens and Scott Lash joined Beck in expanding his theories of reflexive modernization in which citizens are expected to reflect on risk and make choices on food and health, decisions once made by governments in the twentieth century. So how is it that social groups construct or discard perceptions of dangers such as BSE? Examples of mad cow scares help us understand this process. As the BSE saga unfolded anyone exposed to news media from Germany to Ghana, learnt of BSE.[26] But, just as at the time of this writing, January 2007, reports of avian flu in Asia do not induce panic in Europe, reports of BSE in the UK in the 1990s did not induce widespread fear in the USA.

Of the litany of food scares in the 1980s and 1990s, including salmonella, listeria, E.coli, and BSE, many British consumers considered the last the worst, as they turned to diets perceived as more natural and organic.[27] Atkins and Bowler found a high incidence of vegetarianism among young UK consumers, especially women who eschewed beef in the same way as their US counterparts rejected milk produced with recombinant bovine growth hormone (rBGH).[28] Patricia Caplan describes how, as beef sales plunged in the 1996 scare in Britain, consumers in rural Wales sought beef from trusted farms, while many Londoners turned to vegetarianism or other meats.[29] Some consumers knew bone meal was recycled in cattle feed, but few knew that meat was too. Public consternation prompted bans on animal renderings in bovine feed in the UK, USA and other countries. In this ethical domain, the place of morality, prohibitions against animals foraging on animals may be challenged on zoological, historic, economic, environmental and health grounds. After all, the displacement of beef upon cropland for human food was ameliorated by recycling meat and bone meal in cows' fodder.[30] To some this was a virtuous circle of sustainability. But many others deemed animal matter out of place in a cow's manger.[31]

Food panics in the UK and European countries generally spur initial disruption of attitudes and behaviour, followed by a gradual return to the previous consumption equilibrium.[32] It seems that food scares must be severe

193

and lengthy before they permanently alter food systems. In Newcastle, two decades of familiarity with mad cow disease have permanently conditioned large swathes of people to put BSE on their risk map. Whenever they get complacent the tragedy is repeated, and media trumpet another case where someone, vegetarian or not, succumbs to vCJD. Some consumers remain fatalistic about BSE, but others buy safer food if it is available and affordable.

Yet the spectre of mad cow was less frightening in the USA than the UK, supporting the theory that risks are socially constructed and that we are largely unaware of them until experts alert us, or symptoms appear locally. At Christmas 2003, a few months after completion of my fieldwork, the first US case of the disease was identified at a slaughterhouse in Mabton, a rural town east of Seattle – making my study a time capsule of pre-BSE attitudes and behaviour. The animal's origin was Canada. When I called back in 2004–5, one respondent discounted mass conversion to organics, saying 'as long as BSE is still contained to one cow and blamed on Canada, people won't change.' Assumptions about cleanliness in the food system run deep. Two consumers of organic food were asked if they expected mad cow to hit the USA. One answered simply, 'Um, no.' The other a young convert to organics said, 'No. Um, I wouldn't be surprised, given enough time [laughs]. But it's not something I worry about.'

The disparity, in UK and US awareness of BSE as a danger in meat contaminated by rogue prions is apparent in responses to one question posed to 404 people: 'Please number top five risks in the UK or US food system'. Respondents chose from a list including BSE, CJD, E.coli, gluten intolerance, lactose intolerance, heart disease, listeria, obesity and salmonella.[33] The proportion of respondents listing BSE or vCJD as top risks is lower in the USA than the UK. Of all 178 Seattle respondents, just 19 per cent showed what can be called fear of BSE, whereas of the 226 Newcastle respondents, 44 per cent listed BSE as a top risk. Yet, most of those who forsook beef in the 1990s have resumed consumption, perhaps replacing fears of BSE with other worries about food. As one respondent commented: 'I stopped eating it [beef] for a while, but don't think of it now. Guess I'm more aware of "dirty" meat, chopped and reformed, mechanically separated, etc. and try not to eat it but invariably end up eating it every now and then.'

Focus groups in the UK revealed the long-term pall of BSE, as one participant put it, 'the BSE scare *has happened*.' Another participant, who moonlighted as an organic butcher but did not feed UK beef to his own family out of fear of BSE, said:

Particularly on the lines of mad cow disease and foot and mouth, I think it's come more into the forefront for media attention. And with genetically modified foods, you know, we've heard a lot about

194

companies like Monsanto, you know, global international companies. You know – do we really want to go down that line ... or is it just a way of maximizing profits of, you know, global companies?

However, not everyone responds to the perceived risks of dirty food by avoiding those foods, and it is worth placing consumers' constructions of dirt and purity in the food chain in the context of more general views and the practicalities of life. As one Newcastle-based participant explained:

I stopped buying red meat ... for the children 'cause they're most important. I did stop eating beef for about two months and about a year longer for the children. We made a long-term change away from beef. But I absolutely adore steak. ... It's like everything else in the world – you minimize your risks but you can't let it change your life. [BSE did not change] many people I knew. Don't know anyone who actually changed, maybe they cut down on beef, not too many. And the vegetarians I know, they were already away from beef.

One US respondent, a retired conventional farmer, judged quibbles on food safety as the carping of urbanites out of touch with the land. He knew BSE was a concern in Europe but that more people die falling down stairs. He saw longevity data as empirical proof of the safety of the food system, 'People complain about food risks, but every year statistics show they live longer than in the past.' A similar position is taken by Edward Morse [34] an academic who says domestic beef sales have risen since 2003 because the US Department of Agriculture (USDA) 'has required extensive changes in the manner in which beef is processed and its byproducts are used, which are designed to provide further protections against BSE risks. BSE may still occur, but it appears that the marketplace is becoming informed.'

For these two BSE is just one of many bio-security risks mitigated by training, science and technology. Most remarkable is that *after* the appearance of BSE on the US horizon there may have been a hardening of attitudes to BSE among consumers fed up with food scares. This trend is hard to quantify, but was conveyed in comments hinting at American exceptionalism, an assumption that its sophisticated food system grants it immunity from contagion rampant elsewhere. Morse notes that a couple of mad cows born in the USA have not cut domestic consumption to the extent seen in other places, and that the USDA estimates that between 2003 and 2006 domestic beef consumption rose in the USA, compared with falls in Australia, the EU, South Korea, and Japan.

This socially constructed attitude of immunity to BSE seemed palpable in call-backs with respondents in 2004–5. Why? Deborah Lupton argues that, 'transgression is a potent source of pleasure as well as fear and anxiety. It is a risky activity because it calls into question accepted conceptual boundaries, threatening self-integrity by allowing the Other into the self.'[35] This flirtation with risk was exemplified by a well educated manager at a Seattle motorcycle dealership who offered to 'lead a ride to a barbeque' in the town where BSE arose. My results suggest that others would be tempted to ride along. Lupton takes up Douglas's ideas on the social construction of risk, danger and dirt, describing how motor racers, surfers and night club goers who voluntarily embrace danger construct risk differently from outsiders. Lupton observes how a sense of health and liberation can follow confrontations with such dangers, risk and even dirt. In noting Douglas's comments on the paradoxical nature of our desire for purity and our repudiation of dirt, Lupton notes 'secular rituals [that] may also seek to overturn the negative meanings associated with the impure by revelling in its very prohibited nature'.[36] Such factors were apparent when some people celebrated cheap beef at barbeque parties after BSE was found in the USA in 2003.[37]

Conclusion

Douglas writes, 'We must, therefore, ask how dirt, which is normally destructive, sometimes becomes creative.'[38] Is a little of what we fancy good for us, even a barbecued steak that might contain dirty prions or a dirty weekend of dancing and casual sex? The fact that many people – for reasons ranging from convenience, to peer pressure and to raw thrills – occasionally cross the line from purity to danger suggests an exercise of the will in recognizing the two possibilities: first that there is no complete safety from danger, and second that what does not kill us might make us strong, or at least excite us. Such contemporary experiences may represent *ad hoc* rites of communion akin to examples given by Douglas, such as the use of cow dung in some Brahmin purification rituals, or cults of the Lele that 'allow their initiates to eat what is normally dangerous', and even 'St Francis of Assisi rolling naked in the filth and welcoming his Sister Death'.[39]

This is not to say that contaminated food has a conscious place in many people's diets. Occasional dietary irrationalities vis-à-vis dirt and con-tamination, such as a few well-publicized BSE barbecues, should not obscure greater truths, for example that most people avoid demonstrable risks. A forthcoming study by researchers at Washington State University found that soon after the 2003 BSE outbreak, about three-quarters of consumers in one Seattle study were willing to pay more for beef tested for BSE.[40] Yet, as I have shown in this chapter, we do need to understand the complex and context bound ways in which people respond to 'polluted' matter.

It may be three more decades before we can better quantify the contamination of the biosphere by BSE prions, but each additional discovery of the disease in the USA will set more consumers against practices that encourage the proliferation of such anthropogenically caused diseases. Meanwhile, the rising consumption of organic and local food, in places as geographically distant as Seattle and Newcastle, indicates the strength of countervailing trends toward cleanliness and purification via alternative food networks. That is because increasing numbers of people believe that intensive farming methods and globalized food systems expose them to dirty practices and dirty cows.

Contributors

Johan Andersson is completing doctoral research at the Bartlett School of Planning, University College London, on the commercialization of queer space in London since the 1990s. He works for UCL's Urban Laboratory – a cross faculty initiative for interdisciplinary research and teaching – and recently co-authored *Planning on the Edge: The Context for Planning at the Rural–Urban Fringe* (London: Routledge, 2006).

Lívia Barbosa is associate professor at Fluminense Federal University in Rio de Janeiro, Brazil, and research director of the Research Centre in Marketing and Consumption of the ESPM, São Paulo. She has published several articles and books about consumption, business anthropology and political anthropology. Her latest work is a book, *Cultura, Consumo e Identidade* (Rio de Janeiro: Fundação Getulio Vargas, 2006) published together with Professor Colin Campbell, Department of Sociology, University of York.

Alyson Brody lived and worked in Thailand for six years, mainly in the field of development. She received her doctorate in social anthropology from the School of Oriental and African Studies in 2003. She is currently employed as a research officer at the Institute of Development Studies in Brighton.

Ben Campkin is lecturer in architectural history and theory at the Bartlett School of Architecture, UCL. Recent publications include a co-edited special journal issue, 'Architecture and dirt', *The Journal of Architecture*, vol. 12, no. 4, September 2007; and 'Down and out in London? Photography and the politics of representing *Life in the Elephant*, 1948 and 2005', in Mark Swenarton *et al.* (eds) *The Politics of Making* (Abingdon: Taylor & Francis, 2007). Ben's research focuses on urban regeneration; the representation of blighted urban districts; and the aesthetics of hygiene and recycling, particularly in ex-industrial architecture.

Rosie Cox is senior lecturer in London studies at Birkbeck, University of London. She has a long-standing research interest in the organization of paid domestic employment and is author of *The Servant Problem: Paid Domestic Work in a Global Economy* (London: I.B.Tauris, 2006). She has recently been working with colleagues on a project examining producer/consumer relationships in 'alternative food networks'.

Paul Dobraszczyk is a research fellow in the department of typography and graphic communication at the University of Reading. His doctoral research examined the design, construction and reception of London's main drainage system. Recent publications include 'Historicizing iron: Charles Driver and the Abbey Mills pumping station (1865–68)', *Architectural History*, vol. 49, 2006, pp. 223–56; and 'Sewers, wood engraving and the sublime: picturing London's main drainage system in the *Illustrated London News*, 1859–62', *Victorian Periodicals Review*, vol. 38, no. 4, winter 2005–6, pp. 349–78.

Elizabeth Dowler is a reader in food and social policy in the department of sociology, University of Warwick. She works on poverty, food, nutrition and public health; evaluating policy and local initiatives; and people's perspectives. Her publications include E. Dowler and N. Spencer (eds) *Challenging Health Inequalities* (London: Policy Press, 2007); chapters in C. Dora (ed.) *Health, Hazards and Public Debate: Lessons for Risk Communication from the BSE/CJD Saga* (Copenhagen: World Health Organization, 2006); E. Dowler and C. Jones Finer (eds) *The Welfare of Food: Rights and Responsibilities in a Changing World* (Oxford: Blackwell, 2003); Paul Mosley and Elizabeth Dowler (eds) *Poverty and Social Exclusion in North and South: Essays on Social Policy and Global Poverty* (London: Routledge, 2003).

Gareth Enticott is a research fellow at the School of City and Regional Planning, Cardiff University. His research interests include nature–society relations, rural community studies and the sociology of science. He is currently leading an ESRC funded project to investigate farmers' attitudes to biosecurity and the social consequences of outbreaks of bovine tuberculosis in England and Wales.

Pamela K. Gilbert is professor of English at the University of Florida. Her books include *Disease, Desire and the Body in Victorian Women's Popular Novels* (Cambridge: Cambridge University Press, 1997), and *Mapping the Victorian Social Body* (New York: SUNY Press, 2004). Her new books, *The Citizen's Body*, and *Doctoring the Social Body*, will be out in 2007 (and published by Ohio State University Press and SUNY Press respectively). She has published an edited collection entitled *Imagined Londons* (New York: SUNY Press, 2002), and has co-edited, along with Marlene Tromp and Aeron Haynie, *Beyond Sensation: Mary Elizabeth Braddon in Context* (New York:

SUNY Press, 1999). She is also editor of a SUNY Press series entitled Studies in the Long Nineteenth Century.

Lewis Holloway is a lecturer in human geography in the Department of Geography, University of Hull, UK. He has research interests in food, farming and the countryside, focusing particularly on 'alternative' modes of food provisioning and rural lifestyles, and on the implications of 'high-tech' interventions in livestock farming for human–nonhuman relations in agriculture.

Dominic Janes has undertaken research on British visual and material culture during the nineteenth century, on the body and commodification, and on medievalism and the reception of antiquity. He is a lecturer in the history of art at Birkbeck College, London and is currently completing his third book, a study of discourses of idolatry in Victorian England.

Moya Kneafsey is a research fellow in human geography at Coventry University. She has published research on 'alternative' food networks and rural tourism, especially in remote and peripheral areas.

Lydia Martens is a senior lecturer in sociology at Keele University. She is co-editor, with Emma Casey, of *Gender and Consumption: Domestic Cultures and the Commercialisation of Everyday Life* (Aldershot: Ashgate, 2007) and co-author, with Alan Warde, of *Eating Out: Social Differentiation, Consumption and Pleasure* (Cambridge: Cambridge University Press, 2000). Her research interest is in the connections between consumption practices and domestic life, and she is also interested in qualitative research practice.

David L. Pike is associate professor of literature at American University. His books include *Metropolis on the Styx: Underground Space, the Devil, and Urban Culture in London and Paris* (Ithaca, NY: Cornell University Press, 2007); *Subterranean Cities: The World Beneath Paris and London, 1800–1945* (Ithaca, NY: Cornell University Press, 2005), and *Passage through Hell: Modernist Descents, Medieval Underworlds* (Ithaca, NY: Cornell University Press, 1997). He is co-editor, with David Damrosch, April Alliston, Marshall Brown, Page duBois, Sabry Hafez, Ursula K. Heise, Djelal Kadir, Sheldon Pollock, Bruce Robbins, Haruo Shirane, Jane Tylus and Pauline Yu, of the *Longman Anthology of World Literature* (London: Longman, 2007).

Bruce A. Scholten is a doctoral researcher and tutor in the geography department at Durham University, UK. He is researching food and risk in Europe, India, the UK and the USA. His research findings have recently been published in the *Scottish Geographical Journal* and in G. Holt and M. Reed (eds) *Sociological Perspectives of Organic Agriculture: from Pioneer to Policy* (Wallingford: CABI, 2006).

Kyro Selket is currently a doctoral candidate in human geography at Victoria University, Aotearoa New Zealand. In her forthcoming Ph.D. she explores abject space, embalming rooms, exiled corpses and post-death decomposition within the funeral industry in Aotearoa New Zealand. Her research interests include death; feminist and cultural geography; and the production of bodies, spaces and practices of exclusion.

Helena Tuomainen is a research fellow in the department of sociology at the University of Warwick. Her research interests include the sociology and anthropology of food, diet and culture, and the sociology of health and illness. Her recent research examines the relationship between migration, foodways, ethnic identities and gender through a case study of Ghanaians in London. She specializes in qualitative, ethnographic research and has previously worked on a number of health-related projects.

Laura Venn works as a cultural research analyst at the West Midlands Regional Observatory. With a background in qualitative social research she is responsible for collating and coordinating research and intelligence in relation to the scope and significance of the cultural and creative sectors in the West Midlands and for feeding this into evidence-based regional policy.

Paul Watt is lecturer in social policy at Birkbeck, University of London and a visiting fellow at the London East Research Institute, University of East London. He is interested in the interrelationships between the social and spatial parameters of inequality, exclusion and difference. Recent publications include a paper on the London working class in the *International Journal of Urban and Regional Research* (2006), and a co-authored book with Tim Butler, *Understanding Social Inequality* (London: Sage, 2007).

Carol Wolkowitz is an associate professor in the department of sociology, University of Warwick. She is the author of *Bodies at Work* (London: Sage, 2006) and a co-author, with Sonya Andermahr and Terry Lovell, of the *Glossary of Feminist Theory* (Oxford: Oxford University Press, 2000). She teaches courses on sexualities, work and employment, and visual methods.

201

Notes

Introduction: Materialities and Metaphors of Dirt and Cleanliness
Ben Campkin and Rosie Cox

1. For recent work on dirt in relation to architecture, cities and space see also Ben Campkin and Paul Dobraszczyk (eds) 'Architecture and dirt: special issue', *The Journal of Architecture*, vol. 12, no. 4, September 2007.
2. Elizabeth Shove, *Comfort, Cleanliness and Convenience: The Social Organization of Normality* (Oxford, Berg, 2003).
3. Adrian Forty, *Objects of Desire: Design and Society since 1750* (London, Thames & Hudson, 1986) p. 161.
4. Georges Vigarello, *Concepts of Cleanliness: Changing Attitudes in France since the Middle Ages* (Cambridge: Cambridge University Press, 1998).
5. See Shove, *Comfort, Cleanliness and Convenience*, pp. 86–7.
6. For a recent cultural history of smell that is partly framed in relation to the history of hygienism, see Anna Barbara and Anthony Perliss, *Invisible Architecture: Experiencing Places through the Sense of Smell* (Milan: Skira, 2006).
7. Alain Corbin, *The Foul and the Fragrant: Odour and the French Imagination* (Cambridge, MA: Harvard University Press); and Shove, *Comfort, Cleanliness and Convenience*.
8. Forty, *Objects of Desire*, p. 175.
9. Shove, *Comfort, Cleanliness and Convenience*, pp. 87–8.
10. Forty, *Objects of Desire*, p. 180; Shove, *Comfort, Cleanliness and Convenience*; and Susan Strasser, *Never Done: A History of American Housework* (New York: Pantheon Books, 1982).
11. Dominique Laporte, *History of Shit*, translated by Nadia Benabid and Rodolphe el-Khoury (Cambridge, MA: MIT Press, 2000) p. 32.
12. Caroline Davidson, *A Woman's Work is Never Done: A History of Housework in the British Isles 1650–1950* (London: Chatto & Windus, 1982).
13. Laporte, *History of Shit*, p. 32.
14. Pamela Sambrook, *A Country House Servant* (Stroud: Sutton Publishing, 2002) p. 130.
15. Note the title of Shove's book, *Comfort, Cleanliness and Convenience: The Social Organization of Normality*.
16. New editions were reprinted in 1970, 1984, 1991 and 2002. The 2002 edition was prefaced with a new introductory essay by the author. See discussion in Ben Campkin, 'Degradation and regeneration: theories of dirt and the contemporary city' in this volume.
17. Douglas attributes the phrase to Lord Chesterfield.

18. Joseph A. Amato, *Dust: A History of the Small and Invisible* (Berkeley: University of California Press, 2000); Barbara and Perliss, *Invisible Architecture*; William B. Logan, *Dirt: The Ecstatic Skin of the Earth* (New York: Riverhead Books, 1995); John Scanlan, *On Garbage* (London, Reaktion, 2005).
19. Steve Pile gives a useful definition of the process of abjection in *The Body and the City: Psychoanalysis, Space and Subjectivity* (London: Routledge, 1996) p. 90.
20. For example, see Mike Kelley, *The Uncanny* (Cologne: König, 2004); and Anthony Vidler, *The Architectural Uncanny: Essays in the Modern Unhomely* (Cambridge, MA: The MIT Press, 1992)
21. On disgust, see William I. Miller, *The Anatomy of Disgust* (Cambridge, MA: Harvard University Press, 1997).
22. Kristeva quoted in Victor Buchli and Gavin Lucas (eds) *Archaeologies of the Contemporary Past* (London: Routledge, 2001) p. 10.
23. Jenny Robinson, 'Feminism and the spaces of transformation', *Transactions of the Institute of British Geographers: New Series*, vol. 25, no. 3, pp 285–301; David Sibley, *Geographies of Exclusion: Society and Difference in the West* (London: Routledge, 1995).
24. Nadir Lahiji and Daniel S. Friedman, 'At the sink: architecture in abjection', in Nadir Lahiji and Daniel S. Friedman (eds) *Plumbing: Sounding Modern Architecture* (New York: Princeton Architectural Press, 1997).
25. Shove, *Comfort, Cleanliness and Convenience*, p. 88.
26. Anne McClintock, *Imperial Leather: Race, Gender and Sexuality in the Colonial Contest* (London: Routledge, 1994).
27. Timothy Burke, *Lifebuoy Men and Lux Women: Commodification, Consumption and Cleanliness in Modern Zimbabwe* (London: Leicester University Press, 1996).
28. William A. Cohen, 'Introduction: locating filth', in William A. Cohen and Ryan Johnson (eds) *Filth: Dirt, Disgust, and Modern Life* (Minneapolis: University of Minnesota Press, 2005) p. viii. This collection examines 'filth', focusing on the contexts of London and Paris and their colonial territories in the nineteenth and early twentieth centuries, through an exploration of mainly literary representations and other forms of cultural production. Cohen's introduction, wide ranging in its scope, provides a major new contribution to understandings of dirt.
29. On the transformative possibilities of interdisciplinary work, and the distinction between 'interdisciplinary' and 'multidisciplinary', see Jane Rendell, 'Architectural research and disciplinarity', *Architectural Research Quarterly*, vol. 8, no. 4, 2004, pp. 141–7.
30. Many of the chapters in this collection were first given as papers at the Association of American Geographers Annual Meeting in Denver, 5–9 April 2005. Laura Venn and Rosie Cox organized two sessions titled 'Geographies of Dirt and Purity'.

Section 1 Home: Domestic Dirt and Cleaning
Introduction *Rosie Cox*

1. See for example Lindsey German, *Sex, Class and Socialism* (London: Bookmarks 1989); Ellen Malos (ed.) *The Politics of Housework* (Cheltenham: New Clarion Press, 1995); Ann Oakley, *Housewife* (London: Penguin Books, 1972).
2. See for example Isabella Bakker and Stephen Gill (eds) *Power, Production and Social Reproduction: Human In/security in the Global Political Economy*

(Basingstoke: Palgrave Macmillan, 2003); Nancy Folbre, *Who Pays for the Kids: Gender and the Structures of Constraint* (London: Routledge, 1994); Arlie Hochschild, *The Second Shift* (London: Penguin, 1983, reprinted 2003); and Arlie Hochschild, *The Time Bind: When Work becomes Home and Home becomes Work* (New York: Henry Holt, 1997) to cite just a few.

3. See, among others, Barbara Ehrenreich and Arlie R. Hochschild (eds) *Global Woman: Nannies, Maids and Sex Workers in the New Economy* (London: Granta Books, 2003) and Janet H. Momsen (ed.) *Gender Migration and Domestic Service* (London: Routledge, 1999) for global overviews; Bridget Anderson, *Doing the Dirty Work: The Global Politics of Domestic Labour* (London: Zed Books, 2000) for Europe; Grace Chang, *Disposable Domestics: Immigrant Women Workers in the Global Economy* (Cambridge, MA: South End Press, 2000) and Pierette Hondagneu-Sotelo, *Doméstica: Immigrant Workers Cleaning and Caring in the Shadows of Affluence* (London: University of California Press, 2001) for the USA; and Rosie Cox, *The Servant Problem: Paid Domestic Work in a Global Economy* (London: I.B.Tauris, 2006) for the UK.

4. Quoted in Pamela Horn, *The Rise and Fall of the Victorian Servant* (Stroud: Sutton Publishing, 2004) p. 19.

5. Pamela Sambrook, *A Country House Servant* (Stroud: Sutton Publishing, 2002) p. 222.

6. See also Anderson, *Doing the Dirty Work*, p. 124, who refers to domestic workers as the 'status givers and myth makers' of their employers.

Chapter 1 Linguistic Leakiness or Really Dirty? Dirt in Social Theory
Carol Wolkowitz

1. I thank Terry Lovell and the editors of this volume for comments on an earlier draft.

2. Mick Smith and Joyce Davidson, '"It makes my skin crawl ...": the embodiment of disgust in phobias of "nature"', *Body & Society*, vol. 12, no. 1, 2006, p. 44.

3. Valerie Curtis and Adam Biran, 'Dirt, disgust, and disease: is hygiene in our genes?' *Perspectives in Biology and Medicine*, vol. 44, no. 1, 2001, p. 21.

4. American Association for the Advancement of Science, 'The yuck response', vol. 290, no. 5492, 27 October 2000. http://www.sciencemag.org/content/vol290/issue 5492/r-samples.dtl, accessed 15 August 2006.

5. Mary Douglas, *Purity and Danger: An Analysis of Concepts of Purity and Taboo* (London: Routledge & Kegan Paul, 1969, first published 1966).

6. Tim Dant and David Bowles, 'Dealing with dirt: servicing and repairing cars', *Sociological Research Online*, vol. 8, no. 2, 2003 http://www.socresonline.org.uk/8/2/dant.html

7. Andrew Sayer, *Realism and Social Science* (London: Sage, 2000).

8. Sayer, *Realism and Social Science*, p. 13.

9. Diana Coole, 'Dialectical realism and existential phenomenology: a dialogue', *New Formations*, vol. 58, 2005, pp. 121–32.

10. Daniel M. T. Fessler and Kevin J. Haley, 'Guarding the perimeter: the outside-inside dichotomy in disgust and bodily experience', *Cognition and Emotion*, vol. 20, no. 1, 2006, pp. 3–19; Drew Leder, *The Absent Body* (Chicago: University of Chicago Press, 1990).

11. Douglas, *Purity and Danger*; Elizabeth Grosz, *Sexual Subversions: Three French Feminists* (Sydney: Allen and Unwin, 1989); Elizabeth Grosz, *Volatile Bodies:*

Toward a Corporeal Feminism (Bloomington: University of Indiana Press, 1994); Julia Kristeva, *Powers of Horror: An Essay on Abjection*, translated by L. Roudiez (New York: Columbia University Press, 1982).

12. Simon J. Williams and Gillian Bendelow, *The Lived Body: Sociological Themes, Embodied Issues* (London: Routledge, 1998).
13. Kristeva, *Powers of Horror*.
14. Grosz, *Volatile Bodies*, p. 192.
15. Christina Hughes, *Women's Contemporary Lives: Within and Beyond the Mirror* (London: Routledge, 2002).
16. Alexandra Howson, *Embodying Gender* (London: Sage, 2005).
17. Howson, *Embodying Gender*, p. 2.
18. Robyn Longhurst, *Bodies: Exploring Fluid Boundaries* (London: Routledge, 2001) p. 23.
19. Carol Wolkowitz, *Bodies at Work* (London: Sage, 2006).
20. Everett Cherrington Hughes, *The Sociological Eye* (New Brunswick: Transaction Books, 1984).
21. Dant and Bowles, 'Dealing with dirt'.
22. Tony Horowitz, 'Inside a "dirty MuRF": the offal part of the recycling boom', *The Wall Street Journal*, 1 December 1994 http://www.pulitzer.org/year/1995/national-reporting/works/horowitz3.html, Accessed accessed 3 July 2006
23. Grosz, *Volatile Bodies*, p. 201.
24. Lise Widding Isaksen, 'Masculine dignity and the dirty body', *NORA*, vol. 10, no. 3, 2002, p. 137.
25. For a more extensive discussion, see Wolkowitz, *Bodies at Work*.
26. Widding Isaksen, 'Masculine dignity and the dirty body', pp. 139 and 143.
27. Solari, Cinzia, 'Professionals and saints: how immigrant careworkers negotiate gender identities at work', *Gender and Society*, vol. 20, no. 3, 2006, pp. 301–31.
28. Barbara Ehrenreich, 'Maid to order', in Barbara Ehrenreich and Arlie Hochschild (eds) *Global Woman: Nannies, Maids and Sex Workers in the Global Economy* (London: Granta Books, 2003) p.102.
29. Debra Hopkins, Linda McKie, Nick Watson and Bill Hughes, 'The problem of emotion in care: contested meanings from the disabled people's movement and feminist movement', in Helena Flam and Deborah King (eds) *Emotion and Care* (London: Routledge, 2005).
30. Lynn May Rivas, 'Invisible labours: caring for the independent person', in Barbara Ehrenreich and Arlie Hochschild (eds) *Global Woman: Nannies, Maids and Sex Workers in the Global Economy* (London: Granta Books, 2003).
31. Grosz, *Volatile Bodies*, p. 197.
32. Martha Nussbaum, *Hiding from Humanity: Disgust, Shame and the Law* (New Jersey: Princeton University Press, 2004).
33. McKeganey and Barnard (1996) p. 11, cited by Sheila Jeffreys, *The Idea of Prostitution* (Melbourne: Spinflex, 1997) p. 349.
34. Cecilie Hoigard and Liv Finstad, *Backstreets: Prostitution, Money and Love* (University Park: The Pennsylvania State University Press, 1992) p. 108.
35. Hoigard and Finstead, *Backstreets*, p. 92.
36. Kelly Holsopple, *Strip Club Testimony* (Minneapolis, MN: The Freedom and Justice Centre for Prostitution Resources, n.d.) retrieved on 10 January 2004, from http://www.ccv.org/images/strip_club_testimony_and_study.PDF) p. 14.

37. Wendy Chapkis, *Live Sex Acts: Women Performing Erotic Labour* (London: Cassell 1997).
38. Joanna Brewis and Stephen Linstead, *Sex, Work and Sex Work* (London: Routledge, 2000).
39. Shannon Bell, *Reading, Writing, and Rewriting the Prostitute Body* (Bloomington, IN: Indiana University Press, 1994).
40. Julia O'Connell Davidson, *Prostitution, Power and Freedom* (Cambridge: Polity, 1998) pp. 9–10.
41. O'Connell Davidson, *Prostitution, Power and Freedom*, p. 188.
42. Bridget Anderson, *Doing the Dirty Work: The Global Politics of Domestic Labour* (London: Zed Books, 2000).
43. Teela Sanders, *Sex Work: A Risky Business* (Cullompton, Devon: Willan Publishing, 2004).
44. Anderson, *Doing the Dirty Work*.
45. Douglas, *Purity and Danger*, p. 2.

Chapter 2   Domestic Workers and Pollution in Brazil Lívia Barbosa

1. The total number of household servants in Brazil, according to the Departamento Intersindical de Estatística e Estudos Econômicos, is six and half million people, 93 per cent of whom are female servants. Some 25 per cent have formal, legal relations with their employees, while 75 per cent have informal working ties. This means that they are not protected by any kind of legislation. Domestic servants, of all categories, are not a privilege of middle- and upper-income people. There are also lots of domestic workers among the working class and even among maids themselves. This type of servant is usually used as nanny for the young children of working-class mothers and maids when they go to work. They usually help with household tasks. There are no statistics on them.
2. These include protection from arbitrary lay-off, an eight-hour working day, a five-day working week, 30 days vacation with one-third additional pay, transport paid from home to workplace, 'thirteenth month' salary in December and a warranty fund.
3. Ricardo Paes de Barros et al. (n.d.) *O trabalho doméstico infanto-juvenil no Brasil*, www.ilo.org/public/english/standards/ipec/publ/policy/papers/brasil/oitrbarros.pdf, accessed 15 December 2006; Departamento Intersindical de Estatística e Estudos Econômicos, *O emprego doméstico: uma ocupação tipicamente feminina.* (Secretaria Internacional do Trabalho, Brasil, 2006) www.planalto.gov.br/seppir/acoes_afirmativas/genero/Trabalho%20Doméstico-DIEESE%20e%20OIT.pdf, accessed 15 December 2006; Marcelo Medeiros and Rafael Osorio, *Arranjos domiciliares e arranjos nucleares no Brasil: classificação e evolução de 1977 a 1998* (Brasília. Text for discussion no. 788, 2001; www.ipea.gov.br/pub/td/td_2001/td_788.pdf, accessed 15 December 2006; Elizabeth Bortolaia Silva, *Teorias sobre trabalho e tecnologias domésticas: implicações para o Brasil*, (n.d.) http://www.ige.unicamp.br/site/publicacoes/dpct/ Texto-19.doc, accessed 14 December 2006.
4. Lívia Barbosa, 'Cultura, consumo e identidade: limpeza e poluição na sociedade brasileira contemporânea', in Lívia Barbosa and Colin Campbell, *Cultura, Consumo e Identidade* (Rio de Janeiro: Fundação Getulio Vargas, 2006); Lívia Neves, 'Cleanliness, pollution and disgust in modern industrial societies: the Brazilian case', *Journal of Consumer Culture*, vol. 4, no. 3, 2004, pp. 385–405.

5. Ruth S. Cowan, *More Work for Mother: The Ironies of Household Technology from the Open Hearth to the Microwave* (New York: Basic Books, 1983); Adrian Forty, *Objects of Desire: Design and Society since 1750* (London: Thames & Hudson, 1986).

6. Lucinda Lambton, *Temples of Convenience and Chambers of Delight* (London: Pavilion Books, 1997); Reginald Reynolds, *Cleanliness and Godliness* (London: George Allen & Unwin, 1943); Lawrence Wright, *Clean and Decent: The Fascinating History of the Bathroom and the Water Closet, and of the Sundry Habits, Fashions and Accessories of the Toilet, principally Great Britain, France, and America* (New York: Viking Press, 1960).

7. Pat Thomas, *Cleaning Yourself to Death: How Safe is your Home* (Dublin: Newleaf, 2001).

8. Elisabeth Shove, *Comfort, Cleanliness + Convenience: The Social Organization of Normality* (Oxford: Berg, 2003). New technologies/new cultures series.

9. Georges Vigarello, *Concepts of Cleanliness: Changing Attitudes in France since the Middle Ages* (Cambridge: Cambridge University Press, 1998).

10. Norbert Elias, *The Civilizing Process* (Oxford: Blackwell, 1979).

11. Christine M. Bose, Philip Bereano and Mary Malloy, 'Household technology and the social construction of housework', *Technology and Culture*, vol. 25, no.1, January 1984, pp. 53–82; Ruth S. Cowan, 'Two washes in the morning and a bridge party at night: the American housewife between the wars, *Women Studies*, vol. 3, 1976, pp. 147–72; Jonathan M. Godwin, Michael Gershuny and Sally Jones, 'The domestic labour revolution: a process of lagged adaptation', in Michael Anderson, Frank Bechhofer and Jonathan Gershuny (eds) *The Social and Political Economy of the Household* (Oxford: Oxford University Press, 1994); Arwen P. Mohun, *Steam Laundries: Gender, Technology and Work in the United States and Great Britain, 1880–1940* (Baltimore: The Johns Hopkins University Press, 1999); Silva, *Teorias sobre trabalho e tecnologias domésticas*; Nancy Tomes, *The Gospel of Germs: Man, Women, and the Microbe in American Life* (Cambridge, MA: Harvard University Press, 1999).

12. Jeanne Boydston, *Home and Work: Housework, Wages and Ideology of Labor in the Early Republic* (New York: Oxford University Press, 1990); Steven Mintz, *Domestic Revolutions: A Social History of American Family Life* (New York: Free Press, 1988).

13. Rosie Cox, 'What about the dirt in dirty work? Exploring the status of domestic employment', paper presented at the Association of American Geographers Annual Meeting, Denver, March 2005.

14. Pierre Bourdieu, *Esboço de uma teoria da prática: precedido de três estudos de etnologia Kabila* (Oeiras: Celta, 1972, reprinted 2002)

15. Gilberto Freyre, *The Masters and the Slaves (Casa Grande and Senzala): A Study in the Development of Brazilian Civilization* (New York: Alfred A. Knopf, 1956); Gilberto Freyre, *The Mansions and the Shanties (Sobrados e Mucambos): The Making of Modern Brazil* (Berkeley: University of California Press, 1987)

16. Roberto Da Matta, *A casa e a rua: espaço, cidadania, mulher e morte no Brasil* (Rio de Janeiro: Editora Guanabara, 1987).

17. Monique Eleb and Anne Dabarre, *L'Invention de l'habitation moderne, Paris, 1880–1914* (Paris: Hazan, 1995); Sharon Marcus, *Apartment Stores: City and Home in Nineteenth-century Paris and London* (Berkeley: University of California Press, 1999).

18. De Matta, *Casa e a Rua*.

19. Mike Featherstone, *Cultura de consumo e pós-modernidade* (São Paulo: Nobel, 1996).
20. Buckets, brooms, pressing iron, soap and industrial cleaning products also received their share of aesthetic attention. New types of cabinets were developed with the function of hiding all the cleaning utensils. Ironing boards emerge as if by magic from closed doors and bucket, water basin and brushes now come in new colours that remind us of candy bars.
21. Luis Dumont, *Homo hierarchicus: o sistema de castas e suas implicações*, translated by Carlos Alberto da Fonseca (São Paulo: Editora Universidade de São Paulo, 1992).
22. When visiting the poor areas of Brazil during election time, the candidates always try to eat among people. The point behind this kind of behaviour is explicitly to show that they do not feel any disgust for them or their food. The importance of demonstrating that, as a politician and an important person, he or she does not entertain that kind of feeling lies in the fact that not to feel disgust for others is a demonstration of an egalitarian ideology. The same is true of the practice of letting people kiss you or holding poor infants in their laps. See Roberto Pompeu Loureiro, 'Dos pasties a poltrona de couro', *Veja*, 8 November 2006.
23. Mary Douglas, *Implicit Meaning: Essays in Anthropology by Mary Douglas* (London: Routledge & Kegan Paul, 1975).

Chapter 3 The Visible and the Invisible: (De)regulation in Contemporary Cleaning Practices *Lydia Martens*

1. Hoy, Suellen, *Chasing Dirt: The American Pursuit of Cleanliness* (Oxford: Oxford University Press, 1997) p. 179.
2. See also Caroline Bird, *The Two-Paycheck Marriage* (New York: Rawson Wade, 1979); Anne Oakley, *Housewife* (Harmondsworth: Penguin, 1972); Anne Oakley, *The Sociology of Housework* (Bath: Robertson, 1973); John P. Robinson and Melissa A Milkie, 'Back to the basics: trends in and role determinants of women's attitudes toward housework', *Journal of Marriage and the Family*, vol. 60, no. 1, 1998, pp. 205–18.
3. Lisa Ackerley, 'Consumer awareness of food hygiene and food poisoning', *Environmental Health*, March, 1994, pp. 69–74; Guliz Ger and Baskin Yenicioglu, 'Clean and dirty: playing with boundaries of consumer's safe havens', *Advances in Consumer Research*, vol. 31, 2004, pp. 462–7; Richard W. Lacey, 'Food poisoning: the rise continues', *British Food Journal*, vol. 95, no. 3, 1993, pp. 25–31; Lydia Martens and Sue Scott, 'The unbearable lightness of cleaning: representations of domestic practice and products in *Good Housekeeping* magazine (UK) 1951–2001', *Consumers, Markets and Culture*, vol. 8, no. 4, 2005, pp. 379–402; Keith C. Meldrum, 'Food safety: whose responsibility is it?' *PHLS Microbiology Digest*, vol. 11, 1994, pp. 194–8.
4. See for instance Ulrich Beck, *Risk Society: Towards a New Modernity* (London: Sage, 1992); Ulrich Beck, Anthony Giddens and Scott Lash, *Reflexive Modernization: Politics, Tradition and Aesthetics in the Modern Social Order* (Cambridge: Polity Press/Blackwell, 1994); Anthony Giddens, *Modernity and Self-Identity: Self and Society in The Late Modern Age* (Cambridge: Polity Press, 1991). For an instructive interpretation of this literature, see Alan Warde,

Consumption, Food and Taste: Culinary Antinomies and Commodity Culture (London: Sage, 1997).

5. The ESRC funded the project, *Domestic Kitchen Practices*, and I thank the council for its financial support (RES–000–22–0014). Other members of the research team were Professor Sue Scott (co-applicant) and Dr Matt Watson (research associate) and I am very grateful to them for their input into this project. For a detailed discussion of the methodology of this project, please refer to the ESRC's end of award report (Lydia Martens and Sue Scott, 'Domestic kitchen practices: routines, risks and reflexivity – end of award report', *Economic and Social Research Council*, Swindon (UK), 2004, pp. 1–28).

6. The Rayburn is a brand name for a traditional type stove that offered all-in-one facilities for cooking, baking, water and house heating. The Findley's Rayburn used coal as fuel and was a central discussion point among all the family members during our research with them.

7. Nancy Tomes, *The Gospel of Germs: Men, Women and the Microbe in American Life* (London: Harvard University Press, 1998) p.7. For a discussion about germs as a social anxiety and for the way in which germs became the target of an expanding consumer culture, see Richard L. Bushman and Claudia L. Bushman, 'The early history of cleanliness in America', *Journal of American History*, vol. 74, no. 4, 1988, pp. 1213–8; Andrew McClary, 'Germs are everywhere: the germ threat as seen in magazine articles 1890–1920', *Journal of American Culture*, vol. 3, no. 1, 1980, pp. 33–46; Juliann Sivulka, *Stronger than Dirt: A Cultural History of Advertising Personal Hygiene in America, 1875 to 1940* (Amherst, NY: Humanity Books, 2001); Vincent Vinikas, 'Lustrum of the cleanliness institute, 1927–1932', *Journal of Social History*, vol. 22, no. 4, 1989, pp. 613–30; and Vincent Vinikas, *Soft Soap, Hard Sell: American Hygiene in an Age of Advertisement* (Iowa: Iowa State University Press, 1992).

8. For the debate on efficiency in the home, see Irene Cieraad, '"Out of my kitchen!" Architecture, gender and domestic efficiency', *Journal of Architecture*, vol. 7, 2002, pp. 263–79; Christine Frederick, *Household Engineering: Scientific management in the home* (Chicago: American School for Home Economics, 1920); Lillian Gilbreth, *Management in the Home: Happier Living through Saving Time and Energy* (New York: Dodd, Mead, 1954); Ellen Richards, *Euthenics: The Science of Controllable Environment* (Boston: Barrows, 1929). For discussions on women's organizations, the rise of home economics in the early twentieth century, the decline in servants and the significance of the *Good Housekeeping* magazine as an informant of domestic efficiency, see Dena Attar, *Wasting Girls' Time: The History and Politics of Home Economics* (London: Virago Press, 1990); Caitriona Beaumont, 'Citizens not feminists: the boundary negotiated between citizenship and feminism by mainstream women's organisations in England, 1928–39', *Women's History Review*, vol. 9, no. 2, 2000, pp. 411–29; Catherine Horwood, 'Housewives' choice + launching of the British version of *Good Housekeeping*, March 1922: women as consumers between the wars', *History Today*, vol. 47, no. 3, 1997, pp. 23–8; Phyllis Palmer, *Domesticity and Dirt: Housewives and Domestic Servants in the United States, 1920–1945* (Philadelphia: Temple University Press, 1989).

9. Martens and Scott, 'The unbearable lightness of cleaning'.

10. See Hoy, *Chasing Dirt*.

11. It could be argued that scholars have been primarily interested in this factor of domestic cleanliness, as the whiteness, brightness and sparkle induced by cleaning has been connected with 'othering' practices. This has been the focus of some interesting work on the symbolic meanings of cleanliness. See for example Anders Linde-Laursen, 'The nationalization of trivialities: how cleaning becomes an identity marker in the encounter of Swedes and Danes', *Ethnos*, vol. 58, nos 3–4, 1993, p. 275; and Lisa Saugeres, 'Of tidy gardens and clean houses: housing officers as agents of social control', *Geoforum*, vol. 31, no. 4, 2000, pp. 587–599, which theoretically come close to Mary Douglas's theory on the role of purity and danger in the construction of culture (Mary Douglas, *Purity and Danger: An Analysis of Concepts of Pollution and Taboo*, London: Routledge & Kegan Paul, 1966). In this chapter, I do not really address this perspective in preference for a focus on the cultural meanings of cleanliness practices associated with domestic cultures.

12. A reading of Tomes, *The Gospel of Germs*, suggests that aesthetic concerns were the focus of cleanliness in Victorian households before germ consciousness spread, and she identifies this with status struggles. See also Boel Berner, 'The meaning of cleaning: the creation of harmony and hygiene in the home', *History and Technology*, vol. 14, 1998, pp. 312–52; Adrian Forty, *Objects of Desire: Design and Society since 1750* (New York: Pantheon, 1986); Ellen Lupton and J. Abbott Miller, 'Hygiene, cuisine and the product world of early twentieth-century America', in Jonathan Crary and Sanford Kwinter (eds) *Incorporations* (Cambridge, MA: Zone Books/MIT Press, 1992) for discussions on transformations of domestic aesthetics and the linking of domestic cleanliness with the creation of a safe domestic haven.

13. Martens and Scott, 'The unbearable lightness of cleaning'.

14. From a pull out supplement published in association with Hoover entitled 'Take Time to be Young'.

15. See Marjorie DeVault, *Feeding the Family* (Chicago: University of Chicago Press, 1991); Dorothy Smith, *The Everyday Life as Problematic* (Milton Keynes: Open University Press, 1987); Alan Warde and Lydia Martens, *Eating Out: Social Differentiation, Consumption and Pleasure* (Cambridge: Cambridge University Press, 2000).

16. Margaret Horsfield, *Biting the Dust: The Joys of Housework* (London: Fourth Estate, 1998).

17. Grant David McCracken, *Culture and Consumption: New Approaches to the Symbolic Character of Consumer Goods and Activities* (Bloomington: Indiana University Press, 1988).

18. Alain Corbin, *The Foul and the Fragrant: Odour and the French Imagination* (Cambridge, MA: Harvard University Press, 1986); Sarah Pink, 'The sensory home as a site of consumption: everyday laundry practices and the production of gender', in Emma Casey and Lydia Martens (eds) *Gender and Consumption: Domestic Cultures and the Commercialisation of Everyday Life* (Aldershot: Ashgate, 2007) pp. 163–80.

19. Madelaine Akrich, 'The de-scription of technical objects', in Wiebe E. Bijker and John Law (eds) *Shaping Technology/Building Society: Studies in Sociotechnical Change* (Cambridge, MA: MIT Press, 1992).

20. Other participants also felt carpets were inappropriate floor cover for a kitchen.

21. Hoy, *Chasing Dirt*.

22. Mike Featherstone, *Consumer Culture and Postmodernism* (London: Sage, 1991); Celia Lury, *Consumer Culture* (Cambridge: Polity Press, 1996).
23. For an interesting take on the invisible dimensions of the home, see Maria Kaïka, 'Interrogating the geographies of the familiar: domesticating nature and constructing the autonomy of the modern home', *International Journal of Urban and Regional Research*, vol. 28, no. 2, 2004, pp. 265–86.

Chapter 4   Bring Home the Dead: Purity and Filth in Contemporary Funeral Homes *Kyro Selket*

1. Alan Ball, *Six Feet Under. Episode One: The Pilot* (Home Box Office: United States of America, 2000–2005).
2. Aotearoa New Zealand weaves together both the Māori and Pakeha names for what has become known as New Zealand. This is in recognition of Te Triti o Waitangi, the bicultural accord signed by Māori and Pakeha in 1840.
3. Deathscape is a term Elizabeth K. Teather coined in 'Themes from complex landscapes: Chinese cemeteries and columbaria in urban Hong Kong', *Australian Geographical Studies*, vol. 36, no. 1, 1998, pp. 21–36.
4. Don Sawyer, 'The contagious case part III', *The Dodge Magazine*, vol. 1, no. 9, 1994, pp. 17–28.
5. Clarence G. Strub and Lawrence G. Fredrick (eds) *The Principles and Practices of Embalming* (Dallas: Professional Training Schools, 1967, 4th edition) p. 1.
6. Paul W. Cleaver, 'Dealing with death: the Pakeha treatment of death, 1859–1910' (unpublished Masters thesis, Victoria, University of Wellington, 1996).
7. Tony Walter, 'Three ways to arrange a funeral: mortuary variation in the modern West', *Mortality*, vol. 10, no. 3, 2005, pp. 173–92
8. Lindsay Prior, *The Social Organization of Death: Medical Discourse and Social Practices in Belfast* (London: Macmillan Press, 1989); Nancy Tomes, *The Gospel of Germs: Men and Women and the Microbe in American Life* (London: Harvard University Press, 1998).
9. Philippe Aries, *Western Attitudes Toward Death: From the Middle Ages to the Present*, translated by Patricia M. Ranum (Baltimore: Johns Hopkins University Press, 1974); Philippe Aries, *The Hour of our Death*, translated by Helen Weaver (New York: Alfred A. Knopf, 1981) and G. Gorer, *Death, Grief and Mourning in Contemporary Britain* (London: Cresset, 1965).
10. Alison Bashford, *Purity and Pollution: Gender, Embodiment and Victorian Medicine* (New York: St Martin's Press, 1998); Prior, *The Social Organization of Death*; Tomes, *The Gospel of Germs*.
11. Bashford, *Purity and Pollution*; Constance Classen, David Howes and Anthony Synnott, *Aroma: The Cultural History of Smell* (London: Routledge, 1994); Alain Corbin, *The Foul and the Fragrant: Odour and the Social Imagination* (Cambridge, MA: Harvard University Press, 1986); Deborah Lupton, *The Imperative of Health: Public Health and the Regulated Body* (London: Sage, 1995); Tomes, *The Gospel of Germs*.
12. Morris, E. and J. Flyger and Company, *Sanitary Funerals in New Zealand* (Wellington: Funeral Directors Association, 1930) p. 2.
13. Robert W. Habenstein, 'Sociology of occupations: the case of the American funeral director', in Arnold Rose (ed.) *Human Behaviour and Social Processes* (London: Routledge & Kegan Paul, 1972) pp. 225–46.

14. Gaston Bachelard, *The Poetics of Space* (New York: Orion Press, 1964).
15. David Seamon and Robert Mugerauer (eds) *Dwelling, Place, and Environment: Towards a Phenomenology of Person and World* (Dordrecht: Martinus Nijhoff, 1985).
16. Linda McDowell, *Gender, Identity and Place: Understanding Feminist Geographies* (Minneapolis: University of Minnesota Press, 1999); Gillian Rose, *Feminism and Geography: the Limits of Geographical Knowledge.* (Cambridge: Polity Press, 1993); Peter Saunders and Peter Williams, 'The constitution of the home: towards a research agenda', *Housing Studies*, vol. 3, no. 2, 1988, pp. 81–93; Gill Valentine, *Social Geographies: Space and Society* (New York: Prentice Hall, 2001).
17. Saunders and Williams, 'The constitution of the home', p. 91.
18. Even warehouses that have been refurbished as funeral homes attempt to create a warm and inviting homely environment.
19. Lychgate Funeral Home 2006.
20. Strub and Fredrick, *The Principles and Practices of Embalming.*
21. Margrit Shildrick, *Leaky Bodies and Boundaries: Feminism, Postmodernism and (Bio)ethics* (London: Routledge, 1997).
22. Robyn Longhurst, *Bodies: Exploring Fluid Boundaries* (London: Routledge, 2001).
23. Julia Kristeva, *Powers of Horror: An Essay on Abjection*, translated by Leon S. Roudiez (New York: Columbia University Press, 1982) p. 4.
24. Jean Baudrillard, *Symbolic Exchange and Death*, translated by Iain Hamilton Grant, (London: Sage Publications, 1993) p.181.
25. Barbara Creed, *Monstrous-Feminine: Film, Feminism, Psychoanalysis* (London: Routledge, 1993) p. 10.
26. Akiko Busch, *Geography of Home: Writings on Where We Live* (New York: Princeton Architectural Press, 1999).
27. Mary Douglas, *Purity and Danger: An Analysis of Concepts of Pollution and Taboo* (London: Routledge & Kegan Paul 1969); Arnold van Gennep, *Rites of Passage*, translated by Monika B. Vizedom and Gabrielle L. Caffee with an introduction by Solon T. Kimball (London: Routledge & Kegan Paul, 1960).
28. Jane Gallop, *Feminism and Psychoanalysis: The Daughter's Seduction* (London: Macmillan, 1982).
29. van Gennep, *Rites of Passage.*
30. Céline Rosselin, 'The ins and outs of the hall: a Parisian example', in Irene Cieraad (ed.) *At Home: Anthropology of Domestic Space* (Syracuse, NY: Syracuse University Press, 1999) p. 55.
31. Rosselin, 'The ins and outs of the hall'.
32. Strub and Fredrick, *The Principles and Practices of Embalming.*
33. While the Victorian era is associated with clutter, it is not this particular aspect that funeral directors embrace when designing their viewing rooms. Instead, they embody notions of 'family', of 'home' and the presence of comfort, which is seen as being part of the Victorian era.
34. Penny Sparke, 'Studying the modern home', *The Journal of Architecture*, vol. 9, Winter, 2004.

Section 2: City and Suburb: Urban Dirt and Cleansing
Introduction *Ben Campkin*

1. For example Nicholas Barton, *The Lost Rivers of London* (London: Phoenix

House, 1962, reprinted 1992 by Historical Publications); Stephen Halliday, *The Great Stink of London: Sir Joseph Bazalgette and the Cleansing of the Victorian Capital* (Stroud, Sutton Publishing Ltd, 1999); Christopher Hamlin, *Public Health and Social Justice in the Age of Chadwick: Britain, 1800–1854* (Cambridge: Cambridge University Press, 1998); Martin V. Melosi, *The Sanitary City: Urban Infrastructure in America from Colonial Times to the Present* (Baltimore: Johns Hopkins University Press, 2000).

2. Paul Griffiths and Mark Jenner, *Londinopolis: Essays in the Social and Cultural History of Early Modern London* (Manchester: Manchester University Press, 2000)
3. This is in contrast to other aspects of architectural and urban history that in the last two decades of the twentieth century have gradually widened in scope from pure formal analyses, or analyses of designers and their intentions, to explorations of the wider economic, political, social and historical contexts of individual buildings and urban places. See Nan Ellin, *Postmodern Urbanism* (Oxford: Blackwell, 1996) p. 2.
4. Melosi, *The sanitary city*, 2000, p. 12.
5. William A. Cohen and Ryan Johnson, *Filth: Dirt, Disgust, and Modern Life* (Minneapolis: University of Minnesota Press, 2005) p. ix.
6. Matthew Gandy, 'Review of Martin V. Melosi, *The Sanitary City: Urban Infrastructure in America from Colonial Times to the Present*', H-Urban, H-Net Reviews, February 2001. http://www.h-net.org/reviews/showrev.cgi?path=13074983817017, p. 2.
7. Peter Stallybrass and Allon White, *The Politics and Poetics of Transgression* (London: Methuen, 1986) p. 145.
8. Stallybrass and White, *The Politics and Poetics of Transgression*, p. 127.
9. Steve Pile, 'The un(known) city … or, an urban geography of what lies buried below the surface', in Iain Borden, Joe Kerr, Jane Rendell with Alicia Pivaro (eds) *The Unknown City: Contesting Architecture and Social Space* (Cambridge, MA: MIT Press, 2001).

Chapter 5 Degradation and Regeneration: Theories of Dirt and the Contemporary City *Ben Campkin*

1. William A. Cohen, and Ryan Johnson (eds) *Filth: Dirt, Disgust, and Modern Life* (Minneapolis: University of Minnesota Press, 2005) p. viii.
2. Douglas attributes the phrase to Lord Chesterfield.
3. Richard Fardon, 'Obituary: Dame Mary Douglas', *Guardian*, Friday 18 May 2007.
4. It is not intended to provide a comprehensive survey of responses to or applications of Douglas's theory, but rather to highlight some indicative examples.
5. Maria Kaïka and Eric Swyngedouw, 'Fetishizing the modern city: the phantasmagoria of urban technological networks', *International Journal of Urban and Regional Research*, vol. 24, no. 1, 2000, p. 136.
6. Julian Stallabrass, *High Art Lite: The Rise and Fall of Young British Art* (London: Verso, 1999, revised edition 2006) p. 259.
7. Mary Douglas, *Purity and Danger: An Analysis of Concepts of Pollution and Taboo* (London: Routledge & Kegan Paul, 1966) p. 75.
8. Jonathan Culler, 'Junk and rubbish: a semiotic approach', *Diacritics*, vol. 15, no 3, Fall, 1985, p. 2; Elizabeth Shove, *Comfort, Cleanliness and Convenience: The Social Organization of Normality* (Oxford: Berg, 2003) p. 84. Douglas's pre-

occupation with cultural ordering systems, space and signification continued to occupy a central position in more recent work that bridged the methodologies of anthropology and literary criticism. This was evident, for example, in her reading of the structure of the text of Leviticus as a spatial 'picture poem' representing the proportions of the Tabernacle and Mount Sinai. Douglas, Mary, 'How I got to where I am: from anthropology to 'literary criticism', *Mary Douglas Seminar Series*, Institute of Archaeology, unpublished seminar paper, University College London, 26 May 2005.

9. Douglas, *Purity and Danger*, p. xiii.
10. Douglas, *Purity and Danger*, p. 2.
11. Thompson was a student of Douglas's in the department of anthropology at University College, London.
12. Zygmunt Bauman, *Wasted Lives: Modernity and its Outcasts* (Oxford: Polity, 2004); Mark Cousins, (1996) 'The ugly', *AA Files*, no. 28; Adrian Forty, *Objects of Desire: Design and Society since 1750* (London: Thames & Hudson, 1986) pp. 156–81; Katherine Shonfield, 'Dirt is matter out of place', in Jonathan Hill (ed.) *Architecture: The Subject is Matter* (London: Routledge, 2001) pp. 29–44; David Sibley, *Geographies of Exclusion: Society and Difference in the West* (London: Routledge, 1995); Michael Thompson, *Rubbish Theory* (Oxford: Oxford University Press, 1979); Patrick Wright, *Journey through Ruins: The Last Days of London* (London: Radius, 1991), extract reprinted in Patrick Wright, 'Down in the dirt', in Joe Kerr and Andrew Gibson (eds) *London from Punk to Blair* (London: Reaktion, 2003) pp. 353–61.
13. Richard Fardon, *Mary Douglas: An Intellectual Biography* (London: Routledge, 1999) p. 76. Douglas describes the book's argument as 'convoluted'. See Douglas, *Purity and Danger*, p. xi.
14. James Wuthnow, Davison Hunter, Albert Bergesen and Edith Kurzweil, *Cultural Analysis: The Work of Peter L. Berger, Mary Douglas, Michel Foucault, and Jurgen Habermas* (London: Routledge & Kegan Paul, 1984) p. 78. Wuthnow et al. identify these interests as characteristics of Douglas's approach to culture.
15. Douglas, *Purity and Danger*, p. xvii.
16. For a survey of theories and meanings of 'order' in relation to architectural and urban modernism, see Adrian Forty, *Words and Buildings: A Vocabulary of Modern Architecture* (London: Thames & Hudson, 2000) pp. 240–8. David Sibley's work on 'landscapes of exclusion' illustrates the potential of examining linguistic images of dirt and cleanliness through the rhetoric of public debate in media representations of stigmatized places and communities, drawing both on Douglas and the work of Foucault. In this account the spatial marginalization of matter becomes inextricably linked with the spatial marginalization of groups of people who, for one reason or another, do not fit comfortably within society's dominant bourgeois social or cultural values. See Sibley, *Geographies of Exclusion*.
17. She writes (Douglas, *Purity and Danger*, p. xi) that 'The background of daily life in nursery and kitchen may explain why the metaphors are homely.'
18. Wuthnow et al, *Cultural Analysis*, p. 79. For example, see Douglas's domestic references to shoes, cooking utensils and bathrooms in her *Purity and Danger*, pp. 47–8.

19. Jonathan Culler, 'Junk and rubbish: a semiotic approach', *Diacritics*, vol. 15, no. 3, Fall 1985, p. 2; Douglas, *Purity and Danger*, p. xvii. Wuthnow et al, put this argument forward in *Cultural Analysis*, p. 83.

20. For example, the beliefs and practices associated with the cleanliness or dirtiness of certain foods, governed through a combination of spiritual beliefs, practical understanding and medical knowledge

21. See Shove, *Comfort, Cleanliness and Convenience*, p. 82; and Wolkowitz in this volume, pp. 15–17.

22. Wuthnow et al., *Cultural Analysis*, p. 79.

23. Culler, 'Junk and rubbish', p. 2.

24. Sibley, *Geographies of Exclusion*, p. 38.

25. Fardon, *Mary Douglas*, p. 100, note 9. Fardon does not cite any specific authors.

26. William Cohen, 'Introduction: locating filth', in William A. Cohen and Ryan Johnson, *Filth: Dirt, Disgust, and Modern Life* (Minneapolis: University of Minnesota Press) p. xii.

27. Cohen, 'Introduction', p. xiii.

28. Cohen, 'Introduction', p. xi. See also Nadir Lahiji and Daniel S. Friedman, 'At the sink: architecture in abjection', in Nadir Lahiji and Daniel S. Friedman (eds) *Plumbing: Sounding Modern Architecture* (New York, Princeton Architectural Press, 1997). 'Behind every cleanliness resides an execrable uncleanliness – clean dissimulates unclean. Clean and unclean do not exist in real opposition as two positive facts. Rather they are two poles in a relationship of logical contradiction' (p. 36).

29. Wright, 'Down in the dirt', pp. 241, 237.

30. Wright, 'Down in the dirt', p. 241.

31. Dalston is an area of northeast London currently subject to gentrification.

32. Wright, 'Down in the dirt', pp. 238, 241.

33. Douglas, *Purity and Danger*.

34. Bauman, *Wasted Lives*, p. 27.

35. See Ben Campkin, 'Ornament from grime: David Adjaye's Dirty House, the "architectural aesthetic of recycling" and the gritty Brits', in Ben Campkin and Paul Dobraszczyk (eds) 'Architecture and dirt', *The Journal of Architecture*, special issue, vol. 12, no. 4, September 2007.

36. Steve Pile, *The Body and the City: Psychoanalysis, Space and Subjectivity* (London: Routledge, 1996). Steve Pile provides a useful summary of the process of abjection (p. 90): 'Children learn to displace dangerous or unwanted feelings onto others – others who are perceived to be different. These feelings are simultaneously social, bodily and spatial. ... In abjection, senses of revulsion over bodily materials and feelings are established. The subject wants to expel whatever is reviled, but is powerless to achieve it: thus, for example, the desire to be completely clean all the time cannot be achieved, purity cannot be maintained. Abjection, then, is a perpetual condition of surveillance, maintenance and policing of impossible "cleanliness".'

37. Cohen, 'Introduction', p. xxvi.

38. For example, Guy Baeten, 'Hypochondriac geographies of the city and the new urban dystopia', *CITY: Analysis of Urban Trends, Theory, Culture, Policy, Action*, vol. 6, no. 1, April 2002, pp. 103–15; Matthew Gandy, 'The Paris sewers and the rationalization of urban space', *Transactions of the Institute of British Geographers*,

vol. 24, no. 1, 1999, pp. 23–44; Maria Kaïka, *City of Flows: modernity, nature and the city* (London: Routledge, 2004); Maria Kaïka and Eric Swyngedouw, 'Fetishizing the modern city: the phantasmagoria of urban technological networks', *International Journal of Urban and Regional Research*, vol. 24, no. 1, 2000, pp. 120–38; Antoine Picon, 'Anxious landscapes: from the ruin to rust', *Grey Room*, no. 1, Fall 2000, pp. 64–83; Stallabrass, *High Art Lite*; Eric Swyngedouw and Maria Kaïka, 'The environment of the city … or the urbanization of nature', in Gary Bridge and Sophie Watson (eds) *The Blackwell Companion to the City* (Oxford: Blackwell, 2000) pp. 567–80.

39. Stallabrass, *High Art Lite*, p. 256. On images of neglect, decay and ruin in contemporary art and on Rut Blees Luxemburg's photography, see also Jane Rendell, *Art and Architecture: A Place Between* (London: I.B.Tauris, 2006) pp. 89–90.
40. Kaïka and Swyngedouw, 'Fetishizing the modern city', p. 136.
41. Wuthnow et al. (*Cultural Analysis*, p. 85) write: 'For Mary Douglas the artifact is simple, obvious and everyday, much like Marx's commodity and Durkheim's totem.'
42. Swyngedouw and Kaïka, 'The environment of the city', p. 570.
43. Swyngedouw and Kaïka, 'The environment of the city', p. 574.

Chapter 6   From the Dirty City to the Spoiled Suburb *Paul Watt*

1. See the spatial revision to the sociology of Pierre Bourdieu made by Mike Savage, Gaynor Bagnall and Brian Longhurst, 'Local habitus and working-class culture', in Fiona Devine, Mike Savage, John Scott and Rosemary Crompton (eds) *Rethinking Class: Culture, Identities and Lifestyles* (Basingstoke: Palgrave Macmillan, 2005).
2. For a discussion of place in the geographical and psychological literatures, see Per Gustafson, 'Meanings of place: everyday experience and theoretical conceptualizations', *Journal of Environmental Psychology*, vol. 21, no. 1, 2001, pp. 5–16.
3. Rob Shields, *Places on the Margins* (London: Routledge, 1991) p. 60.
4. Mark Clapson, *Suburban Century* (Oxford, Berg, 2003).
5. David Sibley, 'The racialization of space in British cities', *Soundings*, vol. 10, no. 1, 1998, pp. 119–27.
6. Mary Douglas, *Purity and Danger* (London: Routledge & Kegan Paul, 1966) p. 2.
7. David Sibley, *Geographies of Exclusion* (London: Routledge, 1995).
8. Julia Kristeva, *Powers of Horror: An Essay on Abjection* (New York: Columbia University Press) p. 4.
9. Sibley, *Geographies of Exclusion*, p. 78.
10. Mary P. Baumgartner, *The Moral Order of a Suburb* (Oxford: Oxford University Press, 1988) p. 104.
11. Richard Sennett, *The Uses of Disorder* (London: Faber & Faber, 1996).
12. Sibley, *Geographies of Exclusion*, pp. 38–9.
13. Annamarie Jagose, Fran Martin and Chris Healy, 'At home in the suburb', in Fran Martin (ed.) *Interpreting Everyday Culture* (London: Arnold, 2003).
14. Zygmunt Bauman, *Liquid Life* (Cambridge: Polity, 2005) pp. 76–7.
15. Tim Butler with Garry Robson, *London Calling: The Middle Classes and the Remaking of Inner London* (Oxford: Berg, 2003); Paul Watt, 'Respectability, roughness and "race": neighbourhood place images and the making of working-class social distinctions in London', *International Journal of Urban and Regional Research*, vol. 30, no. 4, 2006, pp. 776–97.

16. Stephen J. Ball, *Class Strategies and the Education Market* (London: RoutledgeFalmer, 2003).
17. Michael Keith, *After the Cosmopolitan? Multicultural Cities and the Future of Racism* (London: Routledge, 2005).
18. Clapson, *Suburban Century*.
19. Mike Savage and Andrew Miles, *The Remaking of the British Working Class, 1840–1940* (London: Routledge, 1994) p. 62.
20. Alan A. Jackson, *Semi-Detached London: Suburban Development, Life and Transport, 1900–39* (London: George Allen & Unwin, 1973); Peter Willmott and Michael Young, *Family and Class in a London Suburb* (London: New English Library, 1967).
21. Simon Naylor and James R. Ryan, 'The mosque in the suburbs: negotiating religion and ethnicity in South London', *Social & Cultural Geography*, vol. 3, no. 1, 2002, pp. 39–59; Roger Silverstone, *Visions of Suburbia* (London: Routledge, 1997).
22. Mark Clapson, *Invincible Green Suburbs, Brave New Towns* (Manchester: Manchester University Press, 1998); see also Clapson, *Suburban Century*.
23. Michael Young and Peter Willmott, *Family and Kinship in East London* (London, Routledge & Kegan Paul, 1957).
24. Clapson, *Invincible Green Suburbs*, p. 73.
25. Clapson, *Invincible Green Suburbs*.
26. John Rex and Robert Moore, *Race, Community and Conflict* (Oxford: Oxford University Press, 1967).
27. Peter Jackson, *Maps of Meaning* (London: Routledge, 1989) pp. 145–6.
28. Sibley, 'The racialization of space', p. 122.
29. Eric Avila, *Popular Culture in the Age of White Flight: Fear and Fantasy in Suburban Los Angeles* (Berkeley: University of California Press, 2004) p. 1.
30. Geoff Dench, Kate Gavron and Michael Young, *The New East End: Kinship, Race and Conflict* (London: Profile Books, 2006) pp. 142–7; Paul Watt, 'Narratives of urban decline and ethnic diversity: white flight and the racialisation of space in London and south east England', paper presented at the Countering Urban Segregation Conference, Free University, Amsterdam, 14–15 October 2004.
31. Clapson, *Suburban Century*; Watt, 'Narratives of urban decline'.
32. Paul Watt, 'Going out of town: youth, "race" and place in the south east of England', *Environment and Planning D: Society and Space*, vol. 16, no. 6, 1998, pp. 687–703.
33. Les Back, 'Inside out: racism, class and masculinity in the inner city and the English suburbs', *New Formations*, vol. 33, 1998, pp. 59–76.
34. Thanks to Shirley Koster for both devising the area pseudonyms in this chapter and commenting on drafts.
35. The survey involving 140 residents was undertaken during 2004. A sub-sample of survey respondents was followed up and 42 semi-structured interviews were carried out in 2004–5. The project was funded by the British Academy, grant LRG–35374.
36. Chris Hamnett, *Unequal City: London in the Global Arena* (London: Routledge, 2003); Vikki Rix, 'Social and demographic change in East London', in Michael Rustin and Tim Butler (eds) *Rising in the East* (London: Lawrence & Wishart, 1996).
37. 'S.63' refers to the survey respondent identifying number.

217

38. In *Tales of the City* (Cambridge: Cambridge University Press, 1998) pp. 153–64, Ruth Finnegan is sceptical about whether any claims to a past 'community' have credence given their nostalgic mythical content.

39. Watt, 'Respectability, roughness and race'. See also Les Back, *New Ethnicities and Urban Culture* (London: UCL Press, 1996); Karen Wells and Sophie Watson, 'A politics of resentment: shopkeepers in a London neighbourhood', *Ethnic and Racial Studies*, vol. 28, no. 2, 2005, pp. 261–77.

40. Watt, 'Respectability, roughness and race'; Sophie Watson and Karen Wells, 'Spaces of nostalgia: the hollowing out of a London market', *Social & Cultural Geography*, vol. 6, no. 1, 2005, pp. 17–30.

41. Wells and Watson, 'A politics of resentment', p. 265.

42. Douglas, *Purity and Danger*.

43. For a discussion of the racialized significance of the 'cockroach invasion' in Tower Hamlets, see Paul Hoggett, 'A place for experience: a psychoanalytic perspective on boundary, identity and culture', *Environment and Planning D: Society and Space*, vol. 10, 1992, pp. 345–56. The racist association of dirt with forms of food and cooking specific to minority religions (notably Islam) in London is discussed in Wells and Watson, 'A politics of resentment', pp. 269–70.

44. Exclusionary racist discourses tended to be most overtly expressed by the white working class, although they also appeared in some interviews with the white middle class. Race and white flight, as well as the place images of the small number of black and Asian interviewees, will be discussed in greater detail in future papers.

45. Ball, *Class Strategies and the Education Market*.

46. Diane Reay, 'Mostly roughs and toughs: social class, race and representation in inner city schooling', *Sociology*, vol. 38, 2004, pp. 1005–23.

47. Clapson, *Suburban Century*.

48. James S. Duncan and Nancy G. Duncan, *Landscapes of Privilege* (London: Routledge, 2004).

49. Clapson, *Suburban Century*.

Chapter 7   Dangers Lurking Everywhere: The Sex Offender as Pollution
Pamela K. Gilbert

1. Anon., *Coral Gables: An Exceptional City*, brochure published by the City Manager of Coral Gables, http://64.233.187.104/search?q=cache:Z-4k1RV faoOJ: www.citybeautiful.net/CGWeb/documents/city_manager_docs/CGAnnual Report 04_05.pdf+%22city+of+miami%22+sex+dirt&hl=en&gl=us&ct=clnk&cd=3, accessed 1 August 2006, p. 12.

2. Anon., *Coral Gables*, p. 3.

3. Ronald Reagan, 'City upon a hill' http://www.presidentreagan.info/speeches/city_upon_a_hill.cfm, accessed 17 September 2006.

4. The 'Cities of the Plains', such as Sodom and Gomorrah, were the cities destroyed by God in the biblical book of Genesis (see especially Chapter 19) for unspecified sins that have usually been interpreted as sexual, and often as homosexual (for example, sodomy). For the interpretation of New Orleans as a latter day Sodom, see David Crowe, 'Katrina: God's judgment on America', http://www.beliefnet.com/story/174/story_17439_1.html, accessed 8 September 2006, for a representative statement.

5. See Daniel M. Filler, 'Silence and the racial dimension of Megan's law', *Iowa Law Review*, vol. 89, 2004, pp. 1535–94, available at SSRN: http://ssrn.com/abstract= 648261, for a detailed summary, see especially, pp. 1541–9.

6. Steve Macek, *Urban Nightmares: The Media, the Right, and the Moral Panic over the City* (Minneapolis: University of Minnesota Press, 2006) p. xvii.

7. Macek, *Urban Nightmares*; Peter Stallybrass and Allon White, *The Politics and Poetics of Transgression* (London: Methuen, 1986).

8. For a representative example, see Robert Santiago and Sara Olkon, 'Molester ban poses risks, some say', *Miami Beach Herald*, Monday 19 September 2005.

9. Mike Peringer, 'South End is not a dumping ground for what the city doesn't want', *The Seattle Post Intelligencer*, 4 May 2006, p. B7.

10. Anon., 'Comment on proposal could send sex offenders outside the Lawrence city limits', by Scott Rothschild, *Lawrence Journal World*, Tuesday, 1 November 2005, http://www2.ljworld.com/news/2005/nov/01/proposal_could_send_sex_ offenders_outside_lawrence/?sexual_predator_law#comments, accessed 9 September 2006.

11. For a full discussion of the history of these laws and their racial implications, see Filler, 'Silence'.

12. Filler, 'Silence,' p. 1538.

13. The language of the Louisiana criminal code defines a 'crime against nature' as the following: 'A. Crime against nature is: (1) The unnatural carnal copulation by a human being with another of the same sex or opposite sex or with an animal, except that anal sexual intercourse between two human beings shall not be deemed as a crime against nature when done under any of the circumstances described in R.S. 14:41, 14:42, 14:42.1 or 14:43. Emission is not necessary; and, when committed by a human being with another, the use of the genital organ of one of the offenders of whatever sex is sufficient to constitute the crime. (2) The solicitation by a human being of another with the intent to engage in any unnatural carnal copulation for compensation. B. Whoever violated the provisions of this Section shall be fined not more than two thousand dollars, or imprisoned, with or without hard labor, for not more than five years, or both.'

14. Filler, 'Silence', p. 1548.

15. Mona Lynch, 'Pedophiles and cyber-predators as contaminating forces: the language of disgust, pollution, and boundary invasions in federal debates on sex offender legislation', *Law and Social Inquiry*, vol. 27, no. 3, Summer 2002, p. 545.

16. See Phillip Jenkins, *Moral Panic: Changing Concepts of the Child Molester in Modern America* (New Haven: Yale University Press, 1998).

17. Tiffany Pakkala, 'School bus stop was at sex offender's home', *Gainesville Sun*, 10 August 2006, http://gainesville.com/apps/pbcs.dll/article?AID=/20060810/LOCAL/ 208100330&SearchID=73257054135918.

18. Wes Smith, 'Church foes cite sex offenders' proximity: a proposed complex in Edgewood shouldn't be able to displace residents, opponents say', *The Orlando Sentinel*, 8 September 2006, Associated Press, Lexis-Nexis database.

19. Laura Bauer, 'Houses off-limits to sexual predators: a planned Lenexa subdivision will ban registered sex offenders from buying there', *The Kansas City Star*, Tuesday 13 June 2006, http://www.kansascity.com/mld/kansascity/news/local/ 14804143.htm, accessed 2 August 2006.

20. Jenkins, *Moral Panic*, p. 2.

21. Jenkins, *Moral Panic*, p. 190.
22. Jenkins, *Moral Panic*, p. 200.
23. Robert E. Freeman-Longo, 'Revisiting Megan's law and sex-offender registration: prevention or problem', *American Probation and Parole Association*, 2000, http://www.appa-net.org/revisitingmegan.pdf, accessed 5 September 2006, p. 13.
24. Lynch, 'Pedophiles and cyberpredators', p. 532.
25. Lynch, 'Pedophiles and cyberpredators, p. 543.
26. Lynch, 'Pedophiles and cyberpredators, p. 544.
27. Lynch, 'Pedophiles and cyberpredators, pp. 544–5.
28. Joyce Carol Oates, 'Imaginary cities: America', in Michael C. Jaye and Ann Chalmers Watts (eds) *Literature and the Urban Experience: Essays on the City and Literature* (New Brunswick: Rutgers University Press, 1981) p. 11.
29. Giorgio Agamben, *Homo Sacer* (Chicago: University of Chicago Press, 1998); Lauren Berlant, *The Queen of America Goes to Washington City: Essays on Sex and Citizenship* (Durham: Duke University Press, 1997).
30. Mary Douglas, *Purity and Danger: An Analysis of Concepts of Pollution and Taboo* (London: Routledge & Kegan Paul, 2002) pp. 3–5 and *passim*.
31. As many scholars have noted. See especially James R. Kincaid, *Erotic Innocence: The Culture of Child Molesting* (Durham: Duke University Press, 1998).
32. Winfried Menninghaus, *Disgust: Theory and History of a Strong Sensation*, translated by Howard Eiland and Joel Golb (Albany: SUNY Press, 2003) p. 357.
33. Menninghaus, *Disgust*, p. 52.
34. Stallybrass and White, *The Politics and Poetics of Transgression*, p. 136.
35. Stallybrass and White, *The Politics and Poetics of Transgression*, pp. 125–6.
36. See Pamela K. Gilbert, *Mapping the Victorian Social Body* (Albany: SUNY Press, 2004).
37. See Paul Dobraszczyk's chapter on Victorian sewer maps in this volume.
38. Giorgio Agamben, *Homo Sacer*, p. 105.
39. Agamben, *Homo Sacer*, p. 105.
40. Agamben, *Homo Sacer*, p. 106.
41. In fact, it undercuts its effectiveness, distracting communities with the spectacle of multiple 'threats' from the few genuine dangers it might highlight.
42. Berlant, *Queen of America*, pp. 1–6.
43. Kincaid, *Erotic Innocence*.

Chapter 8   Hygiene Aesthetics on London's Gay Scene: The Stigma of AIDS
Johan Andersson

1. Two recent historical books on London have highlighted the relationship between male homosexuality and spaces perceived as physically and metaphorically dirty. Matt Houlbrook's *Queer London: Perils and Pleasures in the Sexual Metropolis, 1918–1957* (Chicago: University of Chicago Press, 2005) focuses on London's hidden homosexual geography while sex between men was still a criminal offence. Key sites for anonymous sexual encounters were London's public urinals – spaces whose association with bodily fluids also stigmatized homosexual men as 'dirty'. As Houlbrook (*Queer London*, p. 63) puts it: 'The discursive production of person and place was a mutually constitutive process, in which notions of the queer's character were derived from the nature of that site at which he was most often arrested.' Gradually, as a result of increased legal and societal acceptance of homosexuality,

there has been a shift in gay meeting places from the public spaces of the city (such as after-dark parks and public urinals) to a commercial scene primarily consisting of pubs and clubs: while these gay venues are less associated with 'dirt' than public urinals, gay pubs and clubs are frequently portrayed as contaminated with perversion or moral corruption and, during the AIDS crisis in the 1980s, with contagious sexual disease. Another book, Seth Koven's *Slumming: Sexual and Social Politics in Victorian London* (Princeton: Princeton University Press, 2004) has shown how temporary accommodation for the homeless in London's Victorian slums – the so-called workhouses – were seen as not only physically dirty, but also as breeding grounds for homosexuality and disease. This equation between home-lessness and homosexuality survived long into the twentieth-century and was famously depicted in George Orwell's *Down and Out in London and Paris* (London: Victor Gollancz, 1933), which 'marked the culmination of a long history of Victorian and Edwardian social reporting in Britain that imagined the slums of London not only as sites of physical and social disorder – "dirt" – but as spaces hospitable to "queer" lives and "queer" sexual desires' (Koven, *Slumming*, p. 183).

2. Jon Binnie, 'Trading places: consumption, sexuality and the production of queer space', in David Bell and Gill Valentine (eds) *Mapping Desire: Geographies of Sexualities* (London: Routledge 1995); Frank Mort, *Cultures of Consumption: Masculinities and Social Space in Late Twentieth-Century Britain* (London: Routledge 1996); Mark W. Turner, 'Gay London', in Joe Kerr and Andrew Gibson (eds) *London: From Punk to Blair* (London: Reaktion Books, 2003).

3. Richard Dyer, *The Matter of Images: Essays on Representation* (London: Routledge, 1993) p 56.

4. A later British example of film noir aesthetics can be seen in Basil Dearden's *Victim* (1961), which highlights how the association with crime was forced upon homosexual men by the law that criminalized homosexual behaviour.

5. Interview cited in Neil McKenna, 'Fleet Street's perverse cocktail of kinky sex and serial killer', *The Independent*, 20 June 1993.

6. Gordon Douglas (1968) *The Detective* (dvd).

7. Vito Russo, *The Celluloid Closet: Homosexuality in the Movies* (New York: Harper & Row Publishers, 1987, revised edition) p. 238.

8. Brian Masters, *Killing for Company: The Case of Dennis Nielsen* (London: Arrow Books, 1985) p. 84.

9. Masters, *Killing for Company*.

10. Masters, *Killing for Company*, p. 85.

11. Masters, *Killing for Company*, p. 109.

12. Masters, *Killing for Company*, p. 89.

13. Anon., 'Aids sufferer haunted bars in war against homosexuals' *The Times*, 11 July 1987.

14. Anon., 'Gay cruiser who strangled four men in a "cold rage" – Michael Lupo', *Guardian*, 11 July 1987.

15. Anon., 'Victim helped detectives capture killer on pub dance floor', *Guardian*, 11 July 1987.

16. Anon., 'Man killed male lover who said he had Aids', *Independent*, 15 February 1990.

17. Anon., 'Masochistic homosexual was kicked and punched to death', *Independent*, 15 March 1990.

18. McKenna, 'Fleet Street's perverse cocktail'.

19. Christopher Lloyd, 'Pub where three murderers hunted victims', *Sunday Times*, 26 December 1993.

20. Lloyd, 'Pub where three murderers hunted victims'.

21. Paul Brown, Police raid gay pub', *Guardian*, 26 January 1987.

22. Polly Toynbee, 'Thursday women (behind the lines): freedom's roadblock', *Guardian*, 14 January 1988.

23. Rupert Haselden, 'Gay abandon: many gay men now see Aids not as death but destiny', *Guardian*, 7 September 1991.

24. Haselden, 'Gay abandon'.

25. Haselden, 'Gay abandon'.

26. Binnie, 'Trading places'.

27. A. Tuck, 'In the pink', *Time Out*, exact date missing, 1994.

28. Mark Simpson, 'Hello boys! Soho turns pink', *Independent*, 23 May 1994.

29. Beverly Skeggs, Leslie Moran, Paul Tyrer and Jon Binnie, 'Queer as folk: producing the real of urban space', *Urban Studies*, vol. 41, no 9, 2004, p. 1843.

30. Stephen Quilley, 'Constructing Manchester's "new urban village": gay space in the entrepreneurial city', in Gordon Ingram, Anne-Marie Bouthillette and Yolanda Retter (eds) *Queers in Space: Communities, Public Places, Sites of Resistance* (Seattle: Bay Press, 1997) p. 278.

31. Gary Henshaw, private interview, 25 April 2002.

32. Paul Gould, 'The love that dares not forget its brand name', *Financial Times,* 7 March 1998, p. 22.

33. Jean Baudrillard, *The System of Objects*, translated by J. Benedict (London: Verso, 1996) p. 33.

34. Adrian Forty, *Objects of Desire: Design and Society since 1750* (London: Thames & Hudson, 1986) p. 173.

35. Henshaw, private interview.

36. Henshaw, private interview.

37. *Capital Gay*, 8 March 1992, p. 9.

38. *Capital Gay*, 6 December 1991, p. 14.

39. Henshaw, private interview.

40. Lynn Hettinger, 'Brand culture and branded workers: service work and aesthetic labour in fashion retail', *Consumption, Markets and Culture*, vol. 7, no. 2, 2004, p. 179.

41. *Pink Paper*, 20 August 1993, p. 3.

42. Rupert Smith, 'Join the club: Duckie began as a group of drag artists and drunken admirers. Now this 'post-gay' phenomenon is going national', *Guardian*, 14 May 2002, p. 15.

43. Forty, *Objects of Desire*.

Chapter 9 Spiritual Cleaning: Priests and Prostitutes in Early Victorian London
Dominic Janes

1. John Maynard, *Victorian Discourses on Sexuality and Religion* (Cambridge: Cambridge University Press, 1993).

2. Lynda Nead, *Myths of Sexuality: Representations of Women in Victorian Britain* (Oxford: Blackwell, 1988) p. 121.

3. Philip Hubbard, *Sex and the City: Geographies of Prostitution in the Urban West* (Aldershot: Ashgate, 1999) p. 31. See also Matt Houlbrook, 'Toward a historical geography of sexuality', *Journal of Urban History*, vol. 27, 2001, pp. 497–504.

4. Christopher Otter, 'Cleansing and clarifying: technology and perception in nineteenth-century London', *Journal of British Studies*, vol. 43, 2004, pp. 40–65.

5. Warwick Anderson, 'Excremental colonialism: public health and the poetics of pollution', *Critical Inquiry*, vol. 21, 1995, pp. 640–69.

6. Anderson, 'Excremental colonialism', pp. 668–9.

7. Dominique Laporte, *History of Shit*, translated by Nadia Benabid and Rudolphe el-Khoury (Cambridge, MA: MIT Press, 1993) p. 40.

8. Henry Mayhew, *London Labour and the London Poor* (London: Constable, 1968).

9. William Bennett, *Letters to my Children on Moral Subjects* (London: W. J. Cleaver, 1850) p. 150.

10. Mary Douglas and David Hull (eds) *How Classification Works: Nelson Goodman among the Social Sciences* (Edinburgh: Edinburgh University Press, 1992) p. 265. The key earlier presentation of ideas on danger and boundary transgression is Mary Douglas, *Purity and Danger: An Analysis of Concepts of Pollution and Taboo* (London: Routledge & Kegan Paul, Ark reprint edition, 1984).

11. Valerio Valeri, *The Forest of Taboos: Morality, Hunting, and Identity among the Huaulu of the Moluccas* (Madison: University of Wisconsin Press, 1999) p. 102.

12. Valeri, *The Forest of Taboos*, p. 43.

13. Boyd Hilton, *The Age of Atonement: The Influence of Evangelicalism on Social and Economic Thought, 1795–1865* (Oxford: Clarendon Press, 1988).

14. Nead, *Myths*, p. 129 and plate 22; Linda Nochlin, 'Once more the fallen woman', *The Art Bulletin*, vol. 60, 1978, p. 148. An online reproduction of the painting can be viewed at http://www.rossettiarchive.org/docs/s100.rap.html, accessed 31 January 2007.

15. Judith R. Walkowitz, *Prostitution and Victorian Society: Women, Class and the State* (Cambridge: Cambridge University Press, 1980) p. 49.

16. Ralph Wardlaw, *Lectures on Female Prostitution: Its Nature, Extent, Effects, Guilt, Causes and Remedy* (Glasgow: J. Maclehose, 1843, 3rd edition) p. 162.

17. Alfred C. C. List, *The Two Phases of the Social Evil* (Edinburgh: Oliver & Boyd, 1861) p. 32.

18. William Tait, *Magdalenism: An Inquiry into the Extent, Causes, and Consequences of Prostitution in Edinburgh* (Edinburgh: P. Rickard, 1842, 2nd edition) p. 250.

19. Nead, *Myths*, p. 121.

20. Alexander Penrose Forbes, *A Sermon Preached at the Chapel Royal, Savoy Street, Strand, Before the Church Penitentiary Association on Thursday, May 12, 1864* (London: Spottiswoode & Co., 1864) p. 9.

21. Wardlaw, *Prostitution*, p. 43.

22. William Acton, *The Functions and Disorders of the Reproductive Organs in Youth, in Adult Age, and in Advanced Life: Considered in their Physiological, Social and Psychological Relations* (London: John Churchill, 1857) p. 9.

23. Thomas Thellusson Carter, *Mercy for the Fallen: Two Sermons in Aid of the House of Mercy, Clewer. To Which is Added an Appeal for the Completion of the House* (London: Joseph Masters, 1856) p. 6.

24. Acton, *Functions and Disorders*, pp. 163–4.

25. Anon. [Thomas Vincent], *Some Account of St Mary's Home for Penitents at Wantage … by the Chaplain* (Oxford: John Henry Parker, 1852, 2nd edition) p. 22.

26. William Bevan, *Prostitution in the Borough of Liverpool: A Lecture Delivered in the Music Hall, June, 3, 1843* (Liverpool: B. Smith, 1843) p. 5.

27. Bevan, *Prostitution*, p. 22.

28. Liddon, Henry Parry, *Active Love a Criterion of Spiritual Life: A Sermon* (London: Spottiswoode & Co., 1862) p. 14.

29. Amanda Anderson, *Tainted Souls and Painted Faces: The Rhetoric of Fallenness in Victorian Culture* (Ithaca: Cornell University Press, 1993) p. 65.

30. Edward J. Bristow, *Vice and Vigilance: Purity Movements in Britain since 1700* (Totowa: Rowman & Littlefield, 1977) p. 69.

31. Anon., *A Proposal for the Establishment of a Female Penitentiary in Norfolk or Suffolk in Connexion with the Church Penitentiary Association* (Norwich: Charles Muskett, 1853) p. 6.

32. Anon., *A Proposal*, pp. 10–11.

33. Thomas Thellusson Carter, *To a Friend of the Church of England House of Mercy, Clewer* (Windsor: no publisher, 1852) p. 3.

34. Robert Liddell, *A Pastoral Letter to the Parishioners of St Paul's, Knightsbridge and St Barnabas', Pimlico* (London: J. T. Hayes, 1858) pp. 26–9.

35. Robert Liddell, *A Pastoral Letter to the Parishioners of S. Paul's, Knightsbridge, and S. Barnabas', Pimlico* (London: J. T. Hayes, 1853) pp. 20–3.

36. Robert Liddell, *An Account of the House of Refuge in Commercial Road, Pimlico: Addressed to the Church Penitentiary Association* (London: J. H. Parker, 1854) p. 3.

37. Anon. [Vincent], *Some Account of St Mary's Home*, p. 4.

38. Liddell, *An Account of the House of Refuge*, p. 9.

39. Liddell, *An Account of the House of Refuge*, p. 15.

40. Robert Liddell, *Christ the Caster-out of Unclean Spirits: A Sermon Preached at St Paul's, Knightsbridge, on the Fourth Sunday after Epiphany in Behalf of the Church Penitentiary Cause [on Matt. viii. 29]* (London: J. T. Hayes, 1854) p. 6.

41. Liddell, *Christ*, p. 7.

42. Liddell, *Christ*, p. 11.

43. Liddell, *Christ*, p. 11.

44. William Ian Miller, *The Anatomy of Disgust* (Cambridge, MA: Harvard University Press, 1997) p. 204.

45. Nead, *Myths*, p. 112.

46. James Miller, *Prostitution Considered in Relation to its Cause and Cure* (Edinburgh: Sutherland & Knox, 1859).

47. Marcia Werner, *Pre-Raphaelite Painting and Nineteenth-Century Realism* (Cambridge: Cambridge University Press, 2005) pp. 193, 199. An online reproduction can be viewed at: http://www.liverpoolmuseums.org.uk/walker/exhibitions/rossetti/works/love.asp, accessed 31 January 2007.

48. See the interesting interpretation of verticality and dirt in David L. Pike, 'Sewage treatments: vertical space and waste in nineteenth-century Paris and London', in William A. Cohen and Ryan Johnson (eds) *Filth: Dirt, Disgust and Modern Life* (Minneapolis: University of Minnesota Press, 2005) pp. 51–76.

49. Elizabeth Grosz, 'Bodies-cities', in Beatriz Colomina (ed.) *Sexuality and Space* (Princeton: Princeton University Press, 1992) pp. 246, 248.

Chapter 10 Mapping Sewer Spaces in mid-Victorian London Paul Dobraszczyk

1. John Brian Harley, 'Maps, knowledge and power', in Stephen Daniels and Denis Cosgrove (eds) *The Iconography of Landscape: Chapters on the Symbolic Representation, Design and Use of Past Environments* (Cambridge: Cambridge

University Press, 1988) p. 278. Other significant sources for radical cartography include Michel de Certeau, *The Practice of Everyday Life*, translated by Steven Rendall (Berkeley: University of California Press, 1984, first published in 1974); Henri Lefebvre, *The Production of Space*, translated by Donald Nicholson-Smith (Oxford: Blackwell, 1991, first published in 1974); and Louis Marin, *Utopics: Spatial Play*, translated by Robert A. Vollrath (London: Macmillan, 1984, first published in 1973).

2. Ida Darlington, 'Edwin Chadwick and the first large-scale Ordnance Survey of London', *Transactions of London and Middlesex Archaeological Society*, vol. 22, 1969, pp. 58–63; Lynda Nead, *Victorian Babylon: People, Streets and Images in Nineteenth-century London* (New Haven: Yale University Press, 2000) pp. 18–22; and Rosa Lynn B. Pinkus, 'The conceptual development of London, 1850–1855', Ph.D. dissertation (Buffalo: State University of New York, 1974) pp. 124–34.

3. Ida Darlington and James Howgego, *Printed Maps of London, c.1553–1850* (London: George Philip & Son, 1964). Darlington and Howgego's catalogue of London maps, by no means exhaustive, lists 422 separate maps produced from 1553 to 1850, 222 of which cover the period from 1800 to 1850.

4. Pinkus, 'The conceptual development of London', p. 108.

5. On the history of the Ordnance Survey see Colonel Sir Charles Close, *The Early Years of the Ordnance Survey* (Newton Abbot: David & Charles, 1969); Tim Owen and Elaine Pilbeam, *Ordnance Survey: Map Makers to Britain since 1791* (Southampton: Ordnance Survey, 1992); and Raleigh A. Skelton, 'The origins of the Ordnance Survey in Great Britain', *Geographical Journal*, vol. 128, 1962, pp. 415–16.

6. Pamela K. Gilbert, *Mapping the Victorian Social Body* (Albany: SUNY Press, 2004) pp. 13–14, 16.

7. *Parliamentary Papers*, 1847–48, vol. 32, 'First report of the commissioners appointed to inquire whether any and what special means may be requisite for the improvement of the health of the metropolis' (London: HMSO) p. iii.

8. Stephen Halliday, *The Great Stink of London: Sir Joseph Bazalgette and the Cleansing of the Victorian Metropolis* (Stroud: Sutton Publishing Ltd, 1999) pp. 32–4. The seven amalgamated commissions of sewers were: the Crown-appointed Commissions of Westminster, Surrey and Kent, Holborn and Finsbury, Poplar, St Katherine's, Tower Hamlets, and Greenwich. The eighth – the City Commission appointed by the City Corporation – remained independently governed.

9. *Parliamentary Papers*, 'First report of the commissioners', pp. 3–47.

10. *Parliamentary Papers*, 'First report of the commissioners', pp. 48–52.

11. Metropolitan Commissions of Sewers, MCS/481, London Metropolitan Archives, minutes of proceedings, 6 December 1847, p. 2.

12. MCS/481, 13 January 1848, pp. 7–8.

13. MCS/481, 27 January 1848, p. 2.

14. For the origins of the corps of Royal Sappers and Miners, see T. W. J. Connolly, *The History of the Corps of Royal Sappers and Miners*, 2 vols (London: Longman, Brown, Green and Longmans, 1855).

15. Anon., 'Ordnance Survey of London and the environs', *Illustrated London News*, 24 June 1848, p. 414.

16. Anon., 'What are the crows' nests for? Ordnance Survey of the metropolis',

Builder, 17 June 1848, pp. 291–2; and Anon., 'The trigonometrical survey of London', *The Times*, 4 November 1848, p. 5

17. David Owen, *The Government of Victorian London: 1855–1889: The Metropolitan Board of Works, the Vestries, and the City Corporation* (Cambridge, MA: Harvard University Press, 1982) p. 33. Owen uses the parish of St Pancras as an illustration: in 1855, 19 separate boards administered the parish, 16 for lighting and paving alone. The 19 boards comprised 427 commissioners, 255 of them self-elected.

18. *Parliamentary Debates*, 3rd Series, vol. 97, 24 March 1848, p. 1016.

19. Parliamentary Acts, 6 & 7 Will. IV, *c*.96.

20. MCS/476/16, p. 1.

21. Parliamentary Acts, 11 & 12 Vict., *c*.112.

22. David L. Pike, *Subterranean Cities: The World Beneath Paris and London, 1800–1945* (Ithaca: Cornell University Press, 2005) pp. 8–12. On the Colosseum panorama see Stephen Oettermann, *The Panorama: History of a Mass Medium* (New York: Zone Books, 1997) pp. 132–40.

23. Oettermann, *The Panorama*, pp. 135–7.

24. MCS/481, 13 January 1848, pp. 7–8.

25. Pike, *Subterranean Cities*, pp. 9–10.

26. MCS/481, 13 January 1848, pp. 1–2.

27. MCS/487, 21 August 1855, p. 374.

28. Darlington, 'Edwin Chadwick', p. 62.

29. MCS/498/1–1384. The 1384 notebooks held at the London Metropolitan Archives are an invaluable record of the levellers' surveying techniques. Similar notebooks produced by the Ordnance Survey's levellers in 1848 and 1849 were destroyed when the Ordnance Survey's offices in Southampton were bombed during the Second World War.

30. MCS/498/45, Westminster Levels, Book 45, p. 11.

31. MCS/477/31, p. 1.

32. MCS/477/31, p. 1.

33. MCS/477/32, 28 October 1848, p. 9.

34. MCS/477/32, 7 December 1848, p. 11.

35. During 1849, the Metropolitan Commission of Sewers experimented in producing plans at a scale of ten feet to one mile to map the information collected in the subterranean survey. The areas eventually mapped were the City of Westminster and a small area of Kensington, with 28 sheets being produced in total – 13 for Westminster and 15 for Kensington (see MCS/P/25/ pp. 1–15). However, all the maps remained as base plans with none of the details of house drainage inserted; in 1849 this survey was abandoned. Sewer information was eventually hand drawn onto the five feet to one mile sheets of the Ordnance Survey (as seen in Figure 10.3). This process occurred at a later date than the subterranean survey, probably during or after the mid-1850s. Over 300 of these maps are currently held in the Thames Water archive at the Abbey Mills pumping station in London.

Chapter 11 The Cinematic Sewer *David L. Pike*

1. See Michelle Allen, *Cleansing the City: Sanitary Geographies in Victorian London* (Athens, OH: Ohio University Press, 2007); the essays in William Cohen and

Ryan Thompson (eds) *Filth: Dirt, Disgust, and Modern Life* (Minneapolis: University of Minnesota Press, 1995); and David L. Pike, *Subterranean Cities: The World Beneath Paris and London, 1800–1945* (Ithaca: Cornell University Press, 2005) pp. 190–269.

2. My language references Mary Douglas's celebrated formulation in *Purity and Danger* (London: Routledge & Kegan Paul, 1966) pp. 35–6 that dirt is 'matter out of place'. Douglas tends to underplay the complex identities retained by the detritus of any social system; nevertheless, her structural analysis correctly draws out the crucial point that, as categories, filth and pollution are wrought with contradiction rather than existing in static opposition to one another.

3. On the cultural resonance of the Paris sewers, see Matthew Gandy's analysis of the 'urban uncanny' in Nadar's photographs in 'The Paris sewers and the rationalization of urban space', *Transactions of the Institute of British Geographers*, vol. 24, no. 1, 1999, pp. 23–44; Pike, *Subterranean Cities*, pp. 229–51; and Donald Reid, *Paris Sewers and Sewermen: Realities and Representations* (Cambridge, MA: Harvard University Press, 1991).

4. Kevin Hayes documents Guy's fascination with rats, and the underground spaces associated with them, and links this fascination to the Paris of Nadar and Hugo, in 'Alice Guy's *The Pit and the Pendulum*', *The Edgar Allan Poe Review*, vol. 2, no. 1, Spring 2001, pp. 40–1; http://www.lv.psu.edu/PSA/EAPRspring2001.pdf, accessed August 2006.

5. Pike, *Subterranean Cities*, pp. 200–3; see also Fred Radford, '"Cloacal obsession": Hugo, Joyce, and the sewer museum of Paris', *Mattoid*, vol. 48, 1994, pp. 66–85.

6. The TMNT began as a comic book in 1984; it was made into an animated television series (1986–97; revived in 2003) before being adapted to the big-screen (1990, 1991, 1993). A fourth feature was released in 2007. Additional animal characters in the sewers include the New York slum-dwelling family of mice in *An American Tail II* (1991), the fleeing zoo creatures aided by two sewer-dwelling alligators in *The Wild* (2006) and, in London, the arch-villain Ratigan in *The Great Mouse Detective* (1986) and the posh mouse who gets flushed into an anarchic sewer city in *Flushed Away* (2006).

7. For a detailed exposition of this argument, see David L. Pike, 'Urban nightmares and future visions: life beneath New York', *Wide Angle*, vol. 20, no. 4, October 1998, pp. 8–50.

8. David Chute, 'John Sayles: designated writer', *Film Comment*, vol. 17, May/June 1981, p. 58.

9. Some other films of underground sewer mutations not explicitly set in New York include *The Rats*, also known as *Deadly Eyes* (1982); *Mutant* (1983); *Transmutations*, also known as *Underworld* (1985); *Split Second* (1992); and *Monsturd* (2003).

10. Similarly, as the serial killer movie has expanded globally as a genre, it has taken over for itself the monstrousness associated with the sewer space, frighteningly close but irredeemably alien; sewer locations feature prominently in *The Sight* (2000), *Dark Asylum* (2001), *Van Helsing: The London Assignment* (2004), and *Creep* (2005).

Section 3   Country: Constructing Rural Dirt
Chapter 12   Dirt and Development: Alternative Modernities in Thailand
Alyson Brody

1. James Scott, *Weapons of the Weak: Everyday Forms of Peasant Resistance* (New Haven: Yale University Press, 1985).
2. Pasuk Phongpaichit and Chris Baker, *Thailand: Economy and Politics* (Oxford: Oxford University Press, 1995).
3. Phongpaichit and Baker, *Thailand*, p. 153.
4. Jaded Chouwilai, 'Life after redundancy: the effects of the termination of Thai workers', in Alyson Brody (ed.) *Uniting Voices: Asian Women Workers' Search for Recognition in the Global Marketplace* (Bangkok: Committee for Asian Women 2000) p. 85.
5. Wathinee Boonchalaksi and Philip Guest, *Prostitution in Thailand* (Bangkok: Institute for Population and Social Research, Mahidol University, 1994).
6. See, for example, Theodore Fuller and Paul Lightfoot, 'Circular migration in northeastern Thailand', in Han ten Brummelhuis and Jeremy Kemp (eds) *Strategies and Structures in Thai Society* (Amsterdam: University of Amsterdam, 1984) pp. 85–94; Sidney Goldstein, *Migration in Thailand: A 25-Year Review* (Honolulu: Hawaii East–West Center, 1986); Sidney Goldstein and Alice Goldstein, *Differentials in Repeat Return Migration in Thailand* (Bangkok: Chulalongkorn University Institute of Population Studies, 1980); Sidney Goldstein and Pichit Pitaktepsombati, *Migration and Urban Growth in Thailand: An Exploration of Interrelationships among Origin, Recency and Frequency of Moves* (Bangkok: Chulalongkorn University Institute of Population Studies, 1974); Mary Beth Mills, 'Rural women working in Bangkok: modernity and gender vulnerability', in John Van Esterik and Penny Van Esterik (eds) *Gender and Development in Southeast Asia* (London: Centre for Advanced Spatial Analysis, 1992); Mary Beth Mills, '"We are not like our mothers": migrants, modernity and identity in northeastern Thailand', unpublished Ph.D. thesis (Berkeley: University of California, 1993); Mary Beth Mills, 'Contesting the margins of Thai modernity', *American Ethnologist*, vol. 24, no. 1, 1997, pp. 37–61; Mary Beth Mills, *Thai Women in the Global Labour Force: Consuming Desires, Contested Selves* (New Jersey: Rutgers University Press, 1999); Pasuk Phongpaichit, *From Peasant Girls to Bangkok Masseuses* (Geneva: International Labour Organization, 1982).
7. David Harvey, *The Urban Experience* (Oxford: Blackwell, 1989) p. 186.
8. Ara Wilson, *The Intimate Economies of Bangkok: Tomboys, Tycoons and Avon Ladies in the Global City* (Berkeley: University of California Press, 2004).
9. Michel Foucault, *Discipline and Punish: The Birth of the Prison* (Harmondsworth: Penguin, 1975).
10. Foucault, *Discipline and Punish*, p. 138.
11. See for example Scot Barmé, *Luang Wichit Watanagan and the Creation of a Thai Identity* (Singapore: Institute of Southeast Asian Studies, 1993); and Craig J. Reynolds, *National Identity and its Defenders: Thailand 1939–89* (Victoria: Aristoc Press, 1991).
12. Phya Anuman Rajadhon, *Watthanatham* (culture) (Bangkok: Samnakpim Banakarn, 1972) p. 14.

13. Rattana Boonmathaya, 'Contested Concepts of Development in Rural Northeastern Thailand', Ph.D. thesis (University of Washington, 1997) p. 136.

14. Stacy Leigh Pigg, 'Inventing social categories through place: social representations and development in Nepal', *Comparative Studies in Society and History*, vol. 34, 1992, p. 507.

15. Mary Douglas, *Purity and Danger: An Analysis of Concepts of Pollution and Taboo* (London: Routledge & Kegan Paul, 1966) p. 2.

16. Suellen Hoy, *Chasing Dirt: The American Pursuit of Cleanliness* (New York: Oxford University Press, 1995).

17. For example, gangs of prisoners can be seen cleaning out drains and sewers, since this is considered lowly work, worthy of criminals.

18. Krishna Sen, 'Indonesian women at work: reframing the subject', in Krishna Sen and Maila Stivens (eds) *Gender and Power in Affluent Asia* (London: Routledge, 1998) pp. 35–62

19. Pierre Bourdieu, *Outline of a Theory of Practice* (Cambridge: Polity, 1977) p. 3.

20. Scott, *Weapons of the Weak*.

21. Scott, *Weapons of the Weak*.

22. Alyson Brody, 'Agents of change: struggles and successes of Thai women migrants in Bangkok', unpublished Ph.D. thesis (London: School of Oriental and African Studies, 2003).

Chapter 13 Dirty Foods, Healthy Communities? *Gareth Enticott*

1. Jonathan Murdoch and Terry Marsden, *Reconstituting Rurality* (London: UCL Press, 1995); David Sibley, *Geographies of Exclusion* (London: Routledge, 1995); Darren P. Smith and Louise Holt, 'Lesbian migrants in the gentrified valley and "other" geographies of rural gentrification', *Journal of Rural Studies*, vol. 21, no. 3, 2005, pp. 313–22.

2. Paul Cloke and Jo Little (eds) *Contested Countryside Cultures* (London: Routledge, 1997).

3. Bruno Latour, 'Where are the missing masses? A sociology of a few mundane artefacts', in Wiebe E. Bijker and John Law (eds) *Shaping Technology/Building Society* (Cambridge, MA: The MIT Press, 1992) pp. 225–58.

4. Ruth Liepins, 'New energies for an old idea: reworking approaches to "community" in contemporary rural studies – new directions in community studies', *Journal of Rural Studies*, vol. 16, no. 1, 2000, pp. 23–35.

5. Colin Bell and Howard Newby, *Community Studies* (London: Allen & Unwin, 1971); Graham Day and Jonathan Murdoch, 'Locality and community: coming to terms with place', *The Sociological Review*, vol. 41, 1993, pp. 82–111.

6. Gareth Enticott, 'Heterogeneous ruralities: the place of nature and community in the differentiated countryside', unpublished Ph.D. thesis (Cardiff: Cardiff University, 2000).

7. John Law, 'Notes on the theory of the actor-network: ordering, strategy and heterogeneity', *Systems Practice*, vol. 5, no. 4, 1992, pp. 379–93.

8. E. Madeleine DuPuis, *Nature's Perfect Food: How Milk Became America's Drink* (New York: New York University Press, 2002); Keir Waddington, *The Bovine Scourge: Meat, Tuberculosis and the Public's Health, 1860s–1914* (Woodbridge: The Boydell Press, 2006).

9. Gareth Enticott, 'Risking the rural: nature, morality and the consumption of

unpasteurised milk', *Journal of Rural Studies*, vol. 19, no. 4, 2003, pp. 411–24; Gareth Enticott, 'Lay immunology, local foods and rural identity: defending unpasteurised milk in England', *Sociologia Ruralis*, vol. 42, no. 3, 2003, pp. 257–70.

10. Sibley, *Geographies of Exclusion*.
11. Peter Dickens, *Reconstructing Nature: Alienation, Emancipation and the Division of Labour* (London: Routledge, 1996).
12. Jonathan Murdoch, 'Inhuman/nonhuman/human: actor-network theory and the potential for a non-dualistic and symmetrical perspective on nature and society', *Environment and Space D: Society and Space*, vol. 15, no. 6, 1997, pp. 731–56.
13. Ted Benton, 'Biology and social theory in the environmental debate', in Ted Benton and Michael Redclift (eds) *Social Theory and the Environment* (London: Routledge, 1994) p. 29.
14. Benton, 'Biology and social theory in the environmental debate'.
15. Michel Callon and Bruno Latour, 'Don't throw the baby out with the Bath school! A reply to Collins and Yearley', in Andrew Pickering (ed.) *Science as Practice and Culture* (Chicago: Chicago University Press, 1992) p. 359.
16. John Law, 'After ANT: complexity, naming and topology', in John Law and John Hassard (eds) *Actor Network Theory and After* (Oxford: Blackwell Publishers/The Sociological Review, 1999) pp. 1–14.
17. Latour, 'Where are the missing masses?'
18. Bruno Latour, 'On recalling ANT', in John Law and John Hassard (eds) *Actor Network Theory and After* (Oxford: Blackwell Publishers/The Sociological Review, 1999) pp. 15–25.
19. Michel Callon and John Law, 'Agency and the hybrid collectif', *South Atlantic Quarterley*, vol. 94, 1995, pp. 481–508.
20. Bruno Latour, 'Pragmatogonies', *American Behavioural Scientist*, vol. 37, no. 6, 1994, p. 802.
21. Bruno Latour, *We Have Never Been Modern* (Hemel Hempstead: Harvester Wheatsheaf, 1993).
22. Jonathan Murdoch, 'Co-constructing the hybrid countryside: hybrid networks and the extensive self', in Paul Cloke (ed.) *Country Visions* (London: Pearson, 2005) pp 263–82.
23. Murdoch, 'Co-constructing the hybrid countryside'.
24. Murdoch, 'Co-constructing the hybrid countryside', p. 266.
25. For an overview, see Jonathan Murdoch, 'Ecologising sociology: actor-network theory, co-constructionism and the problem of human exemptionalism', *Sociology*, vol. 35, no. 1, 2001, pp. 111–33.
26. Andrew Pickering, 'The mangle of practice: agency and emergence in the sociology of science', *American Journal of Sociology*, vol. 99, no. 3, 1993, p. 565.
27. Murdoch, 'Inhuman/nonhuman/human'.
28. Ian Hacking, *The Social Construction of What?* (Cambridge, MA: Harvard University Press, 1999) p. 32.
29. Karin Knorr-Cetina, 'Sociality with objects: social relations in postsocial knowledge societies', *Theory, Culture and Society*, vol. 14, no. 4, 1997, p. 1.
30. Murdoch, 'Co-constructing the hybrid countryside'.
31. Murdoch, 'Co-constructing the hybrid countryside', p. 276
32. Murdoch, 'Co-constructing the hybrid countryside'.

33. Michael M. Bell, *'Childerley': Nature and Morality in a Country Village* (Chicago: University of Chicago Press, 1994).

34. Jonathan Murdoch, Philip Lowe, Neil Ward and Terry Marsden, *The Differentiated Countryside* (London: Routledge, 2003).

35. Paul Cloke and Owain Jones, *Tree Cultures* (Oxford: Berg, 2002).

36. Murdoch, 'Ecologising sociology', p. 129.

37. Ash Dean and the names of all village residents are pseudonyms for reasons of confidentiality. Further details can be found in Enticott, 'Heterogeneous ruralities'.

38. Murdoch et al., *The Differentiated Countryside*.

39. Charlie Davison, George Davey Smith and Stephen Frankel, 'Lay epidemiology and the prevention paradox: implications of coronary candidacy for health education', *Sociology of Health and Illness*, vol. 13, no. 1, 1991, pp. 1–19.

40. Gareth Enticott, 'Calculating nature: the case of badgers, tuberculosis and cattle', *Journal of Rural Studies*, vol. 17, no.2, 2001, pp.149–64.

41. Brian Wynne, 'Misunderstood misunderstanding: social identities and public uptake of science', *Public Understanding of Science*, vol. 1, 1992, pp. 281–304.

42. Michael Woods, 'Deconstructing rural protest: the emergence of a new social movement', *Journal of Rural Studies*, vol. 19, no. 3, 2003, pp. 309–25.

Chapter 14   Dirty Vegetables: Connecting Consumers to their Food
Lewis Holloway, Laura Venn, Rosie Cox, Moya Kneafsey, Elizabeth Dowler, Helena Tuomainen

1. David Sibley, *Geographies of Exclusion: Society and Difference in the West* (London: Routledge, 1995).

2. Mary Douglas, *Purity and Danger: An Analysis of Concepts of Pollution and Taboo* (London, Routledge Classics, 1969).

3. Sibley, *Geographies of Exclusion*, p. 8.

4. Joanna Blythman, *Shopped: The Shocking Power of British Supermarkets* (London: Harper Perennial, 2004); Terry K. Marsden, Andrew Flynn and Michelle Harrison, *Consuming Interests: The Social Provision of Foods* (London: UCL Press, 2000); Kevin Morgan, Terry Marsden and Jonathan Murdoch, *Worlds of Food: Place, Power and Provenance in the Food Chain* (Oxford: Oxford University Press, 2006).

5. David Goodman, 'Editorial: the quality "turn" and alternative food practices: reflections and agenda', *Journal of Rural Studies*, vol. 19, no. 1, 2003, pp. 1–7; David Goodman, 'Rural Europe redux? Reflections on alternative agro-food networks and paradigm change', *Sociologia Ruralis*, vol. 44, no. 1, 2004, pp. 3–16; Morgan et al., *Worlds of food*; David Watts, Brian Ilbery and Damian Maye, 'Making reconnections in agro-food geography: alternative systems of food provision', *Progress in Human Geography*, vol. 29, no. 1, 2005, pp. 22–40; Sarah Whatmore, Pierre Stassart and Henk Renting, 'Guest editorial: what's alternative about alternative food networks?' *Environment and Planning A*, vol. 35, no. 3, 2003, pp. 389–91.

6. Lewis Holloway, Rosie Cox, Laura Venn, Moya Kneafsey, Elizabeth Dowler and Helena Tuomainen, 'Managing sustainable farmed landscape through "alternative food networks": a case study from Italy', *Geographical Journal*, vol. 172, 2006, pp. 219–29; Helena Norberg-Hodge, Todd Merrifield and Steven

Gorelick, *Bringing the Food Economy Home: Local Alternatives to Global Agribusiness* (London: Zed Books, 2002); Henk Renting, Terry Marsden and Jo Banks, 'Understanding alternative food networks: exploring the role of short food supply chains in rural development', *Environment and Planning A*, vol. 35, 2003, pp. 393–411.

7. Lewis Holloway and Moya Kneafsey, 'Reading the space of the farmers' market: a preliminary investigation from the UK', *Sociologia Ruralis*, vol. 40, no. 3, 2000, pp. 285–99; Lewis Holloway and Moya Kneafsey, 'Producing-consuming food: closeness, connectedness and rurality in four "alternative" food networks', in Lewis Holloway and Moya Kneafsey (eds) *Geographies of Rural Cultures and Societies* (London: Ashgate, 2004) pp. 262–82; Brian Ilbery and Damian Maye, 'Food supply chains and sustainability: evidence from specialist food producers in the Scottish/English borders', *Land Use Policy*, vol. 22, no. 4, 2005, pp. 331–44; James Kirwan, 'Alternative strategies in the UK agro-food system: interrogating the alterity of farmers markets', *Sociologia Ruralis*, vol. 44, no. 4, 2004, pp. 395–415; James Kirwan, 'The interpersonal world of direct marketing: examining conventions of quality at UK farmers markets', *Journal of Rural Studies*, vol. 22, no. 3, 2006, pp. 301–12; Laura Venn, Moya Kneafsey, Lewis Holloway, Rosie Cox, Elizabeth Dowler and Helena Tuomainen, 'Researching European "alternative" food networks: some methodological considerations', *Area*, vol. 38, no. 3, 2006, pp. 248–58.

8. This chapter is based on research funded by the ESRC/AHRC Cultures of Consumption Research Programme, project reference RES–143–25–0005. A version of the chapter was presented at the annual meeting of the Association of American Geographers, Denver, CO, 5–9 April 2005.

9. Erica Rappaport, 'Packaging China: foreign articles and dangerous tastes in the mid-Victorian tea party', paper presented to ESRC–AHRB Cultures of Consumption seminar, Managing Anxiety: Food Scares and the British Consumer in Victorian and Modern Britain, 16 July 2004, Birkbeck, University of London.

10. William Cobbett, *Cottage Economy* (Oxford: Oxford University Press, 1979); Upton Sinclair, *The Jungle* (Harmondsworth: Penguin Classics, 1986).

11. John Burnett, *Plenty and Want: A Social History of Food in England from 1815 to the Present Day* (London: Routledge, 1989, 3rd edition) p. 93.

12. Claude Fischler, 'Food habits, social change and the nature/culture dilemma', *Social Science Information*, vol. 19, no. 6, 1980, pp. 937–53; Claude Fischler, 'Food, self and identity', *Social Science Information*, vol. 27, no. 2, 1988, pp. 275–92.

13. Fischler, 'Food, self and identity', p. 279.

14. Fischler, 'Food, self and identity', p. 282.

15. Felicity Lawrence, *Not on the Label: What Really Goes into the Food on your Plate* (London: Penguin, 2004) p. xiii.

16. Fischler, 'Food habits', p. 945.

17. Gareth Enticott, 'Risking the rural: nature, morality and the consumption of unpasteurised milk', *Journal of Rural Studies*, vol. 19, no. 4, 2003, pp. 411–24; Gareth Enticott, 'Lay immunology, local foods and rural identity: defending unpasteurised milk in England', *Sociologia Ruralis*, vol. 43, vol. 3, 2003, pp. 257–70.

18. Enticott, 'Risking the rural', p.412.

19. Enticott, 'Risking the rural', p.421.

20. Venn et al., 'Researching European "alternative" food networks'.
21. The case studies ranged from a farm shop selling locally grown and processed products, through box delivery schemes, to a community supported agriculture scheme where consumers participate directly in growing their food.
22. Carol Morris and Craig Young, 'New geographies of agro-food chains: an analysis of UK quality assurance schemes', in Alex Hughes and Suzanne Reimer (eds) *Geographies of Commodity Chains* (London: Routledge, 2004) pp. 83–101.

Chapter 15 Dirty Cows: Perceptions of BSE/vCJD *Bruce Scholten*

1. Anon., 'Alzheimer's "seeded" like mad cow disease', *New Scientist*, 30 September 2006.
2. My study focused on how consumer reflections on risks such as BSE materialized in their choice of organic or local foods. Seattle, in northwest USA was chosen because of its similarity to the San Francisco Bay Area as an organic growth pole. Newcastle in northeast UK was chosen to benchmark Seattle data because of its familiarity with food scares. Academics, firefighters and motor-cyclists were targeted to represent a range of relations to risks in food and daily activities. The chief quantitative instrument was a 60 question food and risk survey (www.durham.ac.uk/b.a.scholten), which gathered 226 surveys from Newcastle and 178 from Seattle, totalling 404. Qualitative approaches included focus groups, and additional ethnographic or qualitative data was gleaned from individual interviews, and comments written in survey margins. Quotes perti-nent to our theme of how consumers construct BSE as matter out of place are presented here.
3. For more detail on the study, see Bruce A. Scholten, 'Firefighters in the UK and the US: risk perception of local and organic food', *Scottish Geographical Journal*, vol. 122, no. 2, June 2006, pp.130–48. See also Bruce A. Scholten, 'Motorcyclists in the USA and the UK: risk perception of local and organic food', in Georgina Holt and Matt Reed, *Sociological Perspectives of Organic Agriculture: from Pioneer to Policy* (Wallingford: CABI, July 2006) pp. 107–25.
4. Hugh Pennington, 'The English disease', *London Review of Books*, vol. 22, no. 24, 14 December 2000. See also Hugh Pennington, *When Food Kills: BSE, E. coli, and Disaster Science* (Oxford: Oxford University Press, 2006).
5. Bruce A. Scholten, 'BSE-hurt Brits to start exporting beef', *Hoard's Dairyman*, 25 April 1999. This understanding of the origins of scrapie, BSE and vCJD is the consensus of all knowledgeable observers I have asked, including a former secretary of the World Health Organization (WHO).
6. Anon., 'Hoard's has heard: BSE costs Washington $4.4 billion', *Hoard's Dairyman*, 10 November 2006.
7. J. Gerald Collee, Ray Bradley and Paweł P. Liberski, 'Variant CJD (vCJD) and bovine spongiform encephalopathy (BSE): 10 and 20 years on: part 2', *Folia Neuropathology*, vol. 44, no. 2, 2006, pp. 102–10.
8. John Collinge and Michael P. Alpers, 'Incubation period of human prion disease: author's reply', *The Lancet*, vol. 368, no. 9539, 9–15 September 2006, pp. 914–15.
9. Elizabeth Weise, 'Consumers may have a beef with cattle feed', *USA Today*, 9 June 2003.
10. Sarah Whatmore, *Hybrid Geographies: Natures, Cultures, Spaces* (London: Sage, 2002) p. 163.

11. Mary, Douglas, *Purity and Danger: An Analysis of Concepts of Pollution and Taboo* (London: Routledge, 1966) Preface to Routledge Classics edition, 2002, p. xvii.
12. Douglas, *Purity and Danger*, pp. xviii–xix.
13. Douglas, *Purity and Danger*, p. xix.
14. Douglas, *Purity and Danger*, p. x–xi.
15. Douglas, *Purity and Danger*, p. xi.
16. Douglas, *Purity and Danger*, p. xi.
17. Douglas, *Purity and Danger*, p. xi.
18. Douglas, *Purity and Danger*, p. xiii.
19. Just as Samuel Huntington's influential book *The Clash of Civilizations and the Remaking of the World Order* (New York: Simon & Schuster, 1996) shows that religion remains a force in international relations, it is premature to say that secularism has trumped previous ideas on magic, mythology or religion linked to ideas of purity and danger in food systems.
20. BBC Radio 4 news, 6.15 p.m. Thursday 11 January 2007. Tony Blair's government opined that the prospect of animal/human embryos would meet widespread public opposition.
21. Douglas, *Purity and Danger*, p. xix.
22. Mark Tester, 'The dangerously polarized debate on genetic modification', *British Food Journal*, vol. 103, no. 11, 2001, pp. 785–90. Traditional cattle and plant breeding 'limited modifications to those that occur between closely-related organisms', writes Tester, but in new technologies, 'genes can also be transferred between any two organisms (including between a plant and an organism from another kingdom).'
23. Douglas, *Purity and Danger*, pp. 66–7.
24. Douglas, *Purity and Danger*, p. xix.
25. See Ulrich Beck, *Risk Society: Towards a New Modernity* (London: Sage, 1992, first published 1986). See also Ulrich Beck, Anthony Giddens and Scott Lash, *Reflexive Modernization: Politics, Tradition and Aesthetics in the Modern Social Order* (Cambridge: Polity Press, 1994, reprinted 2004).
26. Internationally, Ghana refused British beef in the late-1990s, fearing BSE would contaminate its food supply. In the UK, BSE ruined the credibility of the Ministry of Agriculture, Fisheries and Forests, and its mantle passed to supermarkets, the new Food Standards Agency and a Department for Environment, Food and Rural Affairs. Neither FSA nor DEFRA mention farms in their titles, a slap at agribusiness perceived responsible for defiling the food chain to the detriment of consumers. See Terry K. Marsden, Andrew Flynn and Michelle Harrison, *Consuming Interests: The Social Provision of Foods* (London: UCL Press, 2000) pp.180–201. See also Kevin Morgan, Terry Marsden and Jonathan Murdoch, *Worlds of Food: Place, Power, and Provenance in the Food Chain* (Oxford, Oxford University Press, 2006).
27. Jonathan Murdoch and Mara Miele, 'Back to nature: changing worlds of production in the food system', *Sociologia Ruralis*, vol. 39, no. 4, 1999, pp. 465–83.
28. Peter Atkins and Ian Bowler, *Food in Society: Economy, Culture, Geography* (London: Arnold, 2001).
29. Patricia Caplan, 'Eating British beef with confidence: a consideration of consumers', in P. Caplan (ed.) *Risk Revisited* (London: Pluto Press, 2000) pp. 114–25.

30. Samuel Fromartz, *Organic, Inc.: Natural Foods and How They Grew* (New York: Harcourt, 2006) pp. 150, 164.
31. Douglas, *Purity and Danger* in Deborah Lupton, *Risk* (London: Routledge, 1999, reprinted 2003).
32. Scholten, 'Firefighters', Figure 1, p. 132.
33. Plague, staphylococcus, and West Nile virus were also listed to test reflection on risks. Several people seemed to object to the inclusion of these as red herrings, including Carmen, an academic who wrote that some 'risks listed are not directly related to the food system'. However, other respondents indicated suspicion that intensive farming was one cause of global warming, which in turn spreads tropical diseases such as WNV, and could also be implicated with contagions such as plague or staphylococcus. Certainly, agribusiness overuse of antibiotics has been linked in a vicious circle with increasing resistance of dangerous micro-organisms to drugs to combat them.
34. Edward E. Morse, 'Where's the beef?' *Creighton Lawyer*, Creighton University, Fall, 2006, p. 17. On the fact that US beef sales rise since 2003 BSE scare, see Http://law.creighton.edu/pdf/publications/morse1.pdf.
35. Lupton, *Risk*, p. 171.
36. Lupton *Risk*, pp. 164–5.
37. Kit Oldham, 'First USA case of mad cow disease', *HistoryLink*, 4 February 2004, Www.historylink.org/essays/output.cfm?file_id=5650
38. Douglas, *Purity and Danger*, p. 196.
39. Douglas, *Purity and Danger*, p. 11.
40. Jill J. McCluskey, Matthew L. Moore and Thomas I. Wahl (forthcoming) *Consumer Response to a BSE Discovery in Washington State*, Washington State University, IMPACT Technical Paper. For another look at BSE in the UK see Patrick van Zwanenberg and Erik Millston, *BSE: Risk, Science and Governance* (Oxford: Oxford University Press, 2005)

References

Ackerley, Lisa (1994) 'Consumer awareness of food hygiene and food poisoning', *Environmental Health*, March, pp. 69–74

Acton, William (1857) *The Functions and Disorders of the Reproductive Organs in Youth, in Adult Age, and in Advanced Life: Considered in their Physiological, Social and Psychological Relations*, London: John Churchill

Agamben, Giorgio (1998) *Homo Sacer: Sovereign Power and Bare Life*, Chicago: University of Chicago Press

Akrich, Madelaine (1992) 'The de-scription of technical objects', in Wiebe Bijker and John Law (eds) *Shaping Technology/Building Society: Studies in Sociotechnical Change*, Cambridge, MA: The MIT Press

Allen, Michelle (2007) *Cleansing the City: Sanitary Geographies in Victorian London*, Athens, OH: Ohio University Press

Amato, Joseph A. (2000) *Dust: A History of the Small and Invisible*, Berkeley: University of California Press

American Association for the Advancement of Science (2000) 'The yuck response', vol. 290, no. 5492, 27 October www.sciencemag.org/content/vol290/ issue5492/r-samples.dtl

Anderson, Amanda (1993) *Tainted Souls and Painted Faces: The Rhetoric of Fallenness in Victorian Culture*, Ithaca: Cornell University Press

Anderson, Bridget (2000) *Doing the Dirty Work: The Global Politics of Domestic Labour*, London: Zed Books

Anderson, Warwick (1995) 'Excremental colonialism: public health and the poetics of pollution', *Critical Inquiry*, vol. 21, pp. 640–69

Anon. (n.d.) *Coral Gables: An Exceptional City*, brochure published by the city manager of Coral Gables http://64.233.187.104/search?q=cache:Z–4k1RVfao0J: www.citybeautiful.net/CGWeb/documents/city_manager_docs/CGAnnualReport 04_05.pdf+%22city+of+miami%22+sex+dirt&hl=en&gl=us&ct=clnk&cd=3, accessed 1 August 2006

Anon. (1848) 'What are the crows' nests for? Ordnance Survey of the metropolis', *Builder*, 17 June, pp. 291–2

Anon. (1848) 'Ordnance Survey of London and the environs', *Illustrated London News*, 24 June

Anon. (1848) 'The trigonometrical survey of London', *The Times*, 4 November, p. 5

Anon. [Thomas Vincent] (1852) *Some Account of St Mary's Home for Penitents at Wantage … by the Chaplain*, Oxford: John Henry Parker, 2nd edition

Anon. (1853) *A Proposal for the Establishment of a Female Penitentiary in Norfolk or Suffolk in Connexion with the Church Penitentiary Association*, Norwich: Charles Muskett

Anon. (1987) 'Aids sufferer haunted bars in war against homosexuals' *The Times*, 11 July.

Anon. (1987) 'Gay cruiser who strangled four men in a "cold rage" – Michael Lupo', *Guardian*, 11 July

Anon. (1987) 'Victim helped detectives capture killer on pub dance floor', *Guardian*, 11 July

Anon. (1990) 'Man killed male lover who said he had Aids', *Independent*, 15 February

Anon. (1990) 'Masochistic homosexual was kicked and punched to death', *Independent*, 15 March

Anon. (2005) 'Comment on proposal could send sex offenders outside the Lawrence city limits', by Scott Rothschild, *Lawrence Journal World*, Tuesday, 1 November 2005, http://www2.ljworld.com/news/2005/nov/01/proposal_could_send_sex_offenders_outside_lawrence/?sexual_predator_law#comments, accessed 9 September 2006

Anon. (2006) 'Alzheimer's "seeded" like mad cow disease', *New Scientist*, 30 September

Anon. (2006) 'Hoard's has heard: BSE costs Washington $4.4 billion', *Hoard's Dairyman*, 10 November 2006

Aries, Philippe (1974) *Western Attitudes Toward Death: From the Middle Ages to the Present*, Translated by Patricia M. Ranum, Baltimore: Johns Hopkins University Press
(1981) *The Hour of our Death*, translated by Helen Weaver, New York: Alfred A. Knopf

Atkins, Peter and Ian Bowler (2001) *Food in Society: Economy, Culture, Geography*, London: Arnold

Attar, Dena (1990) *Wasting Girls' Time: The History and Politics of Home Economics*, London: Virago Press

Avila, Eric (2004) *Popular Culture in the Age of White Flight: Fear and Fantasy in Suburban Los Angeles*, Berkeley: University of California Press

Bachelard, Gaston (1964) *The Poetics of Space*, New York: Orion Press

Back, Les (1996) *New Ethnicities and Urban Culture*, London: UCL Press
(1998) 'Inside out: racism, class and masculinity in the inner city and the English suburbs', *New Formations*, vol. 33, pp. 59–76

Baeten, Guy (2002) 'Hypochondriac geographies of the city and the new urban dystopia', *CITY: Analysis of Urban Trends, Theory, Culture, Policy, Action*, vol. 6, no. 1, April, pp. 103–15

Bakker, Isabella and Stephen Gill (eds) (2003) *Power, Production and Social Reproduction: Human In/security in the Global Political Economy*, Basingstoke: Palgrave Macmillan

Ball, Allan (2000–2005) *Six Feet Under. Episode One: The Pilot*, Home Box Office: United States of America

Ball, Stephen J. (2003) *Class Strategies and the Education Market*, London: RoutledgeFalmer

Barbara, Anna and Anthony Perliss (2006) *Invisible Architecture: Experiencing Places through the Sense of Smell*, Milan: Skira

Barbosa, Lívia (2006) 'Cultura, consumo e identidade: limpeza e poluição na sociedade Brasileira contemporânea', in Lívia Barbosa and Colin Campbell, *Cultura, Consumo e Identidade*, Rio de Janeiro: Fundação Getulio Vargas

Barmé, Scot (1993) *Luang Wichit Watanagan and the Creation of a Thai Identity*, Singapore: Institute of Southeast Asian Studies

Barros, Ricardo Paes de et al. (n.d.) *O trabalho doméstico infanto-juvenil no Brasil*, www.ilo.org/public/english/standards/ipec/publ/policy/papers/brasil/oitrbarros.pdf, accessed 15 December 2006

Barton, Nicholas (1962) *The Lost Rivers of London*, London: Phoenix House, reprinted in 1992 by Historical Publications

Bashford, Alison (1998) *Purity and Pollution: Gender, Embodiment and Victorian Medicine*, New York: St Martin's Press

Baudrillard, Jean (1993) *Symbolic Exchange and Death*, translated by Iain Hamilton Grant, London: Sage Publications

(1996) *The System of Objects*, translated by James Benedict, London: Verso

Bauer, Laura (2006) 'Houses off-limits to sexual predators: a planned Lenexa subdivision will ban registered sex offenders from buying there,' *The Kansas City Star*, Tuesday 13 June, http://www.kansascity.com/mld/kansascity/news/local/ 14804143.htm

Bauman, Zygmunt (2004) *Wasted Lives: Modernity and its Outcasts*, Oxford: Polity

(2005) *Liquid Life*, Cambridge: Polity

Baumgartner, Mary P. (1988) *The Moral Order of a Suburb*, Oxford: Oxford University Press

Beaumont, Catriona (2000) 'Citizens not feminists: the boundary negotiated between citizenship and feminism by mainstream women's organisations in England, 1928–39', *Women's History Review*, vol. 9, no. 2, pp. 411–29

Beck, Ulrich (1992) *Risk Society: Towards a New Modernity*, London: Sage, first published 1986

Beck, Ulrich, Anthony Giddens and Scott Lash (1994) *Reflexive Modernization: Politics, Tradition and Aesthetics in the Modern Social Order*, Cambridge: Polity Press, reprinted 2004

Bell, Colin and Howard Newby (1971) *Community Studies*, London: Allen & Unwin

Bell, Michael M. (1994) *'Childerley': Nature and Morality in a Country Village*, Chicago: University of Chicago Press

Bell, Shannon (1994) *Reading, Writing, and Rewriting the Prostitute Body*, Bloomington, IN: Indiana University Press

Bennett, William (1850) *Letters to my Children on Moral Subjects*, London: W. J. Cleaver

Benton, Ted (1994) 'Biology and social theory in the environmental debate', in Ted Benton and Michael Redclift (eds) *Social Theory and the Environment*, London: Routledge, pp. 28–50

Berlant, Lauren (1997) *The Queen of America Goes to Washington City: Essays on Sex and Citizenship*, Durham: Duke University Press

Berner, Boel (1998) 'The meaning of cleaning: the creation of harmony and hygiene in the home', *History and Technology*, vol. 14, pp. 312–52

Bevan, William (1843) *Prostitution in the Borough of Liverpool: A Lecture Delivered in the Music Hall, June, 3, 1843*, Liverpool: B. Smith

Binnie, Jon (1995) 'Trading places: consumption, sexuality and the production of queer space', in David Bell and Gill Valentine (eds) *Mapping Desire: Geographies of Sexualities*, London: Routledge

REFERENCES

Bird, Caroline (1979) *The Two-Paycheck Marriage*, New York: Rawson Wade

Blythman, Joanna (2004) *Shopped: The Shocking Power of British Supermarkets*, London: Harper Perennial

Boonchalaksi, Wathinee and Philip Guest (1994) *Prostitution in Thailand*, Bangkok: Institute for Population and Social Research, Mahidol University

Boonmathaya, Rattana (1997) 'Contested Concepts of Development in Rural Northeastern Thailand', Ph.D. thesis, University of Washington

Bose, Christine, Philip Bereano and Mary Malloy (1984) 'Household technology and the social construction of housework', *Technology and Culture*, vol. 25, no.1, January, pp. 53–82

Bourdieu, Pierre (1977) *Outline of a Theory of Practice*, Cambridge: Polity
   (1972) *Esboço de uma teoria da prática: Precedido de três estudos de etnologia Kabila*, Oeiras: Celta, reprinted 2002

Boydston, Jeanne (1990) *Home and Work: Housework, Wages and Ideology of Labor in the Early Republic*, New York: Oxford University Press

Brewis, Joanna and Stephen Linstead (2000) *Sex, Work and Sex Work*, London: Routledge

Bristow, Edward J. (1977) *Vice and Vigilance: Purity Movements in Britain since 1700*, Totowa: Rowman & Littlefield

Brody, Alyson (2003) 'Agents of change: struggles and successes of Thai women migrants in Bangkok', unpublished Ph.D. thesis, London: School of Oriental and African Studies

Brown, Paul (1987) 'Police raid gay pub', *Guardian*, 26 January

Buchli, Victor and Gavin Lucas (eds) (2001) *Archaeologies of the Contemporary Past*, London: Routledge

Burke, Timothy (1996) *Lifebuoy Men and Lux Women: Commodification, Consumption and Cleanliness in Modern Zimbabwe*, London: Leicester University Press

Burnett, John (1989) *Plenty and Want: A Social History of Food in England from 1815 to the Present Day*, London: Routledge, 3rd edition

Busch, Akiko (1999) *Geography of Home: Writings on Where We Live*, New York: Princeton Architectural Press

Bushman, Richard L. and Claudia L. Bushman (1988) 'The early history of cleanliness in America', *Journal of American History*, vol. 74, no. 4, pp. 1213–38

Butler, Tim with Garry Robson (2003) *London Calling: The Middle Classes and the Re-making of Inner London*, Oxford: Berg

Callon, Michel and Bruno Latour (1992) 'Don't throw the baby out with the Bath school! A reply to Collins and Yearley', in Andrew Pickering (ed.) *Science as Practice and Culture*, Chicago: Chicago University Press, pp. 343–68

Callon, Michel and John Law (1995) 'Agency and the hybrid collectif', *South Atlantic Quarterley*, vol. 94, pp. 481–508

Campkin, Ben (2007) 'Ornament from grime: David Adjaye's dirty house, the "architectural aesthetic of recycling" and the gritty Brits', in Ben Campkin and Paul Dobraszczyk (eds) 'Architecture and dirt', *The Journal of Architecture*, special issue, vol. 12, no. 4, September

Campkin, Ben and Paul Dobraszczyk (eds) (2007) 'Special issue: architecture and dirt', *The Journal of Architecture*, vol. 12, no. 4, September http://www.tandf.co.uk/journals/routledge/13602365.html

Caplan, Patricia (2000) 'Eating British beef with confidence: a consideration of consumers', in Patricia Caplan (ed.) *Risk Revisited*, London: Pluto Press, pp. 114–25

Carter, Thomas Thellusson (1856) *Mercy for the Fallen: Two Sermons in Aid of the House of Mercy, Clewer. To Which is Added an Appeal for the Completion of the House*, London: Joseph Masters

(1852) *To a Friend of the Church of England House of Mercy, Clewer*, Windsor: n.p.

Chang, Grace (2000) *Disposable Domestics: Immigrant Women Workers in the Global Economy*, Cambridge, MA: South End Press

Chapkis, Wendy (1997) *Live Sex Acts: Women Performing Erotic Labour*, London: Cassell

Chouwilai, Jaded (2000) 'Life after redundancy: the effects of the termination of Thai workers', in Alyson Brody (ed.) *Uniting Voices: Asian Women Workers' Search for Recognition in the Global Marketplace*, Bangkok: Committee for Asian Women, pp. 85–98

Chute, David (1981) 'John Sayles: designated writer', *Film Comment*, vol. 17, May/June, pp. 54–9

Cieraad, Irene (2002) '"Out of my kitchen!" Architecture, gender and domestic efficiency', *Journal of Architecture*, vol. 7, autumn, pp. 263–79

Clapson, Mark (1998) *Invincible Green Suburbs, Brave New Towns*, Manchester: Manchester University Press

(2003) *Suburban Century*, Oxford: Berg

Classen, Constance, David Howes and Anthony Synnott (1994) *Aroma: The Cultural History of Smell*, London: Routledge

Cleaver, Paul W. (1996) 'Dealing with death: the Pakeha treatment of death, 1859–1910', unpublished MA thesis, Victoria, University of Wellington

Cloke, Paul and Owain Jones (2002) *Tree Cultures*, Oxford: Berg

Cloke, Paul and Jo Little (eds) (1997) *Contested Countryside Cultures*, London: Routledge

Close, Colonel Sir Charles (1969) *The Early Years of the Ordnance Survey*, Newton Abbot: David & Charles

Cobbett, William (1979) *Cottage Economy*, Oxford: Oxford University Press, first published 1922

Cohen, William A. (2005) 'Introduction: locating filth', in William A. Cohen and Ryan Johnson (eds) *Filth: Dirt, Disgust, and Modern Life*, Minneapolis: University of Minnesota Press

Cohen, William A. and Ryan Johnson (eds) (2005) *Filth: Dirt, Disgust, and Modern Life*, Minneapolis: University of Minnesota Press

Collee, J. Gerald, Ray Bradley and Paweł P. Liberski (2006) 'Variant CJD (vCJD) and bovine spongiform encephalopathy (BSE): 10 and 20 years on: part 2', *Folia Neuropathology*, vol. 44, no. 2, pp. 102–10

Collinge, John and Michael P. Alpers (2006) 'Incubation period of human prion disease: author's reply', *The Lancet*, vol. 368, no. 9539, 9–15 September, pp. 914–15

Connolly, T. W. J. *The History of the Corps of Royal Sappers and Miners*, 2 vols (London: Longman, Brown, Green and Longmans, 1855)

Coole, Diana (2005) 'Dialectical realism and existential phenomenology: a dialogue', *New Formations*, vol. 58, pp. 121–32

Corbin, Alain (1986) *The Foul and the Fragrant: Odour and the French Imagination*, Cambridge, MA: Harvard University Press

Cousins, Mark (1996) 'The ugly', *AA Files*, no. 28

Cowan, Ruth S. (1976) 'Two washes in the morning and a bridge party at night: the American housewife between the wars', *Women Studies*, vol. 3, pp. 147–72

(1983) *More Work for Mother: The Ironies of Household Technology from the Open Hearth to the Microwave*, New York: Basic Books

Cox, Rosie (2006) *The Servant Problem: Paid Domestic Work in a Global Economy*, London: I.B.Tauris

(2005) 'What about the dirt in dirty work? Exploring the status of domestic employment', paper presented at the Association of American Geographers Annual Meeting, Denver, March

Creed, Barbara (1993) *Monstrous-Feminine: Film, Feminism, Psychoanalysis*, London: Routledge

Crowe, David (n.d.) 'Katrina: God's judgment on America', http://www.beliefnet.com/story/174/story_17439_1.html, accessed 8 September 2006

Culler, Jonathan (1985) 'Junk and rubbish: a semiotic approach', *Diacritics*, vol. 15, no. 3, fall, p. 2

Curtis, Valerie and Adam Biran (2001) 'Dirt, disgust, and disease: is hygiene in our genes?' *Perspectives in Biology and Medicine*, vol. 44, no. 1, pp. 17–31

Da Matta, Roberto (1987) *A casa e a rua: espaço, cidadania, mulher e morte no Brasil*, Rio de Janeiro: Editora Guanabara

Dant, Tim and David Bowles (2003) 'Dealing with dirt: servicing and repairing cars', *Sociological Research Online*, vol. 8, no. 2 http://www.socresonline.org.uk/8/2/dant.html

Darlington, Ida (1969) 'Edwin Chadwick and the first large-scale Ordnance Survey of London', *Transactions of London and Middlesex Archaeological Society*, vol. 22, pp. 58–63

Darlington, Ida and James Howgego (1964) *Printed Maps of London, c.1553–1850*, London: George Philip & Son

Davidson, Caroline (1982) *A Woman's Work is Never Done: A History of Housework in the British Isles 1650–1950*, London: Chatto & Windus

Davison, Charlie, George Davey Smith and Stephen Frankel (1991) 'Lay epidemiology and the prevention paradox: implications of coronary candidacy for health education', *Sociology of Health and Illness,* vol. 13, no. 1, pp. 1–19

Day, Graham and Jonathan Murdoch (1993) 'Locality and community: coming to terms with place', *The Sociological Review,* vol. 41, pp. 82–111

de Certeau, Michel (1984) *The Practice of Everyday Life*, translated by Steven Rendall, Berkeley: University of California Press, first published 1974

Dench, Geoff, Kate Gavron and Michael Young (2006) *The New East End: Kinship, Race and Conflict*, London: Profile Books

Departamento Intersindical de Estatística e Estudos Econômicos (2006) *O emprego doméstico: uma ocupação tipicamente feminina*, Secretaria Internacional do Trabalho, Brasil www.planalto.gov.br/seppir/acoes_afirmativas/genero/Trabalho%20 Doméstico -DIEESE%20e%20OIT.pdf

DeVault, Marjorie (1991) *Feeding the Family*, Chicago: University of Chicago Press

Dickens, Peter (1996) *Reconstructing Nature: Alienation, Emancipation and the Division of Labour*, London: Routledge

Douglas, Gordon (1968) *The Detective* (DVD)

Douglas, Mary (1966) *Purity and Danger: An Analysis of Concepts of Pollution and Taboo*, London: Routledge & Kegan Paul, first published 1966, reprinted 2002

(1975) *Implicit Meaning: Essays in Anthropology by Mary Douglas*, London: Routledge & Kegan Paul

(2005) 'How I got to where I am: from anthropology to "literary criticism", *Mary Douglas Seminar Series*, Institute of Archaeology, unpublished seminar paper, University College London, 26 May

Douglas, Mary and David Hull (eds) (1992) *How Classification Works: Nelson Goodman among the Social Sciences*, Edinburgh: Edinburgh University Press

Dumont, Luis (1992) *Homo hierarchicus: o sistema de castas e suas implicações*, translated by Carlos Alberto da Fonseca, São Paulo: Editora Universidade de São Paulo

Duncan, James S. and Nancy G. Duncan (2004) *Landscapes of Privilege*, London: Routledge

DuPuis, E. Madeleine (2002) *Nature's Perfect Food: How Milk Became America's Drink*, New York: New York University Press

Dyer, Richard (1993) *The Matter of Images: Essays on Representation,* London: Routledge

Ehrenreich, Barbara (2003) 'Maid to order', in Barbara Ehrenreich and Arlie Hochschild (eds) *Global Woman: Nannies, Maids and Sex Workers in the Global Economy*, London: Granta Books

Ehrenreich, Barbara and Arlie Hochschild (eds) (2003) *Global Woman: Nannies, Maids and Sex Workers in the New Economy*, London: Granta Books

Eleb, Monique and A. Dabare (1995) *L'Invention de l'habitation moderne: Paris, 1880–1914*, Paris, Hazan

Elias, Norbert (1979) *The Civilizing Process*, Oxford: Blackwell

Ellin, Nan (1996) *Postmodern Urbanism*, Oxford: Blackwell

Enticott, Gareth (2000) 'Heterogeneous ruralities: the place of nature and community in the differentiated countryside', unpublished Ph.D., Cardiff: Cardiff University

(2001) 'Calculating nature: the case of badgers, tuberculosis and cattle', *Journal of Rural Studies*, vol. 17, no.2, pp.149–64

(2003) 'Risking the rural: nature, morality and the consumption of unpasteurised milk', *Journal of Rural Studies*, vol. 19, no. 4, pp. 411–24

(2003) 'Lay immunology, local foods and rural identity: defending unpasteurised milk in England', *Sociologia Ruralis*, vol. 43, vol. 3, pp. 257–70

Fardon, Richard (1999) *Mary Douglas: An Intellectual Biography*, London: Routledge

(2007) 'Obituary: Dame Mary Douglas', *Guardian*, Friday 18 May

Featherstone, Mike (1991) *Consumer Culture and Postmodernism*, London: Sage

(1996) *Cultura de Consumo e Pós-modernidade*, São Paulo: Nobel

Fessler, Daniel M. T. and Kevin J. Haley (2006) 'Guarding the perimeter: the outside-inside dichotomy in disgust and bodily experience', *Cognition and Emotion*, vol. 20, no. 1, pp. 3–19

Filler, Daniel M. (2004) 'Silence and the racial dimension of Megan's law', *Iowa Law Review*, vol. 89, pp. 1535–94. Available at SSRN: http://ssrn.com/abstract=648261

Finnegan, Ruth (1998) *Tales of the City*, Cambridge: Cambridge University Press

Fischler, Claude (1980) 'Food habits, social change and the nature/culture dilemma', *Social Science Information*, vol. 19, no. 6, pp. 937–53

(1988) 'Food, self and identity', *Social Science Information*, vol. 27, no. 2, pp. 275–92

Folbre, Nancy (1994) *Who Pays for the Kids: Gender and the Structures of Constraint*, London: Routledge

REFERENCES

Forbes, Alexander Penrose (1864) *A Sermon Preached at the Chapel Royal, Savoy Street, Strand, Before the Church Penitentiary Association on Thursday, May 12, 1864*, London: Spottiswoode & Co.

Forty, Adrian (1986) *Objects of Desire: Design and Society since 1750*, London: Thames & Hudson

(2000) *Words and Buildings: A Vocabulary of Modern Architecture*, London: Thames & Hudson

Foucault, Michel (1975) *Discipline and Punish: The Birth of the Prison*, Harmondsworth: Penguin

Frederick, Christine (1920) *Household Engineering: Scientific Management in the Home*, Chicago: American School for Home Economics

Freeman-Longo, Robert E. (2000) 'Revisiting Megan's law and sex-offender registration: prevention or problem', *American Probation and Parole Association*, http://www.appa-net.org/revisitingmegan.pdf, accessed 5 September 2006

Freyre, Gilberto (1956) *The Masters and the Slaves (Casa Grande and Senzala): A Study in the Development of Brazilian Civilization*, New York: Alfred A. Knopf

(1987) *The Mansions and the Shanties (Sobrados e Mucambos): The Making of Modern Brazil*, Berkeley: University of California Press

Fromartz, Samuel (2006) *Organic, Inc.: Natural Foods and How They Grew*, New York: Harcourt

Fuller, Theodore and Paul Lightfoot (1984) 'Circular migration in northeastern Thailand', in Han ten Brummelhuis and Jeremy Kemp (eds) *Strategies and Structures in Thai Society*, Amsterdam: University of Amsterdam, pp. 85–94

Gallop, Jane (1982) *Feminism and Psychoanalysis: The Daughter's Seduction*, London: Macmillan

Gandy, Matthew (1999) 'The Paris sewers and the rationalization of urban space', *Transactions of the Institute of British Geographers*, vol. 24, no. 1, pp. 23–44

Gandy, Matthew (2001) 'Review of Martin V. Melosi *The Sanitary City: Urban Infrastructure in America from Colonial Times to the Present*', H-Urban, H-Net Reviews, February. http://www.h-net.org/reviews/showrev.cgi?path= 13074983817017

Ger, Guliz and Baskin Yenicioglu (2004) 'Clean and dirty: playing with boundaries of consumer's safe havens', *Advances in Consumer Research*, vol. 31, pp. 462–7

German, Lindsey (1989) *Sex, Class and Socialism*, London: Bookmarks

Gershuny, Michael, Jonathan M. Godwin and Sally Jones (1994) 'The domestic labour revolution: a process of lagged adaptation', in Michael Anerson, Frank Bechhofer and Jonathan Gershuny (eds) *The Social and Political Economy of the Household*, Oxford: Oxford University Press

Giddens, Anthony (1991) *Modernity and Self-Identity: Self and Society in the Late Modern Age*, Cambridge: Polity Press

Gilbert, Pamela K. (2004) *Mapping the Victorian Social Body*, Albany: SUNY Press

Gilbreth, Lillian (1954) *Management in the Home: Happier Living through Saving Time and Energy*, New York: Dodd, Mead

Godwin, Jonathan M., Michael Gershuny and Sally Jones (1994) 'The domestic labour revolution: a process of lagged adaptation', in Michael Anderson, Frank Bechhofer and Jonathan Gershuny (eds) *The Social and Political Economy of the Household*, Oxford: Oxford University Press

Goldstein, Sidney (1986) *Migration in Thailand: A 25-Year Review*, Honolulu: Hawaii East–West Center

Goldstein, Sidney and Alice Goldstein (1980) *Differentials in Repeat Return Migration in Thailand*, Bangkok: Chulalongkorn University Institute of Population Studies

Goldstein, Sidney and Pichit Pitaktepsombati (1974) *Migration and Urban Growth in Thailand: An Exploration of Interrelationships among Origin, Recency and Frequency of Moves*, Bangkok: Chulalongkorn University Institute of Population Studies

Goodman, David (2003) 'Editorial: the quality "turn" and alternative food practices: reflections and agenda', *Journal of Rural Studies*, vol. 19, no. 1, pp. 1–7

—— (2004) 'Rural Europe redux? Reflections on alternative agro-food networks and paradigm change', *Sociologia Ruralis*, vol. 44, no. 1, pp. 3–16

Gorer, G. (1965) *Death, Grief and Mourning in Contemporary Britain*, London: Cresset

Gould, Paul (1998) 'The love that dare not forget its brand name', *Financial Times*, 7 March, p. 22

Griffiths, Paul and Mark Jenner (2000) *Londinopolis: Essays in the Social and Cultural History of Early Modern London*, Manchester: Manchester University Press

Grosz, Elizabeth (1989) *Sexual Subversions: Three French Feminists*, Sydney: Allen & Unwin

—— (1992) 'Bodies-cities', in Beatriz Colomina (ed.) *Sexuality and Space* (Princeton: Princeton University Press) pp. 241–54

—— (1994) *Volatile Bodies: Toward a Corporeal Feminism*, Bloomington: University of Indiana Press

Gustafson, Per (2001) 'Meanings of place: everyday experience and theoretical conceptualizations', *Journal of Environmental Psychology*, vol. 21, no. 1, pp. 5–16

Habenstein, Robert W. (1972) 'Sociology of occupations: the case of the American funeral director', in Arnold Rose (ed.) *Human Behaviour and Social Processes*, London: Routledge & Kegan Paul, pp. 225–46

Hacking, Ian (1999) *The Social Construction of What?* Cambridge, MA: Harvard University Press

Halliday, Stephen (1999) *The Great Stink of London: Sir Joseph Bazalgette and the Cleansing of the Victorian Metropolis*, Stroud: Sutton Publishing Ltd

Hamlin, Christopher (1998) *Public Health and Social Justice in the Age of Chadwick: Britain, 1800–1854*, Cambridge: Cambridge University Press

Hamnett, Chris (2003) *Unequal City: London in the Global Arena*, London: Routledge

Harley, John Brian (1988) 'Maps, knowledge and power', in Stephen Daniels and Denis Cosgrove (eds) *The Iconography of Landscape: Chapters on the Symbolic Representation, Design and Use of Past Environments*, Cambridge: Cambridge University Press

Harvey, David (1989) *The Urban Experience*, Oxford: Blackwell

Haselden, Rupert (1991) 'Gay abandon: many gay men now see Aids not as death but destiny', *Guardian*, 7 September

Hayes, Kevin (2001) 'Alice Guy's *The Pit and the Pendulum*', *The Edgar Allan Poe Review*, vol. 2, no. 1, Spring, pp. 38–42 http://www.lv.psu.edu/PSA/EAPRspring 2001.pdf, accessed August 2006

Hettinger, Lynn (2004) 'Brand culture and branded workers: service work and aesthetic labour in fashion retail', *Consumption, Markets and Culture*, vol. 7, no. 2, pp. 165–84

Hilton, Boyd (1988) *The Age of Atonement: The Influence of Evangelicalism on Social and Economic Thought, 1795–1865*, Oxford: Clarendon Press

Hochschild, Arlie (1983) *The Second Shift*, London: Penguin, reprinted 2003

(1997) *The Time Bind: When Work becomes Home and Home becomes Work*, New York: Henry Holt

Hoggett, Paul (1992) 'A place for experience: a psychoanalytic perspective on boundary, identity and culture', *Environment and Planning D: Society and Space*, vol. 10, pp. 345–56

Hoigard, Cecilie and Liv Finstad (1992) *Backstreets: Prostitution, Money and Love*, University Park: The Pennsylvania State University Press

Holloway, Lewis and Moya Kneafsey (2000) 'Reading the space of the farmers' market: a preliminary investigation from the UK', *Sociologia Ruralis*, vol. 40, no. 3, pp. 285–99

(2004) 'Producing-consuming food: closeness, connectedness and rurality in four "alternative" food networks', in Lewis Holloway and Moya Kneafsey (eds) *Geographies of Rural Cultures and Societies*, London: Ashgate, pp. 262–82

Holloway, Lewis, Rosie Cox, Laura Venn, Moya Kneafsey, Elizabeth Dowler and Helena Tuomainen (2006) 'Managing sustainable farmed landscape through "alternative food networks": a case study from Italy', *Geographical Journal*, vol. 172, pp. 219–29

Holsopple, Kelly (n.d.) *Strip Club Testimony*, Minneapolis, MN: The Freedom and Justice Centre for Prostitution Resources. Retrieved on 10 January 2004 from http://www.ccv.org/images/strip_club_testimony_and_study.PDF

Hondagneu-Sotelo, Pierette (2001) *Doméstica: Immigrant Workers Cleaning and Caring in the Shadows of Affluence*, London: University of California Press

Hopkins, Debra, Linda McKie, Nick Watson and Bill Hughes (2005) 'The problem of emotion in care: contested meanings from the disabled people's movement and feminist movement', in Helena Flam and Deborah King (eds) *Emotion and Care*, London: Routledge

Horn, Pamela (2004) *The Rise and Fall of the Victorian Servant*, Stroud: Sutton Publishing, 2004

Horowitz, Tony (1994) 'Inside a "dirty MuRF": the offal part of the recycling boom', *The Wall Street Journal*, 1 December http://www.pulitzer.org/year/1995/national-reporting/works/horowitz3.html, Accessed accessed 3 July 2006

Horsfield, Margaret (1998) *Biting the Dust: The Joys of Housework*, London: Fourth Estate

Horwood, Catherine (1997) 'Housewives' choice + launching of the British version of *Good Housekeeping*, March 1922: women as consumers between the wars', *History Today*, vol. 47, no. 3, pp. 23–8

Houlbrook, Matt (2005) *Queer London: Perils and Pleasures in the Sexual Metropolis, 1918–1957*, Chicago: University of Chicago Press

'Toward a historical geography of sexuality', *Journal of Urban History*, vol. 27, 2001, pp. 497–504

Howson, Alexandra (2005) *Embodying Gender*, London: Sage

Hoy, Suellen (1995) *Chasing Dirt: The American Pursuit of Cleanliness*, New York: Oxford University Press

Hubbard, Philip (1999) *Sex and the City: Geographies of Prostitution in the Urban West*, Aldershot: Ashgate

Hughes, Christina (2002) *Women's Contemporary Lives: Within and Beyond the Mirror*, London: Routledge

Hughes, Everett Cherrington (1984) *The Sociological Eye*, New Brunswick: Transaction Books

Huntington, Samuel (1996) *The Clash of Civilizations and the Remaking of the World Order*, New York: Simon & Schuster

Ilbery, Brian and Damian Maye (2005) 'Food supply chains and sustainability: evidence from specialist food producers in the Scottish/English borders', *Land Use Policy*, vol. 22, no. 4, pp. 331–44

Jackson, Alan A. (1973) *Semi-Detached London: Suburban Development, Life and Transport, 1900–39*, London: George Allen & Unwin

Jackson, Peter (1989) *Maps of Meaning*, London, Routledge

Jagose, Annamarie, Fran Martin and Chris Healy (2003) 'At home in the suburb', in Fran Martin (ed.) *Interpreting Everyday Culture*, London: Arnold

Jeffreys, Sheila (1997) *The Idea of Prostitution*, Melbourne: Spinflex

Jenkins, Phillip (1998) *Moral Panic: Changing Concepts of the Child Molester in Modern America*, New Haven: Yale University Press

Kaïka, Maria (2004) 'Interrogating the geographies of the familiar: domesticating nature and constructing the autonomy of the modern home', *International Journal of Urban and Regional Research*, vol. 28, no. 2, pp. 265–86

(2004) *City Of Flows: Modernity, Nature And The City* (London: Routledge

Kaïka, Maria and Eric Swyngedouw (2000) 'Fetishizing the modern city: the phantasmagoria of urban technological networks', *International Journal of Urban and Regional Research*, vol. 24, no. 1, pp. 120–38

Keith, Michael (2005) *After the Cosmopolitan? Multicultural Cities and the Future of Racism*, London: Routledge

Kelley, Mike (2004) *The Uncanny*, Cologne: König

Kincaid, James R. (1998) *Erotic Innocence: The Culture of Child Molesting*, Durham: Duke University Press

Kirwan, James (2004) 'Alternative strategies in the UK agro-food system: interrogating the alterity of farmers markets', *Sociologia Ruralis*, vol. 44, no. 4, pp. 395–415

(2006) 'The interpersonal world of direct marketing: examining conventions of quality at UK farmers markets', *Journal of Rural Studies*, vol. 22, no. 3, pp. 301–12

Knorr-Cetina, Karin (1997) 'Sociality with objects: social relations in postsocial knowledge societies', *Theory, Culture and Society*, vol. 14, no. 4, pp. 1–30

Koven, Seth (2004) *Slumming: Sexual and Social Politics in Victorian London*, Princeton: Princeton University Press

Kristeva, Julia (1982) *Powers of Horror: An Essay on Abjection*, translated by L. Roudiez, New York: Columbia University Press

Lacey, Richard W. (1993) 'Food poisoning: the rise continues', *British Food Journal*, vol. 95, no. 3, pp. 25–31

Lahiji, Nadir and Daniel S. Friedman (1997) 'At the sink: architecture in abjection', in Nadir Lahiji and Daniel S. Friedman (eds) *Plumbing: Sounding Modern Architecture*, New York: Princeton Architectural Press

Lambton, Lucinda (1997) *Temples of Convenience and Chambers of Delight*, London: Pavilion Books

Laporte, Dominique (2000) *History of Shit*, translated by Nadia Benabid and Rodolphe el-Khoury, Cambridge, MA: The MIT Press

Latour, Bruno (1992) 'Where are the missing masses? A sociology of a few mundane artefacts', in Wiebe E. Bijker and John Law (eds) *Shaping Technology/Building Society*, Cambridge, MA: The MIT Press, pp. 225–58

(1993) *We Have Never Been Modern*, Hemel Hempstead: Harvester Wheatsheaf

(1994) 'Pragmatogonies', *American Behavioural Scientist*, vol. 37, no. 6, pp. 791–808

(1999) 'On recalling ANT', in John Law and John Hassard (eds) *Actor Network Theory and After*, Oxford: Blackwell Publishers/The Sociological Review, pp. 15–25

Law, John (1992) 'Notes on the theory of the actor-network: ordering, strategy and heterogeneity', *Systems Practice*, vol. 5, no. 4, pp. 379–93

(1999) 'After ANT: complexity, naming and topology', in John Law and John Hassard (eds) *Actor Network Theory and After*, Oxford: Blackwell Publishers/The Sociological Review, pp. 1–14

Lawrence, Felicity (2004) *Not on the Label: What Really Goes into the Food on your Plate*, London: Penguin

Leder, Drew (1990) *The Absent Body*, Chicago: University of Chicago Press

Lefebvre, Henri (1991) *The Production of Space*, translated by Donald Nicholson-Smith, Oxford: Blackwell, first published 1974

Liddon, Henry Parry (1862) *Active Love a Criterion of Spiritual Life: A Sermon*, London: Spottiswoode & Co

Liddell, Robert (1853) *A Pastoral Letter to the Parishioners of St Paul's, Knightsbridge, and St Barnabas', Pimlico* (London: J. T. Hayes)

(1854) *An Account of the House of Refuge in Commercial Road, Pimlico: Addressed to the Church Penitentiary Association*, London: J. H. Parker

(1854) *Christ the Caster-out of Unclean Spirits: A Sermon Preached at St Paul's, Knightsbridge, on the Fourth Sunday after Epiphany in Behalf of the Church Penitentiary Cause [on Matt. viii. 29]*, London: J. T. Hayes

(1858) *A Pastoral Letter to the Parishioners of St Paul's, Knightsbridge and St Barnabas', Pimlico*, London: J. T. Hayes

Liepins, Ruth (2000) 'New energies for an old idea: reworking approaches to "community" in contemporary rural studies – new directions in community studies', *Journal of Rural Studies*, vol. 16, no. 1, pp. 23–35

Linde-Laursen, Anders (1993) 'The nationalization of trivialities: how cleaning becomes an identity marker in the encounter of Swedes and Danes', *Ethnos*, vol. 58, nos 3–4, p. 275

List, Alfred C. C. (1861) *The Two Phases of the Social Evil*, Edinburgh: Oliver & Boyd

Lloyd, Christopher (1993) 'Pub where three murderers hunted victims', *Sunday Times*, 26 December

Logan, William B. (1995) *Dirt: The Ecstatic Skin of the Earth*, New York: Riverhead Books

Longhurst, Robyn (2001) *Bodies: Exploring Fluid Boundaries*, London: Routledge

Loureiro, Roberto Pompeu, 'Dos pasties a poltrona de couro', *Veja*, 8 November 2006

Lupton, Deborah (1995) *The Imperative of Health: Public Health and the Regulated Body*, London: Sage

(1999) *Risk*, London: Routledge, reprinted 2003

Lupton, Ellen and J. Abbott Miller (1992) 'Hygiene, cuisine and the product world of early twentieth-century America', in Jonathan Crary and Sanford Kwinter (eds) *Incorporations*, Cambridge, MA: Zone Books/The MIT Press

Lury, Celia (1996) *Consumer Culture*, Cambridge: Polity Press

Lynch, Mona (2002) 'Pedophiles and cyber-predators as contaminating forces: the language of disgust, pollution, and boundary invasions in federal debates on sex offender legislation', *Law and Social Inquiry*, vol. 27, no. 3, summer, pp. 529–67

McClary, Andrew (1980) 'Germs are everywhere: the germ threat as seen in magazine articles 1890–1920', *Journal of American Culture*, vol. 3, no. 1, pp. 33–46

McClintock, Anne (1994) *Imperial Leather: Race, Gender and Sexuality in the Colonial Contest*, London: Routledge

McCluskey, Jill J., Matthew L. Moore and Thomas I. Wahl (forthcoming) *Consumer Response to a BSE Discovery in Washington State*, Washington State University, IMPACT Technical Paper

McCracken, Grant David (1988) *Culture and Consumption: New Approaches to the Symbolic Character of Consumer Goods and Activities*, Bloomington: Indiana University Press

McDowell, Linda (1999) *Gender, Identity and Place: Understanding Feminist Geographies*, Minneapolis: University of Minnesota Press

Macek, Steve (2006) *Urban Nightmares: The Media, the Right, and the Moral Panic over the City*, Minneapolis: University of Minnesota Press

McKenna, Neil (1993) 'Fleet Street's perverse cocktail of kinky sex and serial killer', *Independent*, 20 June

Malos, Ellen (ed.) (1995) *The Politics of Housework*, Cheltenham: New Clarion Press

Marcus, Sharon (1999) *Apartment Stores: City and Home in Nineteenth-century Paris and London*, Berkeley: University of California Press

Marin, Louis (1984) *Utopics: Spatial Play*, translated by Robert A. Vollrath, London: Macmillan, first published 1973

Marsden, Terry K., Andrew Flynn and Michelle Harrison (2000) *Consuming Interests: The Social Provision of Foods*, London, UCL Press

Martens, Lydia and Sue Scott (2004) 'Domestic kitchen practices: routines, risks and reflexivity – end of award report', *Economic and Social Research Council*, Swindon (UK), pp. 1–28

(2005) 'The unbearable lightness of cleaning: representations of domestic practice and products in *Good Housekeeping Magazine* (UK) 1951–2001', *Consumers, Markets and Culture*, vol. 8, no. 4, pp. 379–402

Masters, Brian (1985) *Killing for Company: The Case of Dennis Nielsen*, London: Arrow Books

Mayhew, Henry (1968) *London Labour and the London Poor*, London: Constable

Maynard, John (1993) *Victorian Discourses on Sexuality and Religion*, Cambridge: Cambridge University Press

Medeiros, Marcelo and Rafael Osorio (2001) *Arranjos domiciliares e arranjos nucleares no Brasil: classificação e evolução de 1977 a 1998*, Brasília. Text for discussion no. 788. www.ipea.gov.br/pub/td/td_2001/td_788.pdf, accessed 15 December 2006

Meldrum, Keith C. (1994) 'Food safety: whose responsibility is it?' *PHLS Microbiology Digest*, vol. 11, pp. 194–8

Melosi, Martin V. (2000) *The Sanitary City: Urban Infrastructure in America from Colonial Times to the Present*, Baltimore: Johns Hopkins University Press

Menninghaus, Winfried (2003) *Disgust: Theory and History of a Strong Sensation*, translated by Howard Eiland and Joel Golb, Albany: SUNY Press

Metropolitan Commissions of Sewers, MCS/481 (1847 and 1848) London Metropolitan Archives, minutes of proceedings

Miller, James (1859) *Prostitution Considered in Relation to its Cause and Cure*, Edinburgh: Sutherland & Knox

Miller, William I. (1997) *The Anatomy of Disgust*, Cambridge, MA: Harvard University Press

Mills, Mary Beth (1992) 'Rural women working in Bangkok: modernity and gender vulnerability, in Penny and John Van Esterik (eds) *Gender and Development in Southeast Asia*, London: Centre for Advanced Spatial Analysis

(1993) '"We are not like our mothers": migrants, modernity and identity in Northeastern Thailand', unpublished Ph.D. thesis, Berkeley: University of California

(1997) 'Contesting the margins of Thai modernity', *American Ethnologist,* vol. 24, no. 1, pp. 37–61

(1999) *Thai Women in the Global Labour Force: Consuming Desires, Contested Selves,* New Jersey: Rutgers University Press

Mintz, Steven (1988) *Domestic Revolutions: A Social History of American Family Life,* New York: Free Press

Mohun, Arwen P. (1999) *Steam Laundries: Gender, Technology and Work in the United States and Great Britain, 1880–1940,* Baltimore: The Johns Hopkins University Press

Momsen, Janet H. (ed.) (1999) *Gender Migration and Domestic Service,* London: Routledge

Morgan, Kevin, Terry Marsden and Jonathan Murdoch (2006) *Worlds of Food: Place, Power, and Provenance in the Food Chain,* Oxford: Oxford University Press

Morris, Carol and Craig Young (2004) 'New geographies of agro-food chains: an analysis of UK quality assurance schemes', in Alex Hughes and Suzanne Reimer (eds) *Geographies of Commodity Chains,* London: Routledge, pp. 83–101

Morris, E. and J. Flyger and Company (1930) *Sanitary Funerals in New Zealand,* Wellington: Funeral Directors Association

Morse, Edward E. (2006) 'Where's the beef?' *Creighton Lawyer,* Creighton University, Fall, pp. 13–19, Http://law.creighton.edu/pdf/publications/morse1.pdf

Mort, Frank (1996) *Cultures of Consumption: Masculinities and Social Space in Late Twentieth-Century Britain,* London: Routledge

Murdoch, Jonathan (1997) 'Inhuman/nonhuman/human: actor-network theory and the potential for a non-dualistic and symmetrical perspective on nature and society', *Environment and Space D: Society and Space,* vol. 15, no. 6, pp. 731–56

(2001) 'Ecologising sociology: actor-network theory, co-constructionism and the problem of human exemptionalism', *Sociology,* vol. 35, no. 1, pp. 111–33

(2005) 'Co-constructing the hybrid countryside: hybrid networks and the extensive self', in Paul Cloke (ed.) *Country Visions,* London: Pearson, pp. 263–82

Murdoch, Jonathan and Terry Marsden (1995) *Reconstituting Rurality,* London: UCL Press

Murdoch, Jonathan and Mara Miele (1999) 'Back to nature: changing worlds of production in the food system', *Sociologia Ruralis,* vol. 39, no. 4, pp. 465–83

Murdoch, Jonathan, Philip Lowe, Neil Ward and Terry Marsden (2003) *The Differentiated Countryside,* London: Routledge

Naylor, Simon and James R. Ryan (2002) 'The mosque in the suburbs: negotiating religion and ethnicity in South London', *Social & Cultural Geography,* vol. 3, no. 1, pp. 39–59

Nead, Lynda (1988) *Myths of Sexuality: Representations of Women in Victorian Britain,* Oxford: Blackwell

(2000) *Victorian Babylon: People, Streets and Images in Nineteenth-Century London,* New Haven: Yale University Press

Neves, Lívia (2004) 'Cleanliness, pollution and disgust in modern industrial societies: the Brazilian case', *Journal of Consumer Culture,* vol. 4, no. 3, pp. 385–405

Nochlin, Linda (1978) 'Once more the fallen woman', *The Art Bulletin*, vol. 60, pp. 139–53

Norberg-Hodge, Helena, Todd Merrifield and Steven Gorelick (2002) *Bringing the Food Economy Home: Local Alternatives to Global Agribusiness*, London: Zed Books

Nussbaum, Martha (2004) *Hiding from Humanity: Disgust, Shame and the Law*, New Jersey: Princeton University Press

Oakley, Anne (1972) *Housewife*, Harmondsworth: Penguin
(1973) *The Sociology of Housework*, Bath: Robertson

Oates, Joyce Carol (1981) 'Imaginary cities: America', in Michael C. Jaye and Ann Chalmers Watts (eds) *Literature and the Urban Experience: Essays on the City and Literature*, New Brunswick: Rutgers University Press, pp. 11–13

O'Connell Davidson, Julia (1998) *Prostitution, Power and Freedom*, Cambridge: Polity

Oettermann, Stephen (1997) *The Panorama: History of a Mass Medium*, New York: Zone Books

Oldham, Kit (2004) 'First USA case of mad cow disease', *HistoryLink*, 4 February, Www.historylink.org/essays/output.cfm?file_id=5650

Orwell, George (1933) *Down and Out in London and Paris*, London: Victor Gollancz

Otter, Christopher (2004) 'Cleansing and clarifying: technology and perception in nineteenth-century London', *Journal of British Studies*, vol. 43, pp. 40–65

Owen, David (1982) *The Government of Victorian London: 1855–1889: The Metropolitan Board of Works, the Vestries, and the City Corporation*, Cambridge, MA: Harvard University Press

Owen, Tim and Elaine Pilbeam (1992) *Ordnance Survey: Map Makers to Britain since 1791*, Southampton: Ordnance Survey

Pakkala, Tiffany (2006) 'School bus stop was at sex offender's home,' *Gainesville Sun*, 10 August http://gainesville.com/apps/pbcs.dll/article?AID=/20060810/LOCAL/ 208100330&SearchID=73257054135918

Palmer, Phyllis (1989) *Domesticity and Dirt: Housewives and Domestic Servants in the United States, 1920–1945*, Philadelphia: Temple University Press

Parliamentary Debates (1848) 3rd Series, vol. 97, 24 March

Parliamentary Papers (1847–48) 'First report of the commissioners appointed to inquire whether any and what special means may be requisite for the improvement of the health of the metropolis', vol. 32, London: HMSO

Pennington, Hugh (2000) 'The English disease', *London Review of Books*. vol. 22, no. 24, 14 December
(2006) *When Food Kills: BSE, E. coli, and Disaster Science*, Oxford: Oxford University Press

Peringer, Mike (2006) 'South End is not a dumping ground for what the city doesn't want', *The Seattle Post Intelligencer*, 4 May

Phongpaichit, Pasuk (1982) *From Peasant Girls to Bangkok Masseuses*, Geneva: International Labour Organization

Phongpaichit, Pasuk and Chris Baker (1995) *Thailand: Economy and Politics*, Oxford: Oxford University Press

Pickering, Andrew (1993) 'The mangle of practice: agency and emergence in the sociology of science', *American Journal of Sociology*, vol. 99, no. 3, pp. 559–89

Picon, Antoine (2000) 'Anxious landscapes: from the ruin to rust', *Grey Room*, no. 1, Fall, pp. 64–83

Pigg, Stacy Leigh (1992) 'Inventing social categories through place: social representations and development in Nepal', *Comparative Studies in Society and History*, vol. 34, pp. 491–513.

Pike, David L. (1998) 'Urban nightmares and future visions: life beneath New York', *Wide Angle*, vol. 20, no. 4, October, pp. 8–50

(2005) 'Sewage treatments: vertical space and waste in nineteenth-century Paris and London', in William A. Cohen and Ryan Johnson (eds) *Filth: Dirt, Disgust and Modern Life*, Minneapolis: University of Minnesota Press, pp. 51–76

(2005) *Subterranean Cities: The World Beneath Paris and London, 1800–1945*, Ithaca: Cornell University Press

Pile, Steve (1996) *The Body and the City: Psychoanalysis, Space and Subjectivity*, London: Routledge

(2001) 'The un(known) city … or, an urban geography of what lies buried below the surface', in Iain Borden, Joe Kerr, Jane Rendell with Alicia Pivaro (eds) *The Unknown City: Contesting Architecture and Social Space*, Cambridge, MA: MIT Press, pp. 268–9

Pink, Sarah (2007) 'The sensory home as a site of consumption: everyday laundry practices and the production of gender', in Emma Casey and Lydia Martens (eds) *Gender and Consumption: Domestic Cultures and the Commercialisation of Everyday Life*, Aldershot: Ashgate, pp. 163–80

Pinkus, Rosa Lynn B. (1974) 'The conceptual development of London, 1850–1855', Ph.D. dissertation, Buffalo: State University of New York

Prior, Lindsay (1989) *The Social Organization of Death: Medical Discourse and Social Practices in Belfast*, London: Macmillan Press

Quilley, Stephen (1997) 'Constructing Manchester's "new urban village": gay space in the entrepreneurial city', in Gordon Ingram, Anne-Marie Bouthillette and Yolanda Retter (eds) *Queers in Space: Communities, Public Places, Sites of Resistance*, Seattle: Bay Press

Radford, Fred (1994) '"Cloacal obsession": Hugo, Joyce, and the sewer museum of Paris', *Mattoid*, vol. 48, pp. 66–85

Rajadhon, Phya Anuman (1972) *Watthanatham* (culture), Bangkok: Samnakpim Banakarn

Rappaport, Erica (2004) 'Packaging China: foreign articles and dangerous tastes in the mid-Victorian tea party', paper presented to ESRC–AHRB Cultures of Consumption seminar, Managing Anxiety: Food Scares and the British Consumer in Victorian and Modern Britain, 16 July, Birkbeck College, University of London

Reagan, Ronald (n.d.) 'City upon a hill' (http://www.presidentreagan.info/speeches/city_upon_a_hill.cfm) accessed 17 September 2006

Reay, Diane (2004) 'Mostly roughs and toughs: social class, race and representation in inner city schooling', *Sociology*, vol. 38, pp. 1005–23

Reid, Donald (1991) *Paris Sewers and Sewermen: Realities and Representations*, Cambridge, MA: Harvard University Press

Rendell, Jane (2004) 'Architectural research and disciplinarity', *Architectural Research Quarterly*, vol. 8, no. 4, pp. 141–7

(2006) *Art and Architecture: A Place Between*, London: I.B.Tauris

Renting, Henk, Terry Marsden and Jo Banks (2003) 'Understanding alternative food networks: exploring the role of short food supply chains in rural development', *Environment and Planning A*, vol. 35, pp. 393–411

Rex, John and Robert Moore (1967) *Race, Community and Conflict*, Oxford: Oxford University Press

Reynolds, Craig J. (1991) *National Identity and its Defenders: Thailand 1939–89*, Victoria: Aristoc Press

Reynolds, Reginald (1943) *Cleanliness and Godliness*, London: George Allen & Unwin

Richards, Ellen (1929) *Euthenics: The Science of Controllable Environment*, Boston: Barrows

Rivas, Lynn May (2003) 'Invisible labours: caring for the independent person', in Barbara Ehrenreich and Arlie Hochschild (eds) *Global Woman: Nannies, Maids and Sex Workers in the Global Economy*, London: Granta Books

Rix, Vikki (1996) 'Social and demographic change in East London', in Michael Rustin and Tim Butler (eds) *Rising in the East*, London: Lawrence & Wishart

Robinson, Jenny, 'Feminism and the spaces of transformation', *Transactions of the Institute of British Geographers: New Series*, vol. 25, no. 3, pp 285–301

Robinson, John P. and Melissa A. Milkie (1998) 'Back to the basics: trends in and role determinants of women's attitudes toward housework', *Journal of Marriage and The Family*, vol. 60, no. 1, pp. 205–18

Rose, Gillian (1993) *Feminism and Geography: The Limits of Geographical Knowledge* (Cambridge: Polity Press)

Rosselin, Céline (1999) 'The ins and outs of the hall: a Parisian example', in Irene Cieraad (ed.) *At Home: Anthropology of Domestic Space*, Syracuse, NY: Syracuse University Press

Russo, Vito (1987) *The Celluloid Closet: Homosexuality in the Movies*, New York: Harper & Row Publishers, revised edition

Sambrook, Pamela (2002) *A Country House Servant*, Stroud: Sutton Publishing

Sanders, Teela (2004) *Sex Work: A Risky Business*, Cullompton, Devon: Willan Publishing

Santiago, Robert and Sara Olkon (2005) 'Molester ban poses risks, some say', *Miami Beach Herald*, Monday 19 September

Saugeres, Lisa (2000) 'Of tidy gardens and clean houses: housing officers as agents of social control', *Geoforum*, vol. 31, no. 4, pp. 587–99

Saunders, Peter and Peter Williams (1988). 'The constitution of the home: towards a research agenda', *Housing Studies*, vol. 3, no. 2, pp. 81–93

Savage, Mike and Andrew Miles (1994) *The Remaking of the British Working Class, 1840–1940*, London: Routledge

Savage, Mike, Gaynor Bagnall and Brian Longhurst (2005) 'Local habitus and working-class culture', in Fiona Devine, Mike Savage, John Scott and Rosemary Crompton (eds) *Rethinking Class: Culture, Identities and Lifestyles*, Basingstoke: Palgrave Macmillan

Sawyer, Dan (1994) 'The contagious case part III', *The Dodge Magazine*, vol. 1, no. 9, pp. 17–28

Sayer, Andrew (2000) *Realism and Social Science*, London: Sage

Scanlan, John (2005) *On Garbage*, London: Reaktion Books

Scholten, Bruce A. (1999) 'BSE-hurt Brits to start exporting beef', *Hoard's Dairyman*, 25 April

(2006) 'Firefighters in the UK and the US: risk perception of local and organic food', *Scottish Geographical Journal*, vol. 122, no. 2, June, pp.130–48

(2006) 'Motorcyclists in the USA and the UK: risk perception of local and organic food', in Georgina Holt and Matt Reed, *Sociological Perspectives of Organic Agriculture: from Pioneer to Policy*, Wallingford: CABI, July, pp. 107–25

Scott, James (1985) *Weapons of the Weak: Everyday Forms of Peasant Resistance*, New Haven: Yale University Press

Seamon, David and Robert Mugerauer (eds) (1985) *Dwelling, Place, and Environment: Towards a Phenomenology of Person and World*, Dordrecht: Martinus Nijhoff

Sen, Krishna (1998) 'Indonesian women at work: reframing the subject', in Krishna Sen and Maila Stivens (eds) *Gender and Power in Affluent Asia*, London: Routledge, pp. 35–62

Sennett, Richard (1996) *The Uses of Disorder*, London: Faber & Faber

Shields, Rob (1991) *Places on the Margins*, London: Routledge

Shildrick, Margrit (1997) *Leaky Bodies and Boundaries: Feminism, Postmodernism and (Bio)ethics*, London: Routledge

Shonfield, Katherine (2001) 'Dirt is matter out of place', in Jonathan Hill (ed.) *Architecture: The Subject is Matter*, London: Routledge, pp. 29–44

Shove, Elizabeth (2003) *Comfort, Cleanliness and Convenience: The Social Organization of Normality*, Oxford, Berg

Sibley, David (1995) *Geographies of Exclusion: Society and Difference in the West*, London: Routledge

—— (1998) 'The racialization of space in British cities', *Soundings*, vol. 10, no. 1, pp. 119–27

Silva, Elizabeth Bortolaia (n.d.) *Teorias sobre trabalho e tecnologias domésticas: implicações para o Brasil.* http://www.ige.unicamp.br/site/publicacoes/dpct/Texto-19.doc, accessed 14 December 2006

Silverstone, Roger (1997) *Visions of Suburbia*, London: Routledge

Simpson, M. (1994) 'Hello boys! Soho turns pink', *Independent*, 23 May

Sinclair, Upton (1986) *The Jungle*, Harmondsworth: Penguin Classics, first published 1906

Sivulka, Juliann (2001) *Stronger than Dirt: A Cultural History of Advertising Personal Hygiene in America, 1875 to 1940*, Amherst, NY: Humanity Books

Skeggs, Beverly, Leslie Moran, Paul Tyrer and Jon Binnie (2004) 'Queer as folk: producing the real of urban space', *Urban Studies*, vol. 41, no. 9, p. 1843

Skelton, Raleigh A. (1962) 'The origins of the Ordnance Survey in Great Britain', *Geographical Journal*, vol. 128, pp. 415–16

Smith, Darren P. and Louise Holt (2005) 'Lesbian migrants in the gentrified valley and "other" geographies of rural gentrification', *Journal of Rural Studies*, vol. 21, no. 3, pp. 313–22

Smith, Dorothy (1987) *The Everyday Life as Problematic*, Milton Keynes: Open University Press

Smith, Mick and Joyce Davidson (2006) '"It makes my skin crawl …": the embodiment of disgust in phobias of "nature"', *Body & Society*, vol. 12, no. 1, pp. 43–67

Smith, Rupert (2002) 'Join the club: Duckie began as a group of drag artists and drunken admirers. Now this 'post-gay' phenomenon is going national', *Guardian*, 14 May

Smith, Wes (2002) 'Church foes cite sex offenders' proximity: a proposed complex in Edgewood shouldn't be able to displace residents, opponents say', *The Orlando Sentinel*, 8 September 2006, Associated Press, Lexis-Nexis database

Solari, Cinzia (2006) 'Professionals and saints: how immigrant careworkers negotiate gender identities at work', *Gender and Society*, vol. 20, no. 3, 2006, pp. 301–31.

Sparke, Penny (2004) 'Studying the modern home', *The Journal of Architecture*, vol. 9, Winter, 2004

Stallabrass, Julian (1999) *High Art Lite: British Art in the 1990s*, London: Verso

Stallybrass, Peter and Allon White (1986) *The Politics and Poetics of Transgression*, London: Methuen

Strasser, Susan (1982) *Never Done: A History of American Housework*, New York: Pantheon Books

Strub, Clarence G. and Lawrence G. Fredrick (1967) *The Principles and Practices of Embalming*, Dallas: Professional Training Schools, 4th edition

Swyngedouw, Eric and Maria Kaïka (2000) 'The environment of the city ... or the urbanization of nature', in Gary Bridge and Sophie Watson (eds) *The Blackwell Companion to the City*, Oxford: Blackwell, pp. 567–80

Tait, William (1842) *Magdalenism: An Inquiry into the Extent, Causes, and Consequences of Prostitution in Edinburgh*, Edinburgh: P. Rickard, 2nd edition

Teather, Elizabeth K. (1998) 'Themes from complex landscapes: Chinese cemeteries and columbaria in urban Hong Kong', *Australian Geographical Studies*, vol. 36, no. 1, pp. 21–36

Tester, Mark (2001) 'The dangerously polarized debate on genetic modification', *British Food Journal*, vol. 103, no. 11, pp. 785–90

Thomas, Pat (2001) *Cleaning Yourself to Death: How Safe is your Home*, Dublin: Newleaf

Thompson, Michael (1979) *Rubbish Theory*, Oxford: Oxford University Press

Tomes, Nancy (1998) *The Gospel of Germs: Men, Women and the Microbe in American Life*, London: Harvard University Press

Toynbee, Polly (1988) 'Thursday women (behind the lines): freedom's roadblock', *Guardian*, 14 January

Tuck, A. (1994) 'In the pink', *Time Out*, day and month missing

Turner, Mark W. (2003) 'Gay London', in Joe Kerr and Andrew Gibson (eds) *London: From Punk to Blair*, London: Reaktion Books

Valentine, Gill (2001) *Social Geographies: Space and Society*, New York: Prentice Hall

Valeri, Valerio (1999) *The Forest of Taboos: Morality, Hunting, and Identity among the Huaulu of the Moluccas*, Madison: University of Wisconsin Press

van Gennep, Arnold (1960) *Rites of Passage*, translated by Monika B. Vizedom and Gabrielle L. Caffee with an introduction by Solon T. Kimball, London, Routledge & Kegan Paul

van Zwanenberg, Patrick and Erik Millston (2005) *BSE: Risk, Science and Governance*, Oxford: Oxford University Press

Venn, Laura, Moya Kneafsey, Lewis Holloway, Rosie Cox, Elizabeth Dowler and Helena Tuomainen (2006) 'Researching European "alternative" food networks: some methodological considerations', *Area*, vol. 38, no. 3, pp. 248–58

Vidler, Anthony (1992) *The Architectural Uncanny: Essays in the Modern Unhomely*, Cambridge, MA: The MIT Press

Vigarello, Georges (1998) *Concepts of Cleanliness: Changing Attitudes in France since the Middle Ages*, Cambridge: Cambridge University Press

Vinikas, Vincent (1989) 'Lustrum of the cleanliness institute, 1927–1932', *Journal of Social History*, vol. 22, no. 4, pp. 613–30

(1992) *Soft Soap, Hard Sell: American Hygiene in an Age of Advertisement*, Iowa: Iowa State University Press

Waddington, Keir (2006) *The Bovine Scourge: Meat, Tuberculosis and the Public's Health, 1860s–1914*, Woodbridge: The Boydell Press

Walkowitz, Judith R. (1980) *Prostitution and Victorian Society: Women, Class and the State*, Cambridge: Cambridge University Press

Walter, Tony (2005) 'Three ways to arrange a funeral: mortuary variation in the modern West', *Mortality*, vol. 10, no. 3, pp. 173–92

Warde, Alan (1997) *Consumption, Food and Taste: Culinary Antinomies and Commodity Culture*, London: Sage

Warde, Alan and Lydia Martens (2000) *Eating Out: Social Differentiation, Consumption and Pleasure*, Cambridge: Cambridge University Press

Wardlaw, Ralph (1843) *Lectures on Female Prostitution: Its Nature, Extent, Effects, Guilt, Causes and Remedy*, Glasgow: J. Maclehose, 3rd edition

Watson, Sophie and Karen Wells (2005) 'Spaces of nostalgia: the hollowing out of a London market', *Social & Cultural Geography*, vol. 6, no. 1, pp. 17–30

Watt, Paul (1998) 'Going out of town: youth, "race" and place in the south east of England', *Environment and Planning D: Society and Space*, vol. 16, no. 6, pp. 687–703

(2004) 'Narratives of urban decline and ethnic diversity: white flight and the racialisation of space in London and south east England', paper presented at the Countering Urban Segregation Conference, Free University, Amsterdam, 14–15 October

(2006) 'Respectability, roughness and "race": neighbourhood place images and the making of working-class social distinctions in London', *International Journal of Urban and Regional Research*, vol. 30, no. 4, pp. 776–97

Watts, David, Brian Ilbery and Damian Maye (2005) 'Making reconnections in agro-food geography: alternative systems of food provision', *Progress in Human Geography*, vol. 29, no. 1, pp. 22–40

Weise, Elizabeth (2003) 'Consumers may have a beef with cattle feed', *USA Today*, 9 June

Wells, Karen and Sophie Watson (2005) 'A politics of resentment: shopkeepers in a London neighbourhood', *Ethnic and Racial Studies*, vol. 28, no. 2, pp. 261–77

Werner, Marcia (2005) *Pre-Raphaelite Painting and Nineteenth-Century Realism*, Cambridge: Cambridge University Press

Whatmore, Sarah (2002) *Hybrid Geographies: Natures, Cultures, Spaces*, London: Sage

Whatmore, Sarah, Pierre Stassart and Henk Renting (2003) 'Guest editorial: what's alternative about alternative food networks? *Environment and Planning A*, vol. 35, no. 3, pp. 389–91

Widding Isaksen, Lise (2002) 'Masculine dignity and the dirty body', *NORA*, vol. 10, no. 3, pp. 137–46

Williams, Simon J. and Gillian Bendelow (1998) *The Lived Body: Sociological Themes, Embodied Issues*, London: Routledge

Willmott, Peter and Michael Young (1967) *Family and Class in a London Suburb*, London: New English Library

Wilson, Ara (2004) *The Intimate Economies of Bangkok: Tomboys, Tycoons and Avon Ladies in the Global City*, Berkeley: University of California Press

Wolkowitz, Carol (2006) *Bodies at Work*, London: Sage

Woods, Michael (2003) 'Deconstructing rural protest: the emergence of a new social movement', *Journal of Rural Studies*, vol. 19, no. 3, pp. 309–25

Wright, Lawrence (1960) *Clean and Decent: The Fascinating History of the Bathroom and the Water Closet, and of the Sundry Habits, Fashions and Accessories of the Toilet, principally Great Britain, France, and America*, New York: Viking Press

Wright, Patrick, *Journey through Ruins: The Last Days of London* (London: Radius, 1991)

(2003) 'Down in the dirt', in Joe Kerr and Andrew Gibson (eds) *London from Punk to Blair*, London: Reaktion

Wuthnow, James, Davison Hunter, Albert Bergesen and Edith Kurzweil (1984) *Cultural Analysis: The Work of Peter L. Berger, Mary Douglas, Michel Foucault, and Jurgen Habermas*, London: Routledge & Kegan Paul

Wynne, Brian (1992) 'Misunderstood misunderstanding: social identities and public uptake of science', *Public Understanding of Science,* vol. 1, pp. 281–304

Young, Michael and Peter Willmott, *Family and Kinship in East London* (London: Routledge & Kegan Paul, 1957)

Index

257